D1572472

Champion of the Barrio

SWAIM-PAUP-FORAN SPIRIT OF SPORT SERIES
Focusing on Sport in Modern Society

Sponsored by James C. '74 and Debra Parchman Swaim,
Nancy and T. Edgar Paup '74, and Joseph Wm. and Nancy Foran

Champion
OF THE BARRIO

The Legacy of Coach Buryl Baty

R. Gaines Baty
with a foreword by Raymond Berry

Texas A&M University Press | College Station

LIBRARY OF CONGRESS CATALOGING-IN-PUBLICATION DATA

Baty, R. Gaines, 1950– author.
    Champion of the barrio : the legacy of Coach Buryl Baty / R. Gaines Baty ; with a
foreword by Raymond Berry.—First edition.
        pages cm — (The Swaim-Paup-Foran spirit of sport series)
    Includes bibliographical references and index.
    ISBN 978-1-62349-266-3 (cloth : alk. paper)—
    ISBN 978-1-62349-267-0 (e-book)
    1. Baty, Buryl, 1924–1954. 2. Football coaches—Texas—Biography. 3. Football teams—
Texas—History—20th century. 4. School sports—Texas—History—20th century.
5. Discrimination in sports—Texas—History—20th century. 6. Hispanic American
football players—Texas—El Paso—History—20th century. 7. Bowie High School
(El Paso, Tex.)—Sports—History—20th century. I. Title. II. Series: Swaim-Paup-Foran
spirit of sport series.
    GV939.B387B37 2015
    796.332092—dc23
    [B]
    2014042775

**A portion of proceeds from this book will be donated
to the Buryl Baty Scholarship Fund.**
Your donations to the annual Buryl Baty Scholarship Fund
may be made to:
    Bowie High Alumni Association
    Attn: Scholarship Committee
    (Coach Buryl Baty Memorial Scholarship)
    PO Box 1804
    El Paso, TX 79949

Dedicated to my best friend
and the love of my life.
Keri, thank you for your support and love.

Destiny is no matter of chance. It is a matter of choice.
It is not a thing to be waited for; it is a thing to be achieved.

—WILLIAM JENNINGS BRYAN (1860–1925)

Contents

Foreword

My father, Coach Mark Raymond Berry, was the most influential person in my life.

I confess that I did not fully realize this as a young boy. My father was surely important to me then, but I was mostly in awe of the better players that he coached: Jack White, Buryl Baty, and Bucky Sheffield. Later, I added John Kimbrough, Leroy "Crazy Legs" Hirsch, and Doak Walker to my list of idols. Eventually, other coaches influenced me. I played for and coached under or with a number of the great ones: Rusty Russell, Weeb Eubank, Don Shula, Tom Landry, Frank Broyles, and others. They all left their marks on me. A great leader can influence a young man profoundly, much like a father.

But in hindsight, my father stood above them all, and to him I owe my greatest gratitude. I can't imagine what my life might have been without him. This story about Buryl Baty, one of my dad's best players and one of my childhood heroes, has reminded me of what my dad stood for and what he really meant to me. It has caused dormant emotions, emotions that I didn't realize I had, to rise from deep within. It has touched me. It has also inspired me, as a great coach might have done. And it has reminded me of a few life lessons along the way.

I was drawn into Buryl Baty's story as if I had actually been there. In fact, I was there, and this book has taken me back to those days. I knew or know many of the people mentioned between its covers. And I'll never forget my dad's praise for Buryl Baty. It was a joy to meet him again in this book. His life inspires me, as it did many of those fortunate enough to know him. He left his mark. And he would certainly have left a much greater mark had he lived longer.

This is one of the best books I've read. I will not put it down and forget about it. I'll read it again, and maybe again. I'll think about it for a long time. I want my children and grandchildren to read it.

Thanks for allowing me to be a part of it.
—Raymond Berry
NFL Hall of Fame Player and Coach

Preface

This is the story of my father, but our connection is only slightly relevant to the story. I will address this relationship at the conclusion of the narrative. What is most important now follows.

Buryl Baty was born into "the Greatest Generation." He grew up in a small depression-era town in a family of very modest means. As it did for many boys, athletics played a significant role in his development. As he matured, his successes brought a level of prominence and fame. He followed his dream to become a coach—so that he could teach the same principles that his own athletic and military endeavors had instilled in him: discipline, perseverance, accountability, leadership, respect, integrity, and honor.

His second head-coaching job in El Paso, Texas, presented an unexpected challenge. While the post-WWII era abounded with optimism and opportunity for Anglo-Americans, discrimination soured the times. Shameless acts against people of color, black and brown, were accepted and/or ignored by the Anglo majority. Athletics were mired in this same oppressive state. Buryl Baty did not realize the extent of this phenomenon when he accepted the El Paso job, but his eyes were quickly opened. And he did not like what he saw.

In an inspiring fashion Coach Baty set about the business of building boys into productive citizens and, simultaneously, into a winning team. The football field was a perfect place to prove that his Hispanic players were equal to the Anglos across the line of scrimmage . . . because the evidence was irrefutable. Might it also suggest that they were equal *off* the field as well? At a minimum, the seed was planted. But Anglos did not appreciate this notion.

This young coach dug deep for the courage and conviction to confront his contemporaries, and the world he himself had grown up in, to fight this endless battle. Along the way, his intensity and determination inspired an epiphany for his players: that they had the right and the ability to seek their own dreams. And that they had voices. More seeds were planted.

Buryl Baty was a pioneer, a champion for equality. It would be ten long years after his death before the Civil Rights Act of 1964 outlawed discrimination on the basis of race, color, religion, sex, or national origin.

I interviewed more than one hundred people to document this story—family, friends, teammates, classmates, players, students, fellow coaches, opponents, news reporters, and fans. While a few names have been changed for privacy, every event in the book actually took place—as described by interviewees' firsthand (albeit sometimes hazy) knowledge of the incident, or by written documentation. Most conversations and speeches were "best recollections" of the words spoken—as provided by numerous sources. The transcript of a recorded service is included, and a personal recording of Coach Raymond Berry's comments provided much of his dialogue related in this text. In some cases, dialogue was reconstructed to appropriately represent confirmed circumstances and character. In addition to first hand stories, approximately three hundred newspaper articles, several scrapbooks, and three journals/diaries provided direct and relevant information.

This is a true story of triumph—triumph over hardship, over evil, over discrimination, over tragedy, over one's self. These are lessons for us, for our children, and for our grandchildren.

As for my dad, his memory is secure. A stadium has been dedicated in his name. His Hall of Fame induction plaque hangs on the wall. And people still talk about him.

He lives on.

Champion of the Barrio

1 "No Mexicans Allowed"

Bowie High School's coaches had looked forward to this game. At the same time, they had dreaded going back to Snyder; the trip there two years ago had been a nightmare. But this year, Coach Buryl Baty had prepared his players for some trademark small-town bigotry.

At seven thirty on Thursday morning, the players climbed up into the bus. They were carrying sack lunches and many also carried a second paper sack holding a change of clothes. They were full of energy as the bus accelerated eastward from the barrio and into the sunrise, but their banter and animation waned as the long drive grew hot and tiresome. When the Greyhound stopped to fill up four hours later in Roswell, the boys found a shady spot to eat their sandwiches. The late afternoon sun was dropping in the sky behind them by the time the bus finally slowed into Snyder's central square. Curious boys now sat up to take in the sights of the town they had heard so much about.

As they drove through the square, Big Ernie Perea, the freshman defensive tackle, spotted a sign in a drugstore window.

WELCOME TO SNYDER. NO DOGS OR MEXICANS ALLOWED.

"Hey, guys!" he cried. "There's one of those signs!"

An older teammate laughed. "*One?* You ain't seen nothing, man." Several upperclassmen had been to Snyder before, and the whole team, of course, had heard about the town. But the younger varsity players flew from window to window to gawk at the reappearance of the same sign in different storefronts.

The bus eventually eased into the mostly empty parking lot of the motel that had been reserved for the night.

Coach Baty strode into the lobby to check in. The manager, seeing two, then three boys trailing behind him, swiveled his head around to look out the lobby window at the parking lot, where the rest of the team was already milling.

"There's been a mistake. All my rooms are rented," he said coolly.

Then, perhaps taken aback by the scowl on the coach's face, he added, "There's a place outside the city limits. It may have vacancies."

"Then *dial* them," Baty said, jabbing his finger at the phone. Having confirmed that the rooms could be had, he turned on his heel and left, the uncomfortable boys still in tow.

En route to the second motel outside of town, the coaches stopped to buy sandwiches and snacks for the boys, and the next morning, saving the team's energies for the game, they brought breakfast in from a nearby grocery store. Reservations for lunch, however, had been confirmed at a café, where the players should be able to eat a healthy pre-game meal. Until then they waited in their rooms. Some listened to the radio, over which they heard a local disc jockey say, "Don't miss tonight's game between your Snyder Tigers and the Mexicans from El Paso Bowie High School!"

Early that afternoon, the team's bus rolled past the stately red-bricked courthouse toward a café on the square, and, brakes squealing, pulled to a stop. Players were allowed to get out and stretch their legs, but were told to stay near the bus. Coach Baty walked into the café, then stepped back out and waited by the front door. A huge man wearing a white, food-splattered apron soon followed him and after a short, hushed conversation, burst out with, "Coach, them Meskins are not going inside my place of bui'ness!"

The coach had anticipated just such a reaction. He leaned toward the massive, sweaty café proprietor and glared. "Yes, they are. I made reservations here, and we are gonna eat here. If you don't feed my boys, we are gonna get back in that bus and head back to El Paso. And if we do, *there'll be no football game tonight.*"

The declaration, and the intensity behind it, took the restaurant owner by surprise. Could this coach be serious? The owner winced as he considered the possible repercussions of a canceled ballgame. If he were held responsible, he could well be boycotted by Snyder football fans. While most of his fellow citizens shared his social views, nothing else was as important to them as Friday night football.

Little did he suspect, however, that the only person in town who stood to suffer more than he did over a cancelled football game was standing in front of him.

2   Paris, Texas

1930–1938

Paris was founded in 1844, while Texas was still a republic. It borders Oklahoma on the Red River, just outside the Piney Woods in northeast Texas. By the time of the Civil War, the population had swelled to seven hundred. Fertile red soil, and a railroad depot built in 1876, spurred Paris's growth into a major cotton exchange for the region. And, as in most southern towns of the era, segregation was the norm.

But on the whole, Paris was a nice little town. Rolling countryside bordered by creeks and thickets of huge trees added to the community's charm. Its population in the 1930s approached eighteen thousand citizens, most of whom were down-to-earth, hard working people. Among these good folks were the Batys.

Burton Baty understood hard work. He was a strong, quiet man, whose rough, calloused hands and broken, stained fingernails revealed his lifestyle. Tall and lean, he had a prominent nose, high cheekbones, a dark, receding hairline, and skin weathered from his years of working under a hot Texas sun. In his younger days he had labored in the fields picking cotton, at which a man could earn a dollar a day plus room and board—enough money to make it through the winter. After serving in World War I, Burton tended crops with his father Steve in nearby Deport. Sometimes he travelled farther to earn his living—in the fall of 1924, he took his wife Bobbie and their five-month-old son Buryl to West Texas, where he hired on to harvest cotton.

As his family grew, Burton became more resourceful. He found full-time employment as a "chemist" at the Speas Vinegar plant. He wasn't a chemist by education, of course, but he quickly learned to ferment high-quality vinegar and apple juice. For one hundred dollars a month, he walked over a mile each way to and from work, six days a week. And at least twice a week he walked to the town square to buy bargain groceries and supplies. Like many in this Depression era, Burton also kept chickens and hogs, and he tended a vegetable garden behind the family's rented home.

Burton's wife, Bobbie, spent most of her waking hours in the kitchen, which was a sweatbox during the hot summers. The heat generated by the wood-burning stove was oppressive, and with only an electric fan and a slight breeze through the open windows for relief, she could sometimes hardly catch her breath. But she mopped her face with a towel and carried on. To help out, her boys retrieved vegetables from the garden, mashed potatoes and shelled peas, and occasionally went out into the backyard pen to fetch a couple of fat hens, a task that required fending off the big, protective red rooster. Soon the crackling hot grease and the thick aroma of frying chicken energized the household. Bobbie's announcement of dinner—"Supper's ready!"—would set off a race to the kitchen table.

Outside the kitchen, Bobbie filled her time with other domestic duties—sewing, washing, ironing, cleaning. The covered front porch offered a slight respite from the sweltering heat, and occasionally the semblance of a breeze sifted through it. When she could, it was there that Bobbie sat to snap beans, shuck corn, or mend clothes. And beside her in a washtub lined with a homemade quilt would always be one of her babies. This tub served as a playpen for her succession of infant children until they grew mobile enough to escape it.

The four young Baty brothers roughhoused, teased, and scrapped throughout their childhood. The younger boys idolized their oldest brother, Buryl, and eventually all of them wore his clothes. With the assistance of Bobbie's skilled needle and thread, these patched and faded hand-me-downs had as many lives as a cat. Overalls, shirts, britches, underwear, and socks from older uncles and cousins were passed first to Buryl, then to brothers Earl, Al, and Harold. The only new apparel the boys were likely to get was an occasional pair of shoes and the handmade underwear that Bobbie cut and sewed from smooth cotton flour sacks. The family made the most of every penny, and while they had little to share, guests rarely left the house without a jar of vinegar or apple juice, half a pie or cake, or some leftover fried chicken.

Burton was a strict father and was quick to dispense discipline with a razor strap. Whippings were doled out to the boys for sassing their mother, telling lies, saying dirty words, and any number of other ill-conceived boyish offenses. Burton also vigorously enforced his edict that a person's word, once given, must be kept: "When you say you'll do something, you do it," he pronounced; and as a result of his strong right-handed persuasion, the boys learned their lessons quickly and well.

The youngsters ran freely through the neighborhood, which was full of other children, many of whom were relatives. The continuous sounds of screen doors slamming and kids laughing in the yard created a comforting chaos. Buryl's favorite playmate, Zelma, lived next door with his grandparents (Burton's parents) and several of Burton's other younger siblings (she was his baby sister). Technically Zelma was Buryl's aunt, but he called her "Sister." She was a feisty tomboy and the perfect sidekick. They played ball, floated on the rope swing in the big oak tree, walked through the neighborhood on stilts made by Zelma's older brothers, and shot slingshots at birds in the mulberry tree out back. During the summers, the kids fished for crawdaddies with a small piece of bacon on the end of a string that they fed down into a crawfish hole. When they felt a tug, they pulled the string up firmly and gently until the crawdad, still clamped onto the bacon, emerged.

But of all the fun and frolic with friends, the maturing Buryl most naturally gravitated to games involving some sort of ball, and especially a football.

• • •

In October 1938, a tall, slender man climbed the steps of the covered front porch. Beads of perspiration had accumulated on his balding forehead, and the shade felt good. He knocked on the screen door and nervously waited for a response. From outside, he could see a short, heavy woman with brushed-back, dark blonde hair laboring toward him.

"Well, hello, Mr. Justiss," the woman said as she approached the door.

The high school principal got straight to the point. "Mrs. Baty, why is Buryl not in school?"

Mrs. Baty's eyebrows lifted. "As far as I know, he *is* in school," she replied.

"No, Ma'am, he hasn't been for several days straight," returned Justiss. "Since he hurt his shoulder, he just doesn't seem to care. The coach told him he could play again as soon as it healed, but Buryl says you don't want him on the team."

A frown creased Mrs. Baty's face. The football injury was a sore point for her.

"Frankly," Justiss added, "we're having trouble keeping him in school. But I do have a solution to propose."

"And what's that, Mr. Justiss?"

"Ma'am, the boy loves football, and playing on the team could give him motivation."

Mrs. Baty didn't respond right away. She visualized her son's bright brown eyes and big smile, then blurted out, "I don't want him to get hurt so bad that he can't get a good job later. And I don't want him to get his teeth knocked out . . . he's too good-lookin' a boy."

"I understand," the principal answered. "But football may be the only thing that'll keep him in class. And another thing. Buryl's a fine athlete, and football could be his ticket to college—on a scholarship."

Buryl's mother had never considered college as a possibility for anyone in her family. This was an argument that put an entirely new face on the sport. Football could be his big chance, she figured.

After a few seconds of silence, she nodded. "Okay. If he wants to play, I won't keep him from it."

When Coach Raymond Berry heard the good news, he wanted to talk to Buryl directly. But first he had to find the truant freshman. He asked other boys where Buryl might be, had no luck, and finally just drove around until he found him. He leaned across the passenger seat and opened the door, beckoning Buryl in.

"You haven't been going to class, son. What's going on?"

Reluctant to make eye contact, Buryl hemmed and hawed uncomfortably. "My mother told me I can't play football. She says she doesn't want to see me crippled."

"Well, nobody does," the coach countered. "But she's going to let you play. She's okay with it."

"You talked to her?"

"Mr. Justiss did."

"Swell!"

"You know, son, you can be a great player if you choose to be. You may even have a chance to play college ball."

Buryl sat up a little straighter and looked the coach in the eye. Berry now had his complete attention.

"But if you want to play ball, there'll be a price. You'll have to work hard and press through the tough times. You can never give up. And more important, you'll have to go to school, make good grades, and stay out of trouble. You can't hang around with troublemakers. Do you understand?"

"Yes, sir."

"Good. You think about it, and we'll talk more tomorrow."

For the rest of the semester, Coach Berry talked with the teenager frequently, usually cornering him at the back of freshman study hall. A few weeks later, he noticed that Buryl was absent from school again, and once again he tracked him down and escorted him back to class. But he remained upbeat in reasoning with the boy. "Let me tell you something, Buryl. Anybody that's ever done anything worthwhile has experienced difficulty. Successful people work through those things. Success is always on the other side of discouragement. That's what I'm telling you. Never give up!"

This all sounded easy, but it wasn't. Buryl still hadn't recovered from his shoulder injury and he still couldn't play football, even with his mother's permission. He watched the last few games of the season from the sidelines, in street clothes.

But Coach Berry knew that if he could just keep his young player inspired, great things would come.

3 Coach Raymond Berry and the Seeds of Success

When Buryl reflected on his injury-shortened first season under Coach Berry, he vividly recalled how drained he had felt after that first practice. It had been a scorching hot first of September, 1938. Only days before drills had started, the temperature reached a record high of 115 degrees. Dry, sandy-colored grass, crisped by the summer heat, crunched underfoot everywhere—except on the practice field. That had been watered daily. Its thick green Bermuda turf was freshly mowed and chalk-striped. The smell of cut grass always accompanied the start of football season, the most exciting time of the year. It was as if a magnet had pulled Buryl to the gridiron.

This was Texas, after all. And since the turn of the century, high school football had been its chief form of entertainment—an obsession—in every town across the state. Nothing could equal the thrill of taking the field to the cheers of the hometown crowd, then pushing the football across the goal—or simply knocking an opponent on his butt. Younger boys idolized their town's football players and dreamed of the day when they too could play for the high school team. Fans of all ages filled the stands and shouted encouragement and advice to the hometown heroes, while bands marched and cheerleaders bounced and yelled and waved pompoms. Paris's team was a fixture of community pride—but the town longed for a winner.

That fall of 1938 was significant not only because it was Buryl's first varsity football season at Paris High; it was also Coach Berry's. Raymond Berry was a great hire, one over which the school and the town celebrated. He brought a wealth of experience and, fans hoped, his winning ways. He was an impressive man, hard, lean, nearly six feet tall, with dark eyes and thick dark hair and brows. His presence was calm, his voice deep and commanding. Berry had begun his coaching career under the legendary Pete Shotwell at Breckenridge. There and at Knute Rockne's coaching clinics, he had benefited from excellent mentoring. But he had also witnessed the seedy side of Texas high school football— gambling, cheating, bribing of referees, illegal recruiting, and the worst of town politics. After four years Berry moved on to Corpus Christi High, where he was promoted to head coach the next season. His Buccaneers advanced to the '35 state semi-finals and '36 quarterfinals, but in 1937 they were denied a third consecutive playoff run by losing the final regular season game to undefeated rival Robstown, finishing 9–1. Strangely, despite his stellar record, Berry was fired. According to his son, the termination was orchestrated by angry townsmen, probably including many who had lost money on this one-point defeat. Of course, coaches were always easy scapegoats. Assistant Harry Stiteler succeeded Berry as head coach in Corpus, and Berry went to Paris.

Raymond Berry was a "fundamentals" coach to his core, and he believed that a game was won on the practice field the week before it was played. He was skilled in the motivational power of words, and he got the very best from every player. "There's always a way to beat the other team, and *you* can beat 'em!" he would shout. On the other hand, he didn't tolerate a halfhearted effort from anybody, on or off the field. He personally checked every boy's weekly grade and citizenship reports. Profanity and "smart-talking" were prohibited, and offenders were sternly disciplined. "I'll take care of the heavy cussing," Coach Berry was fond of saying, although actually, he rarely swore.

Buryl and his teammates had never worked so hard as they did in Berry's first year in Paris, and the stifling September heat intensified their misery. At times, painfully sore and drained of energy, the sweaty players could barely muster the strength to jog from the huddle to the line of scrimmage. But when the ball was snapped, Coach Berry accepted nothing less than perfection. "Full speed!" he would yell. He was meticulous and exacting about every aspect of the game. For example, when a particular play didn't work well in a drill, he would shout, "Run it again!" If the boys botched the play a second time, once again they heard, "Run it again!" This pattern continued until the repetition resulted in a successful outcome. Then Berry finished each practice off with a healthy dose of conditioning drills. He knew what it took to build a winner.

Nevertheless, that first, 1938 season of Berry's had not gone well. Buryl had earned a starting backfield position in only his second game, but when he lunged at an opponent for a tackle, his shoulder exploded with pain. It had separated. The coach jerked it back into its socket, but this marked the end of Buryl's season—and the beginning of his truancy. Meanwhile, the team persevered. Despite all its hard work, however, Paris High lost four of its last six games and took a final-game thumping by Sherman to finish the '38 season with a 4–6 record. Players rationalized the final loss in the locker room, dismissing it with, "Oh, well, we've *never* beaten Sherman." In fact, many players acted glad the season was over.

Coach Berry, however, did not so readily resign himself to failure. In his post-game speech, which the team assumed would mark an end to football until spring practice in April, he delivered a surprise.

"Boys," he announced, "we didn't play well at the close of the season, and I don't like to lose. We're gonna fix this problem. I want every underclassman to report to this field house for practice on Monday, immediately after class."

The team showed up and they practiced. They also practiced the next day and the next, and the day after that. At the time there were no restrictions on the number of practice sessions allowed during the off-season, and the Paris Wildcats turned out in full pads every weekday afternoon from that speech in November until school let out in May. Berry pounded fundamental, hard-nosed football into every player on his team. Observers could hear the loud "pop" of pads from clear across the field. "Hit 'em hard and wrap 'em up!" yelled coaches during tackling drills. Coach Berry was planting the seeds of success.

. . .

By the time the '39 season came around, every player knew how to execute the fundamentals of the game. As a sophomore with big-play ability, Buryl made a significant contribution to the team and refined his skills. However, his injured left shoulder frequently popped out of joint, and it would plague him for the rest of his football career.

That second season, 1939, the Wildcats posted a respectable 6–3–1 record. And more importantly, players and townspeople got a taste of winning. It tasted good.

4 Breakout! 1940 Season

"Men, this is a football. Spelled F-O-O-T-B-A-L-L! You older players think you recognize it, but I'm going to formally reintroduce it to you today."

Upperclassmen had heard this exact speech from Coach Berry in each of their two previous seasons, but it still captured their attention.

"This ball is essential to the game. The objectives are simple: you want to carry this football across the opponent's goal line as many times as possible, and you want to prevent the opponent from advancing it across your own goal line. And while the objectives are straightforward, the rules and tactics are more complicated. Therefore, we will now discuss, in detail, the rules of football. And when we start our drills this morning, we will be working on the tactics."

Then, with each regulation, Berry provided an example, referencing two of his best former players, Charlie Haas from Corpus Christi and "Boone" Magness from Breckenridge. He chronicled their exploits in great detail—even embellished them, perhaps—to emphasize each important point. Paris's players were awed by these legendary heroics. "Did Haas and Magness really exist?" they sometimes wondered. (They did; and both are members of the Texas High School Football Hall of Fame.) Berry's boys would hear those hallowed names many more times as their high school careers progressed.

On that first day of camp, Coach Berry also introduced the new team "mascot," his grade-school-aged son. Like most coaches' sons—in fact, like most younger kids generally—Raymond Emmett idolized these big-time varsity players and dreamed of one day suiting up for the Wildcats. He fetched footballs and kicking tees, and in his miniature Wildcat uniform stood on the sidelines next to his favorite players during games, running water to the huddle during timeouts. Young Berry lived and died by the fate of the Wildcats.[1]

The previous year's winning season had generated considerable enthusiasm among Wildcat faithful, and a strong core of talent had returned, including a healthy and more mature Buryl Baty. Hopes ran high. Of course, the more cynical folks doubted that the town could ever field a real winner. "They've always folded under pressure in the past," these naysayers muttered. But the optimism of the steadfast was rewarded as the Wildcats marched through the first two-thirds of the season like the blitzkrieg on the other side of the globe. They scored 157 points against a total of only 6 for all seven opponents combined. Buryl, the junior co-captain, led the team in rushing, passing, and scoring, kicked extra points, and was one of Paris's leading defenders. "Baty's brilliant running and passing dazzled opposing squads," crowed the *Paris News*. Nobody could stop Baty.

He was in a zone.

Next the Wildcats won a close 6–0 contest over Texarkana, where Buryl re-injured his shoulder and sat out the remainder of the game, and they routed Bonham 28–0, in a contest for which Buryl did not suit up.

The next opponent stacked up as the biggest yet. The 8–0 Sherman Bearcats, who were reigning district champs and ranked number one in the state, were favored by two touchdowns over Paris, according to bookies. In the days leading up to the game, no one dared to voice what everyone knew—that Paris had never beaten Sherman. Unless the Wildcats could overcome years of history, the Bearcats would crush them in their quest for a first championship. The stakes were huge, and anxiety intensified by the day. Nevertheless, in the face of all this, Coach Berry kept his team convinced that they could nail down a victory.

On the cool, clear Friday evening of the game, wild yells and clapping echoed off the Paris field house's cinderblock walls as the players lunged out through its metal doors. Standing fans parted to make a path for the Wildcats (including Buryl Baty) to sprint toward the field. Everybody in the stadium had wondered if he would be able to return after his injury. In his mind, however, there had been no doubt. "In the first half," the *Paris News* would report the next day, "tailback Buryl Baty burst through the line for a thirty-four-yard touchdown, setting up his downfield blockers masterfully along the way." Evidently, his shoulder pain was bearable.

At halftime Coach Berry summoned one of his student equipment managers. "Son, run across to the store and buy me some chewin' tobacco!" He had already chewed through his entire tobacco supply during the first two quarters.

Late in the third quarter, Sherman finally pushed the ball across the goal to even the score. At that point, the game could have gone either way. Paris answered to regain the decisive lead, 14–7, and the Wildcats moved one step closer to their dream, the state playoffs.

"This is the finest game you boys have played," Coach Berry told his euphoric team afterwards. Loud whoops and hollers echoed through the locker room. More enthusiastic chatter followed as the guys showered and dressed. Outside, a crowd of fired-up fans waited for the victors. Handshakes and hugs from parents, siblings, and a girlfriend or two greeted the players. Still decked out in her blue satin drum-major uniform, Bo Hutchinson was among many who congratulated Buryl. They had agreed to a date later at the victory party in the gym. "I'll pick you up," he reminded her, as if she needed reminding. Meanwhile, fans paraded through Paris in their cars, honking, hollering, and carrying on in celebration.

Bo and Buryl had known each other for a long time, because in this small town everyone knew everyone else. Bo's earliest memory of Buryl was of a little boy in scruffy overalls, hurling rocks in her direction as she and some friends walked past the park. From Bo's point of view, this was not a favorable beginning. But by the time he was a high school junior, Buryl's persistence had resulted in their dating occasionally.

But Bo was a beautiful and popular girl, and she had many suitors. With her black hair, dark eyes, symmetrical features, and movie-star smile, she stood out in a crowd. She dated Steve Beard (who lived across the street from her), Fred Milsap (a Texas A&M freshman who sent her letter after letter), and Lowry "Louse" Inzer, a senior at PHS. In fact, her diary attests that she regularly fielded several date requests a day. In the early fall of 1940 she had dated Lowry most often. "I really like Lowry," one diary entry from that year read. "He's the nicest boy I've ever known." And "I'm crazy about Louse!"

Buryl had to hustle to get ahead of the pack. He also had a mountain to climb if he was to win over Bo's protective father.

However, for now, Buryl had other things to think about. The final game against Denison's Yellow Jackets (which, according to the *Paris News,* was marked by a "brilliant Baty performance"), resulted in a Wildcat rout, 28–0, clinching the district championship. "On to the state playoffs!" shouted the public address announcer, who then urged students to attend the post-game victory party in the gymnasium.

The next morning it was announced that the Wildcats' bi-district opponent would be the Greenville Lions, former state champions and current winners of the tough Highland Park district.

Assistant Coach Lively's scouting report warned, "This is one of the toughest teams in Texas. It'll take our best game of the year to beat them."

5 The State Playoffs

It was a cold, windy December day in Greenville. A train—the "Wildcat Special"—had transported hundreds of fans to watch the Saturday afternoon game. They were bundled up in their warmest coats, hats, gloves, and blankets and were greeted by Greenville cheerleaders selling game programs inside the front gate. Teenaged girls and boys flirted around the crowded concession stand, where local booster-club volunteers sold snacks, cold drinks, hot chocolate, and coffee. The hot drinks would sell out quickly, so only the fans with thermos jugs would enjoy warming refreshments in the second half.

Paris fans were happy to be here. They hoped for a win, but they would be plenty happy with the season regardless of the outcome. Wildcat players shivered from the cold, and perhaps because they were more nervous than they had ever been before. This was the first playoff game the school's football team had ever qualified for. All week Coach Berry had planted in their brains the thought, "We're gonna win this game, whatever it takes!"

"Remember," he advised the team on game day—"those boys put on their jockey straps the same as you do. They've got nothin' on you. You're here to win. Just play your game."

In the first quarter, Buryl Baty capped an eighty-yard drive with a nine-yard touchdown pass and kicked the extra point to put Paris up 7–0. But Greenville's defense tightened. After two scoreless frames, Greenville finally answered with a touchdown of its own early in the fourth quarter. Celebrating farmers and ranchers honked horns from their pickups outside the end zone fence, all but drowning out cheers from the hometown fans in the bleachers. The racket ceased, however, when the point-after kick failed to go through the uprights. Paris held on to its slim advantage to win 7–6. All of Paris reveled in the victory. On to the quarterfinals!

In the small, isolated town, the bi-district champions were all heroes. But Buryl Baty's performances leading up to this point in the season had drawn the attention of high school fans, news reporters, and college coaches all across Texas. Buryl had piled up rushing and passing yards, rushing and passing touchdowns, points, and school records. He had troubled every opponent and dominated games. He had earned his acclaim.

Meanwhile, the war dominated headlines. Reports of British bombers being repulsed by German anti-aircraft fire and of German air raids on London were coupled with the announcement of the Selective Service and Training Act. This act reinstated the draft for only the second time since the American Civil War. Every male citizen and resident alien between twenty-one and twenty-five years of age was required to register for military service. But twenty-one seemed pretty far away to these boys in Paris, Texas.

With a victory over Dallas's champion, Sunset High, the undefeated Masonic Home had earned the right to face Paris, now ranked number one in the state. Masonic Home had inspired a reputation bordering on the legendary. Coach Rusty Russell had worked his scrappy bunch of orphans year-round, to which rival coaches objected, resulting in a well-drilled and formidable varsity, a farm system of younger boys, and a legacy of successful state playoff campaigns. These Mighty Mites had captured the hearts of Ft. Worth fans and media. Coach Russell won the coin flip and declared his home stadium, the new Farrington Field, as the site of the game.

Excitement over the playoff soared. The *Fort Worth Star-Telegram*'s Frank X. Tolbert wrote, "Buryl Baty is the heart, soul and gizzard of the Paris Wildcats."[1]

Not unexpectedly, Mother Nature's influence intensified. The previous game in Greenville had been a cold one, but an outright blizzard trumped Greenville's weather in spades. Temperatures in the twenties were worsened by biting, howling winds and sleet. Nevertheless, an undaunted contingent of fans rode the train to Fort Worth that morning, and the Wildcats arrived by bus well in advance of the 2 p.m. kickoff.

The team hustled into what they assumed would be a warm locker room. But the visitors' quarters had no heat and provided only sterile wooden benches on a concrete floor in a room that felt like a Deepfreeze. The coaches wondered if the home team had heaters. Despite several layers of t-shirts and sweatshirts under their jerseys, Wildcat players' teeth chattered. Coach Berry plotted a solution. With a few wooden slats from some old pallets in the corner of the locker room and all the paper his equipment managers could gather, he improvised a campfire over a large drain in the middle of the concrete floor, and drew the long benches around it in a circle. Although the fire did begin to warm the room, unanticipated problems presented themselves. First, embers popped onto the players and their clothes, which were hanging from nearby locker hooks. Second, smoke accumulation made it difficult to catch a breath. The boys hurriedly doused the fire and opened every door and window to clear the air—so they could breathe. And shiver.

It was miserably cold on the slushy, slippery field. A blustering wind and freezing rain intensified the chill. Players constantly blew warm breath into their loose fists to regain the feeling in their numbed fingers. In the first quarter, Masonic Home twice mounted drives that were killed by stubborn Paris goal-line stands at the one-yard line. Then, suddenly, the home crowd was shocked and quieted when Baty broke two tackles and burst twenty-two yards for a second-quarter touchdown. His name blared across west Fort Worth as the public address announcer reported the play. The point-after kick, however, went wide in the gusting wind, so the Wildcats settled for a 6–0 lead to close out the half.

With uniforms soaking from the icy rain and wet turf, the locker room seemed even colder at halftime. The boys clinched their teeth against chattering as equipment managers replaced short cleats with longer ones to minimize slipping on the sloppy field. As the players sat trying to gather themselves, they heard their coach say, "It's just as cold for them as it is for us. Play just like you did in the first half and we win!" Then they jogged back onto the field and into the bitter, howling wind.

Early in the second half, huge Masonic end Ray Coulter put a crushing tackle on Baty, twisting his ankle under him. As Buryl limped painfully to the sideline, Paris fans groaned a collective "Oh, no!" And their greatest fear was realized; Paris's best passer, runner, and defensive safety was out of the game.

Once again the determined Wildcat linemen stopped a Mighty Mites drive at the Paris one. Fans marveled at the inspired defense. Then, halfway through the fourth quarter, Masonic Home threatened again. When their fourth-down pass fell harmlessly to the slushy end-zone turf, Wildcat fans began celebrating. Then, suddenly, a red penalty flag flew high in the air. "Pass interference!" yelled the referee. Coach Berry objected to the back judge, but his appeal fell on deaf ears. The penalty put the Mites on the one-yard line, with a first down. This time they punched the ball across the goal for six points. A gust of wind, however, blew the PAT wide of the uprights, and the game remained tied 6–6.

Paris fans were initially relieved that Masonic Home had been unable to forge ahead on the scoreboard, but they soon came to realize what every coach and official already knew—that the Mites had accumulated more penetrations (advances past the opponent's twenty-yard line) than the Wildcats and would advance to the next playoff game if the score remained tied.

"We need to score, boys!" Coach Berry yelled. Their championship hopes depended on it. But the game's remaining few minutes ticked away too quickly. The Mites were declared winners by virtue of penetrations. The Wildcats were stunned.

Players kicked their lockers and slammed their pads to the floor in disgust. Coach Berry seized the team's attention and offered congratulations on a great season: "It hurts right now," he said, "but you can be proud. You went 11–0–1. Most teams *never* experience a season like this." His comments were answered with silence.

After learning that the roads were too slick for a safe return home by bus, Coach Berry arranged for his team to go back on the Wildcat Special. After quick, icy-cold showers in the sullen locker room, the Wildcats rushed to the train depot.

In the passenger cars sat subdued Paris fans, cheerleaders, band members, and students. Bo Hutchinson was among those who had already boarded and claimed a seat. As Buryl passed her on his way to the designated team section, she whispered, "I saved a seat." She knew he would be disappointed about the loss, of course, but mostly, she just wanted to sit with him.

Bo's invitation gave Buryl an immediate rush. "I've got to check in with Coach first," he answered, and he couldn't circle back quickly enough. Still, once he sat down beside her, he had to let off some steam. "I can't believe this," he said. "We were the better team; we should be celebrating now."

"I know." Then, summoning a slight smile, she said, "But y'all just finished the best season Paris ever had." She paused. "Everybody in town is proud of what you've done. Maybe you should be proud, too." Buryl smiled his first smile of the day.

As Bo watched thick snowflakes falling outside her window the next day, she wrote in her diary, "I like Buryl a lot." She later added another entry: "I really do like Buryl. He's really swell. Oh boy!"

· · ·

That week, Buryl asked friends LV Morrow and James Jackson to help him and his father with a "hog killin'." As the old red rooster crowed that cold Saturday morning, the helpers were ready. For a year, Mr. Baty had corn-fed three hogs out in a pen behind his house. It was now time to harvest the crop. Mr. Baty had already built a raging fire to boil water in an old fifty-five-gallon barrel. He made a quick and painless kill on each hog with his .22 rifle, slit its throat to quickly drain the blood, and instructed the boys to "hold 'em one at a time by the hind legs, real tight, and dip 'em in the water till I tell you to pull 'em out." This task required all the endurance the boys could muster; their shoulder muscles burned from holding the suspended animals for what seemed like an eternity. Then, with the boys' help, Mr. Baty butchered the carcasses, cutting them for ham, bacon, pork chops, and other delicacies to be cured or refrigerated. Then he grinned and added, "We'll use everything but the squeal." By the time the guys had washed up, Mrs. Baty's kitchen oozed with the mouthwatering aroma of fresh fried pork chops.

On weekends, Buryl enjoyed driving around town with James Jackson. One of the few boys with access to a car, James was tall, slender, and one of the nicest guys around. He was quite a talker. The two boys spent many an hour cruising up and down the drag, around the square past the Palace, and out to the country and back. And they sometimes hunted in the fields near James's father's farm.

One afternoon an Aggie alum invited Buryl and James to stop by his house. "I have something for you," he said, as he handed Buryl a long, narrow box with a new shotgun inside. "You've done a lot for Paris." The Aggie took a deep breath. "Buryl, do me a favor. Don't let it be known where you got this, because some folks might mistake it as an enticement to go to A&M. And that's just not true." He paused. "Of course, I'd sure be excited to see you in an Aggie uniform. But this shotgun has nothing to do with that."

As spring fever set in, Paris boys did what boys do. Wedged in between track practice, spring training for football, and cruising the town, girls were on their minds. Occasionally a couple of boys would have words over a pretty female classmate and vow to settle the issue by duking it out at the roadside park on the East Highway. They usually arrived to find several cars full of adrenaline-fueled boys waiting to watch the fight. The few punches landed among the loud cheers typically took only a minute or two. Afterward, the victor and his opponent shook hands in a show of magnanimous respect.

Meanwhile, townspeople read accounts of the war in Europe. The Nazis were within seventy-five miles of Paris. Adults understood the implications of these overseas events, but for teenagers, they were scarcely real—they were a world away. The Nazi army was nowhere near Paris, Texas.

Aggie boosters arranged summer jobs on a survey crew for Buryl, James, and Ollie Jack. At three dollars a day for a ten-hour workday, this was a marked improvement over their previous farm jobs, which had required them to work from sunup to sundown for one dollar.

It never occurred to these boys that the carefree summer days might not come again. The threat of war was imminent. But for now they counted the days and could not contain their enthusiasm for football season.

6 Bo and Buryl

Competition was intense, but Buryl would not back down. He had his eye on Bo.

One clear, cold, starry night, Lowry Inzer drove Bo home from a date. He found Buryl waiting quietly on her front porch. Lowry sped away in a huff, leaving Buryl to spend some time with Bo alone.

On another occasion, Bo had accepted Fred Milsap's invitation to a dance party. Buryl pled with her to break the date and go with him instead, but she stubbornly refused. She was not surprised to see Buryl and a friend at the dance. However, she *was* surprised that he and his buddy sat in the booth next to her and her date at the all-night diner, clear up in Hugo, Oklahoma, after the party.

It was easy to understand why these teenagers were becoming an item. Bo Hutchinson, with her magnetic smile, was one of the prettiest and most personable girls in town. Buryl, over six feet tall and with high Cherokee cheekbones, was equally good-looking and popular. They were comfortable with each other and enjoyed each other's company, Bo in her reserved manner and Buryl in his more playful one. And they spent a lot of time on Bo's front porch.

This porch projected from the Hutchinsons' hundred-year-old two-story house on a main thoroughfare between the train depot and the center of town. There was not much happening in Paris, but when excitement did come along, the folks on 6th SE Street were among the first to know. Almost every important visitor to town—and even most of the indigents—passed by this house on the way to or from the train station.

Bo's kind-hearted, soft-spoken mother, Opal, frequently handed sandwiches to scruffy boxcar hoboes who walked past the house. She would quietly wave them around to the back door to shield them from the disapproving stares of two busybody next-door neighbors. Mrs. Logue, on the one side, would not allow kids into her fenced yard to retrieve lost balls. And on the other side Mrs. Gerber, when she saw weekend golfer Mr. Hutchinson happily practicing his chipping in the front yard, would demand from her porch, "Mr. Hutchins, don't you have something better to do?" (She always mispronounced his name.) Opal also, on most days, gave fresh buttermilk to another neighbor's maid.

The house was rather basic by today's standards. With only oscillating fans and screened windows for ventilation, and space heaters and a downstairs fireplace for warmth, the Hutchinson home sweltered in the summers and froze in the winters. It would be decades before the new invention, air conditioning, was available and affordable to average people. During the brutal summers, the Hutchinsons sat in the backyard under the shade of huge pecan trees. On cold nights the family heated bricks in the fireplace, wrapped them in towels, and placed them in their frigid beds.

This family was typical of the era. Albert Hutchinson, a bald, bespectacled banker, a World War I veteran, and a survivor of the Great Depression, was extremely frugal, as the times dictated. He once warned his wife, "Don't be surprised if I come home unemployed one day. Banks are failing everywhere, and I may never find another job in this economy." He taught his five daughters and his son the value of money. When one of them went to the picture show, he provided a dime and demanded a nickel in change upon her return. He paid each of his two oldest daughters twenty-five cents a week for watering the cow, whose daily milking provided not only fresh milk, cream, and buttermilk, but also cheese and, in the hot summers, ice cream. Mr. Hutchinson's matronly wife cooked breakfast every morning, then cleaned the kitchen and washed the dishes, did the laundry, and prepared the next meal before the day got too hot. Every member of the family walked home for a hot lunch, and by mid-afternoon, Mrs. Hutchinson was cooking again. She was afforded one small luxury—ordering groceries by phone for delivery. After lively conversation around the big supper table, the girls washed the dishes and cleaned the kitchen. Later, the adults and older siblings often sat talking on the front porch while the younger children tumbled in the grass, ran through the house, or climbed on the massive banisters.

The Hutchinson children created their own entertainment. They invented games and rode bikes for hours through the neighborhood. They attended Sunday school with friends, they read books, and they never missed mixing with classmates at the local Friday-night football games. They spent countless hours at the roller-skating rink. And they gathered around the radio in the evenings for such programs as *Little*

Orphan Annie, Let's Pretend, The Shadow, and *Jack Armstrong, the All-American Boy.*

As the little girls became young ladies, the Hutchinson home was filled with a different kind of energy. The family phone rang off the hook, and Bo spent a great deal of time talking on it, with the cord pulled down the hall and into the bathroom, door closed. As she spoke softly into the mouthpiece, her little sisters listened as best they could and whispered excitedly to each other, "Who is she talking to? Is it Lowry, or is it Buryl?" But Bo's ears became very sensitive to noises from the hall, and she quickly shooed away all eavesdroppers. She also learned not to say anything she didn't want repeated, as someone might be listening—if not outside the bathroom door, then on the party line. With five sisters in the house, the bathroom was always crowded. And, of course, like most siblings, the Hutchinson offspring occasionally had their conflicts.

Daddy Hutchinson kept a tight rein on his girls and paid close attention to the boys they dated. He imposed a curfew, but allowed the girls to sit on the front porch with their friends or dates if they were home on time. Quietly, however, Mr. Hutchinson was concerned about Bo's apparent infatuation with Buryl. "I think she'll get over him," he whispered to his wife.

Meanwhile, Buryl became very popular with Bo's siblings. Eleven-year-old Jeannie, as many younger sisters are prone to do, developed a crush on her big sister's boyfriend. Anytime Buryl was expected, Jeannie was poised to be the first to greet him. When a knock came at the door, she raced out of the kitchen, down the hall, and around the staircase to open the front door before Bo got there. And, of course, Jeannie and sister Glenda yearned to read Bo's diary. That ambition, however, remained unfulfilled, as Bo kept her memoirs securely locked in her cedar chest. But just before the end of the semester, she brought home her signed Paris High yearbook and accidentally left it on the round kitchen table. Her father could not ignore what was written on one of its pages:

Dear Bo,

To the swellest girl I know. I have really enjoyed your friendship and going with you. You know I wish it could amount to something more than a friendship, but you say you are not ready for any such thing. Wishing you all the success and happiness in

the world. I think you are the tops of them all, and good looking
too. Stay in there and carry that flag for us next year, you have
what it takes.

   Love,
   Buryl Baty

Mr. Hutchinson took alarm. He objected to what he considered the Baty boy's provocative comments. Nobody was good enough for his daughter—and certainly not this blue-collar boy. "Those comments are not appropriate!" he declared.

"I know you don't like him, Daddy, but Buryl is a nice boy," Bo cried.

"I didn't say I don't like him. But I don't want you going with him. I want better for you."

"That's not fair, Daddy!"

• • •

Bo and Buryl frequently double-dated. Moving "picture shows" were a favorite American pastime, and all of the popular films were featured at one or the other of Paris's two downtown theaters. The couple arrived early with their doubling friends to grab good seats, watch the previews and war reports, and share a box of popcorn. Most often, they had planned to see the current movie months in advance, because when the previews ended, Buryl always whispered, "Let's see that show together." Of course, Bo usually answered in the affirmative, brown eyes sparkling. When the lights darkened, Buryl shifted in his seat and moved a little closer to his date.

7 The Mighty Paris Wildcats

FALL 1941

Last year's impressive season had set the stage, and finally the time had arrived. On the last Friday in August, the Wildcat Booster Club sponsored a fund-raising barbeque. All seventy-five players ate for free, and fans paid a dollar each. A huge crowd showed up on a still, hot evening and sat at picnic tables under the park's great trees. The sound of loud talking and laughing carried for blocks, and optimism filled the air; these reigning bi-district champs would be disappointed with anything less than a state title.

Upperclassmen had endured intense two-a-day practices before. In previous years, big LV Morrow had thrown up just about every day. He pledged to himself that this preseason would be different, and he worked out diligently all summer so that he could breeze through the two-a-days. "I'll shine, while the guys who don't work out," LV reasoned, "will puke their guts out!"

Coach Berry kicked off preseason by lecturing about "the rules of the game." Next, fundamental skills were emphasized and seemingly endless conditioning drills were run. To dodge the oppressive heat, the grueling two-a-day practices took place at 7:30 a.m. and 4:30 p.m. LV Morrow, in spite of all his preparation, bent over to heave daily.

During the first week of school, Principal Tom Justiss announced the new class officers, along with officers of the German, Spanish, and Latin Clubs. He also heralded the newly elected football co-captains, Luke Abbett and Buryl Baty.

Buryl's father was especially excited at the arrival of football season. He loved walking to the stadium on Friday nights to watch his son play ball, and his younger children usually accompanied him. Little sister June was enthralled by the cheerleaders, the band music, the fanfare. Burton smiled when he heard her scream, "Look, Daddy, there's Buryl!"

The Wildcats clinched the season opener, and Bo and Buryl attended the victory party in the gym after the game. After a second victory, the Wildcats prepared for the next game in Sulphur Springs. As he closed

Thursday's light workout, Coach Berry blew his shrill whistle to capture everyone's attention. "Listen up! The bus starts loading at one thirty tomorrow. Remember, you're each responsible for your own equipment. If you get to Sulphur Springs without *all* of your gear, you will not play in the game. Normal travel attire: coats and ties as always. And I want everybody to get plenty of sleep tonight." The boys had heard this lecture before.

The coaches began the walk back to the field house while the team held their ground for a bit of traditional pregame inspiration. Suddenly, eyes turned to a co-captain's loud declaration. "Boys, after a shit, shower, and shine, I have a date tonight . . . then we're off to Sulphur Springs tomorrow!" Buryl grinned broadly as the whole team erupted in yelps and laughter.

"Buryl!" A deep voice interrupted the ruckus. Everyone shifted their attention in its direction. "Buryl, you know better than to talk like that. Take five laps," ordered the not-quite-out-of-earshot Coach Berry. "And everybody who laughed—run two laps!" The entire team took off running.

Luke Abbett noticed a slight grin twitching in the corners of Coach Berry's mouth. And Buryl would never live down the incident with his friends.

The following night in the quiet pregame locker room, Buryl and James noticed Ollie moving nervously from teammate to teammate, whispering something. Each inquiry resulted in the teammate's shaking his head. Ollie seemed to be more panicked by the minute. Finally, his predicament became clear as he whispered to Buryl and James, "Do either of you have an extra jock strap?"

"Yep, I do. But I don't think it's been washed," James said. "Do you mind wearing a dirty jock?"

"Nope, I don't care one bit. Coach won't let me play if I don't have a jockey strap."

"Well it's your lucky day, Ollie. And it *has* been washed," James grinned.

"Thank you! I owe you one." Ollie gleefully shook James's hand as Buryl fought to hold back his own laughter.

By the time they started back to Paris, the Wildcats had crushed their third opponent of the season. And according to the *Paris News*, Baty's performances were "spellbinding sportswriters and fans."

The next game was in Sherman. Paris traveled there for the inaugural season in the new Bearcat Stadium. Sherman's welcome, however, was not a friendly one. On the first play of the game, Paris's linemen were slammed in the face with fists and elbows. On the second play, Wildcats caught more slugs and assaults of profanity. Luke Abbett, the quiet co-captain, spoke to his teammates in the huddle. Coolly, in his deep East Texas twang, he said, "They're just trying to distract us. Let's keep our mouths shut and stick our game down their throats." On the next play, the third of the game, Baty ran sixty-five yards to a touchdown, and he later added two more scores.

Paris rolled over the Bearcats for the second consecutive year, 32–6, but Sherman's fans atoned for the loss . . . in the parking lot. After the game, Paris Wildcat fans, many of whom had washed and polished their cars and decorated them with blue and white streamers, met an infuriating sight. Disgruntled local fans had driven shiny new nails into their tires, deflating them. Evidently, the vandals had not enjoyed the game.

Baty led the next victory, over Arlington, with two TD passes and vintage touchdown runs of twenty-five and eighty-four yards. The team was on a roll, and the kids were feeling their oats. After a locker-room celebration and hot showers, players scattered to the square. Several guys were cutting up outside the soda shop, milkshakes in hand, when Coach Lively drove up. He had just scouted Denison, the next opponent, and hadn't heard the results of the Wildcats' game. He knew he would find people congregating on the square. Seeing this group of players under the streetlight, he stopped at the curb, rolled down his window, and asked, "How did we do?"

"We killed 'em, Coach, 40–7," Ollie answered.

Coach Lively exploded out of the car and into the boys' faces. "You let those guys score? What was wrong with you!" he screamed. The boys were speechless. But the following Friday night, they responded with a 24–0 romp over the previously undefeated Denison Yellow Jackets. Statewide acclaim grew.

• • •

Early the next week, the Cole Brothers Circus paraded from the train depot past the Hutchinson family's front porch, en route to their performance site. A lively rhythm first announced the procession from blocks away. Soon a uniformed band marched past with drums beating and trumpets blaring. Then followed colorful jesting clowns with big feet and red noses, beautifully costumed performers on majestic Arabian horses, and horse-drawn wagons with cages housing lions and tigers. And finally several huge elephants trooped past, led by trainers holding long prods. Fortunately, two men followed the procession with shovels and buckets in hand. From the Hutchinson's vantage point, the parade may have been better than the circus itself.

Buryl sprained his ankle again in a midweek practice. But with another Coach Berry tape job, he managed to take the field early in a 44–0 rout of Texarkana. Buryl escorted Bo to the circus that weekend, then led the Wildcats to a 34–0 win over McKinney six days later.

Bo and Buryl dated fairly steadily, but at one point, for some reason, they had broken up. Bill Booth, a fun-loving friend, took it upon himself to set Buryl up with a date. "Come on," he coaxed. "She thinks you're cute, and she likes to have a good time. We'll grab a malt and then go parking."

"I don't know, Bill."

"But Bo has a date. Come on."

"Oh, all right."

The next day, when James Jackson inquired about the date, Buryl shook his head. "Too fast for me!" he said.

At 8–0 for the year, PHS had to survive only Gainesville and Bonham to have a second consecutive undefeated regular season. But Gainesville had other plans. The Leopards' Coach Lindsey aspired to the same district championship and had his team fired up to seize an upset on Thanksgiving Day. "Gainesville is a tough team," Coach Berry warned. "We'll have to play our best game to beat 'em."

Across Paris, signs displayed words of encouragement: "Win district! Win state!"

The night before the big game, Buryl paid a visit to Bo on the Hutchinson's front porch. She had heard about Buryl's date and made her displeasure known. "If you go out with girls like that, people will wonder about the other girls you date. You have to decide which way you want it, because I won't risk ruining my reputation."

Buryl was silent for a moment. "Bo, you're right. I apologize. And just so you know, you're the only one I'm interested in." Bo felt better, although it would take a couple of days' festering for her to completely let it go. They sat on the porch until almost midnight. After this, according to good friend Bill Booth, they dated only each other.

The next day dawned cool and clear. It was Thanksgiving, and lively fans packed Gainesville's stadium. Also attending were scouts from the Highland Park Scots and from several colleges.

All the hype was justified. Gainesville had come to play ball this afternoon, while the favored Wildcats seemed flat and lethargic. After a halftime scoreless tie, the inspired Leopards forged ahead 7–0 early in the third quarter. This was the first time the Wildcats had trailed all season. Gainesville fans celebrated wildly over a possible upset in the making. Paris knew they had to answer.

They answered. Baty ran for a touchdown. This started the fireworks. Red Hudson picked up a Gainesville fumble and ran it back thirty-eight yards for a score. Baty ran in another TD early in the fourth. Gainesville countered to narrow the margin to 21–14 and, after holding the Wildcats, mounted another drive. Momentum seemed to shift. A touchdown would tie the game. Every person in the stadium nervously stood and cheered. Now deep in Paris territory, Gainesville's tailback passed toward an open receiver.

Suddenly, Buryl Baty jumped in front of the receiver to intercept the pass, killing the drive. But he was not finished. His deft running and passing, including a twenty-seven-yard completion to James Jackson, moved the Wildcats into scoring position. Buryl carried the ball to pay dirt for the game-clinching final points.

Sunday's *Paris News* reported, "Buryl Baty played one of the grandest games of his career Thursday. . . ."

"Bullet Buryl scored three touchdowns and kicked four extra points to run his season total to 143 points. Besides this, the All-State candidate completed seven of eleven passes attempted and played a smashing defensive game."

Luke Abbett said about the game later, "I've never seen a player take a team on his shoulders and carry them to victory like Buryl did that day."

On the Monday after that game, *The Paris News* announced that "Buryl Baty accepted an offer to play football at Texas A&M on a full scholarship next season."

Buryl's parents beamed with pride.

The Wildcats next polished off Bonham 35–0 to win their tenth game of the year.

For the second consecutive year, Paris finished the regular season unbeaten. Their first playoff game would pit them against a young Bobby Layne and his Highland Park Scotties. This game would not only serve as the first step on the way to the state championship, it would also represent a clash of cultures—country town vs. affluent suburb. It was the talk of North Texas. Paris storefronts displayed signs of encouragement: "Go Wildcats! Win State!" On a chilly Saturday morning, the nervous Wildcats boarded a bus for Dallas to seize their destiny.

Both teams were ready for a fight. But it seemed as if the Scots had a spy in Paris's huddle, as if they knew every play called before the Wildcats ran it. Baty again sprained his fragile ankle and had to exit the game. Everything went wrong, to the tune of a bitter 19–0 defeat. Paris's exuberance and towering expectations were abruptly replaced with shock and emptiness. Parisians fell into a state of mourning.

The next day, the small town was quiet, stunned, somber. Coach Berry opened the field house early for players to return equipment and clean out their lockers. Young Raymond Emmett Berry, who accompanied his father to every team function, was devastated. He had cried himself to sleep after the game, but tried to hide his tears that morning. Coaches and student managers loaded the washing machines with sweaty uniforms, socks, jocks, and t-shirts, and stacked shoulder pads and helmets on shelves in the rear of the wire-caged storage area. Without the normal, lively chatter, the sounds of these activities echoed loudly through the building.

Later that morning, Burton returned with his boys from Sunday school to an aroma-filled house. "Roast beef, gravy, and all the trimmings—come get it!" Bobbie announced. It was a Sunday dinner to restore the soul, and the boys were always easy to get to the table. Not a leftover could be found after they finished, and a couple of freshly baked cakes waited as desert. "You boys have hollow legs!" their mother marveled. Burton always smiled at this comment.

The boys hurriedly washed the dishes and cleaned the kitchen. They were anxious to settle in the living room—to listen to the Sunday afternoon pro football radio broadcast. The game announcer set the stage, describing the Redskins' red and gold uniforms and the Eagles' bright green and white attire. He began to announce the starting lineups before the kickoff.

Suddenly, the announcer's voice was interrupted by loud static, followed by a different, alarmed voice. It said, "The Japanese have attacked Pearl Harbor, Hawaii, by air."

The next morning, eighty million Americans sat next to their radios as President Roosevelt spoke. "Yesterday, December 7, 1941—a date which will live in infamy—the United States of America was suddenly and deliberately attacked by naval and air forces of the Empire of Japan," he began. And by the time he finished, he had declared war.

Older folks, who carried with them horrendous memories of the Great War, were petrified by this news. The younger generation, on the other hand, had little idea what to expect. But a cloud of uncertainty and fear was cast over Paris and the nation.

Life was about to change.

8 Can't Wait!

Hand-painted royal-blue and white spirit posters covered the auditorium walls. Drums beat and horns blared while cheerleaders jumped in unison for this all-school pep rally honoring the 1941 Wildcats.

Coach Berry took the stage and waved for the boys to stand. "These boys," he said, bending into the microphone and pointing to the dressed-up players behind him, "accomplished what no Paris team has ever accomplished; they went undefeated the past two regular seasons and won two consecutive district championships and one bi-district crown. They are the best team that Paris has ever put on the football field. Let's give 'em a big ovation!" The building seemed to shake as the crowd stood and roared.

When the cheering subsided, the players sat back down, and Berry acknowledged several seniors for their fine season. Then he summoned Buryl and Jack White to stand next to him. "Buryl Baty is the finest all-around tailback that I have ever coached!" he boomed to the crowd. It was no exaggeration. That year alone Buryl had rushed for 1468 yards and 22 touchdowns, passed for 725 yards and 13 TDs, and scored 160 points. He was twice team captain, twice All-District, and twice elected to the All-State team. The coach then added, with a note of unmistakable pride, "And we'll enjoy watching him on Saturdays at Texas A&M!"

Then, putting his arm around Jack's shoulders, Berry said, "And Jack White is the finest guard that I've ever coached." He also was twice All-State and twice All-District. "Jack hasn't decided yet where he's going, but you can bet he'll be a star at some college." Loud applause followed the coach's proclamation.

On that day, Buryl Baty and Jack White officially joined the elite company of Charlie Haas and "Boone" Magness in Coach Berry's traditional lectures and tall tales. They had secured their status as local legends.

Nobody ever played for my dad without a thorough indoctrination to Boone Magness, Charlie Haas, and Bullet Buryl Baty. He talked about Buryl Baty all the time. Any time he talked about football, those three names eventually came up in the conversation.—Raymond Emmett Berry

With the extended season now finished, the players had time to enjoy school activities, their friends, and soon, after completing final exams, the holidays. Buryl, of course, spent all the time he could with Bo over the break. And after they had celebrated at a New Year's Eve party in the junior college gym, they drove to the bridge outside of town on the East Highway to dance in the freezing night air.

Buryl graduated at midterm in January 1942 and waited to start college that next fall. Until then, he worked a well-paying oil field job, courtesy of an Aggie alum. He missed seeing Bo at school, but they got together most evenings. It wasn't long before football letter jackets arrived at the athletic office. "I'll pick it up for you," Bo insisted. Of course, she tried it on and liked the feel of it. That afternoon thirty Wildcat players, and Bo, proudly wore blue and white letter jackets to class.

When she came home wearing the jacket after school, her father shook his head, realizing that he was fighting an uphill battle. That spring, Bo's diary entries documented over eighty-four dates with Buryl from January through May.

Toward the end of the spring semester, yearbooks were delivered. When Buryl thumbed through Bo's annual, he was thrilled to find an empty page with "Reserved for Buryl Baty" written across the top in Bo's handwriting. On it he wrote:

Dear Bo,

About this time last year, I said something that seemed to get you in Dutch somewhere, this time I will try to keep that out.

Deeply Bo, you are the swellest girl I have ever known or met. Your personality is like some dream that came true. It keeps you and everyone around you going, except when you are mad, and then everything goes down. You are a dream girl who always gets the choice of everything.

I have enjoyed the good times we have had together, the bad too (on your side). The things we have done and the places we have been are nothing compared to what they will be someday in the future (college separates us).

I have never enjoyed a girl friendship as I have enjoyed yours. Bo, you are tops in all categories. Always remain the same, please.

It was an honor for us to have you as our Football Queen. You really made a swell one. I could go on talking and writing forever and never tell you any more than you already know. Rather than to mess up your whole book, I will stop here.

> *Je vous aime,*
> *Buryl Baty*

On the other side of the world, the Japanese onslaught in the Pacific seemed unstoppable. Large portions of North Africa, Europe, and Russia were occupied by Nazi forces, and Adolf Hitler labeled Winston Churchill and Franklin Roosevelt "war mongers." In retrospect, the spring of '42 marked the high point of Axis power. War was a dire certainty for these high schoolers as conscription legislation for eighteen-year-olds had begun to make its way through the nation's capitol.

Also that spring, Parisians were relieved that Coach Berry had declined nearby East Texas State College's offer to replace its recently drafted head coach. And Berry was intrigued that his former assistant and successor at Corpus, Harry Stiteler, had accepted the head coaching job at Waco High.

As the dog days of summer passed, the Paris High practice field was a busy place in the afternoons. Buryl, along with almost every other athlete in town, both high school and college, trained there daily for the upcoming football season. He knew the competition would be tough at A&M, and he wanted to be in the best condition possible. He could hardly wait.

Late in the summer, good friend and teammate Ollie Jack announced disappointing news. Although he had committed to go to A&M, he had changed his mind and was going to play ball for Baylor instead. "There's no girls at A&M, Baty!" Ollie explained.

Just before college football camps were to begin, Buryl and Jack White participated in the annual Oil Bowl all-star game in Wichita Falls, featuring the best high school players in Texas. The *Paris News* reported on the game with a headline reading, "Baty Shines as North Texas Team Wins." After both running and passing for touchdowns, Baty was elected Most Valuable Player of the game.

After a quick trip back through Paris on the night before leaving for College Station, Buryl and Bo sat together for several hours on her front porch. The next morning, the morning of his departure, Buryl sported a new haircut and his best Sunday suit. His mother wept as she clung to him a little longer. "I'm just going to college, Mom, and I promise to write," he consoled her.

Buryl and his father, each carrying a suitcase, walked to the train station. "We're proud of you, son," Burton said as they shook hands firmly.

"Thanks, Dad. I'll see you soon." Buryl turned and lifted his two bags up onto the train's second step. His dream was about to come true.

9 Big Time

FALL 1942

Buryl didn't know how long he would be at A&M; the war raging over-seas would eventually call. But for now, he relished the opportunity to play college ball. And he knew that A&M was the perfect place for him. The Aggies had been the best team in the Southwest Conference in 1940 and the National Champions in 1939. They had lost only one game in the previous two years (to their archrival, the University of Texas). The program attracted many of the best high school players in the state.

The A&M campus must have been intimidating to incoming fresh-men. The classical buildings rose grandly from the campus's flat, austere terrain and symbolized the soaring opportunities that education offers to students. About 6,600 young men were in attendance. Although the newcomers among them may not have realized it, Texas A&M was changing. A new curriculum, stricter discipline, and intensified military training were being put into effect. A&M's isolated rural campus was transitioning into a military camp.[1] Administrators were also discouraging certain time-honored traditions—freshman hazing, specifically paddling, had been declared unacceptable. But some things never change.

Football would remain an integral part of the A&M tradition. Each new freshman player was instructed to report first to the "quack shack" for his physical exam and then to the field house to acquire practice gear and instructions for registration and housing. At the football facility, players met briefly with freshman coaches who handed out checklists of items to be completed. These graduate assistants gruffly dictated how "Fish" would proceed through the first day and how they were expected to act in the company of upperclassmen.

These expectations seemed pretty clear. Fish should offer enthusiastic introductions and strong handshakes to every upperclassman they encountered. "Howdy, sir, I'm Fish Baty, from Paris, Texas. I'm glad to meet you, sir. Where are you from, sir? What are you studying, sir?" Afterwards, he was expected to greet each of these upperclassmen by name—"Howdy, Mister Smith!"—and remember every hometown and major. Memory lapses were punished by a motivational encounter with the "board." Most new Fish had heard about these rules but had no idea about the difficulty of the tasks or how painful each mistake might prove to be.

After this orientation, each Fish player went to the administration building where he was assigned to his military unit, issued uniforms, given a military-style buzz haircut, and rushed off to register for classes.

Fish Baty was one of nearly ninety hopefuls who suited up for the first morning practice. Five all-state players highlighted the group. In fact, the first and second teams consisted primarily of all-state and all-district recruits. It seemed an embarrassment of riches. Several unexpected "walk-ons" were also there after being told they had ten days to prove themselves. The odds would be stacked against these guys.

However, as Freshman Coach "Stuttering Lil" Dimmit quickly pointed out, "This first d-d-depth chart is based upon what you d-did in high school, but the d-d-depth chart for the first game will be based upon what you've d-d-done, starting today, since you got to college. Nothing is g-g-g-guaranteed; everybody has to earn his s-spot." It was a battle for every position.

These were tough, strong kids. It was evident from their slim, toned bodies and calloused hands that these boys had grown up working on farms and ranches and in the oil fields. They were as ready for college athletics as they could be.

However, few were ready for cadet life off the field.

• • •

Tradition at the Agricultural and Mechanical College of Texas ran deep. In fact, tradition was part of what had appealed to Buryl about the school. A&M had been founded in 1876 as a public land-grant college and as such was mandated to provide military training. At that time, nostalgia over the Old South and the "Lost Cause" was at an almost religious pitch in Texas. Along with the attachment to Southern sentiments went the idea that the soldier's values were the values of a sound citizenry. Many of A&M's founding administrators had attended military institutions before serving proudly as Confederate officers. In fact, Jefferson Davis, West Point graduate, former US senator, and more recently president of the Confederacy, was offered the first presidency at A&M. He gracefully declined.[2]

The Corps of Cadets was organized to weave military discipline into the education of a new generation of young Texans. Membership in the Corps, along with commitment to its regulations and values, was required of every student. The aim from the beginning was to develop and graduate good men.

In its beginning, the new college had been rugged and its students rough-edged and rowdy, but its sophistication and reputation for excellence increased dramatically over the decades. In 1891, "Sul" Ross, a former Texas Ranger, Confederate general, and governor of Texas, took on the presidency of the college, and his tenure secured A&M's future. He added buildings and raised academic standards, and during his administration, the first intercollegiate football team was formed, the first "Farmer" band was organized, the class ring was redesigned (to become much like today's), the Alumni Association was established, and a few trees were planted to complement the classic architecture on the bare campus.

Another improvement that Ross attempted at A&M met with less success. He tried to eradicate hazing, which had contributed to a freshman fallout rate of over 50 percent in most years. In an attempt to curb the practice, an early 1900's Texas Legislature passed a bill outlawing it as a misdemeanor, punishable by fine or imprisonment. Unfortunately, rapid A&M growth and inadequate oversight allowed the problem to continue unchecked.[3]

Hazing, of course, was never exclusive to Texas A&M. Just down the road, members of a University of Texas service organization (the Texas Cowboys) are known to have paddled their pledges until their posteriors bled, used cattle prods to induce a few more push-ups during intense calisthenics, and literally branded new members with permanent "UT" scars on their chests.[4]

Nonetheless, Sul Ross endeavored to banish the practice at A&M. In the fall of 1912, he dismissed twenty-seven cadets for "strapping" (whipping Fish with leather straps). In protest, over four hundred upperclassmen refused to go to class, resulting in their own dismissal. Eventually, this whole lot of cadets was given amnesty in exchange for their pledge to abstain from all forms of hazing.[5] But the tradition persisted.

In 1942, Aggie Fish were continuously pestered and humiliated by upperclassmen, and they provided a form of indentured servitude during most of their waking hours. They were required to wear raincoats and military-style Stetsons for their every trip to the bathroom down the hall. They were not allowed to walk on the sidewalks. They were forbidden to eat dessert.

Each morning at five thirty, the trumpets of reveille shattered the silence of night. Within twenty minutes, cadets had hurriedly made their beds and prepped their rooms for inspection, donned their uniforms, and raced out of the dorm to fall into shoulder-to-shoulder formation. There, the Fish were scrutinized to ensure that their shoes and brass belt buckles were perfectly polished, their uniforms impeccably ironed, their ties precisely tied, and their braces at attention sufficiently rigid. Anything short of perfection drew the wrath of older cadets. Nose-to-nose with offending Fish, upperclassmen screamed at them at the top of their lungs in the most intimidating manner and demanded motivational appointments (after the noon meal) with the "board." At precisely 6 a.m., bugles designated the call to breakfast formation, and classes started promptly at seven.

With white stripes sewed on their left uniform sleeves, Fish were easy to spot, and they were the objects of incessant attention from vindictive sophomores ("Pissheads"), who, as Fish the previous year, had endured the same persecution. Every day, Fish cleaned upperclassmen's rooms, made their beds, shined their shoes, polished their belt buckles, did their laundry, ironed their uniforms and boxer shorts, and completed countless other petty tasks. With their time consumed by Corps requirements and Pisshead demands, Fish could barely squeeze in their schoolwork and found zero time for relaxation.

A Fish might find himself spending the night polishing Sul Ross's statue or standing at uniformed attention until dawn, "guarding" the flagpole. And many other creative demands were made of underclassmen. For example, one particularly obnoxious sophomore from Amarillo, called "Butthole" in private, forced freshmen to consume entire jars of jalapeño peppers. These unfortunate Fish heaved for several hours, while they seethed with animosity toward the gloating Panhandle Pisshead.

Buryl had looked forward to eating at the mess halls. During his visits as a recruit, the food had seemed to be one of the more attractive benefits of A&M. It was fresh from the agricultural school's own dairy, vegetable farm, and cattle herd.

In reality, when each company marched into the mess hall three times a day, Fish were required to serve food to the upperclassmen, and they were not allowed to eat until the older cadets had finished two helpings. They had to sit at attention on the front six inches of their chairs at all times and request permission to take each bite—of whatever leftovers remained after upperclassmen had stuffed themselves. Poor table manners, a dropped utensil, or a minor spill resulted in swats after the meal. Then Fish cleaned tables and floors and, in fact, the entire mess hall. Buryl and every other freshman on campus quickly realized that, along with the other facets of Fish life, mealtime served up more frustration than satisfaction.

Frequently, at the conclusion of mandatory study time and after taps at 10 p.m., worn-out Fish would hear dreaded screams ringing up and down the dorm halls: "Fish-call! Fish-call! Outside! Now!" Dressed in only boxer shorts and undershirts, Fish, screaming at the top of their lungs and with their hands waving wildly, raced down the stairs and outside the dorms to form rack lines. Within minutes, they were agonizing through sit-ups, push-ups, and leg lifts, and then running innumerable laps, in formation, to and around a distant flagpole. Shouts of "Faster, Fish! Run faster!" sounded in their ears as they struggled to maintain their in-step running pace and the rhythmical chanting of some absurd song or obscene limerick.

On still-hot September nights, these grueling Fish-call exercises were performed half-naked on scorched, prickly grass, and during the cold of winter they were performed in driving, freezing rain. The life of a Fish was miserable in every season.

At any moment, an upperclassman named Smith might yell, "The board for Fish Baty!" The named Fish had no choice but to lean forward and endure a painful whipping. And when these "motivational" licks were delivered, the Fish was expected to offer a firm handshake to the administrator and say, "Damn good, Mr. Smith!" These swats caused blisters and bruises, which were called "blue-butts."

Initially, Fish could only feel confused, helpless, and enraged. But eventually they began to wise up. As the semester progressed, they responded boldly with pranks against those who had made their lives most miserable. The most common prank was the "drown-out," in which Fish filled five-gallon metal trash cans with tap water, ice water, or some combination of bodily fluids, sneaked quietly into compact, unlocked dorm rooms, and drenched Pissheads as they slept.

And they found other ways as well to prank upperclassmen. Some soaked a Pisshead's sheets with a full bottle of syrup, then remade the bed so that its owner would not discover the syrup until he had lain down in it at ten o'clock that night. In other cases, Fish plugged the drain of a dorm room sink, turned on the faucet, and sealed the bottom of the room's door with towels. When the Pisshead returned to open his door later in the day, he was met head-on with a tidal wave of rushing water. The pleasure of watching the upperclassmen's shock was never realized, however, as the avenging Fish had to bolt to protect their anonymity. A heavy price awaited those who were identified, often via punishments as creative as the pranks themselves. For example, one required that an offending Fish sleep on box springs only—no mattress, no sheets, no pillow, no clothes—for a week.

Of course, these payback pranks served immediate purposes. First, they united Fish in spirit; and second, Pissheads tended to moderate their behavior after such incidents. They didn't want to pay such a steep price more than a time or two.

But most alumni look back on Corps of Cadet membership as a shared rite of passage. They laugh off their tough times. Despite the angst and woe associated with Fishhood, most Aggies agree that the experience imposed many of the most valuable lessons in their lives—about strength in the face of adversity, confidence, humility, integrity, leadership, character. The school was tough physically, mentally, and academically, and those who met its challenges together formed lasting bonds of loyalty and brotherhood.

However, not all made it to that brotherhood.

Buryl Baty and his fellow Fish were shell-shocked. They had heard about the hazing, but there was no way to prepare for what it was really like. Fishhood was an unpleasant experience, to say the least, and this sterile, secluded campus offered nothing to relieve it. Getting out of town seemed like a good idea. But how?

Keeping a car was a privilege reserved for upperclassmen. If a Fish didn't have a friend with whom to bum a ride, he was left to catch a train or to "highway it"—that is, hitchhike. On weekends and holidays, hundreds of cadets swarmed the roadsides. It was widely crowed on campus that no driver passed an Aggie without offering him a ride. Clean-cut, with starched, khaki-colored uniforms, perfectly polished shoes, and agreeable manners (outside the dorm, at least), Aggie cadets were considered the epitome of what was good and right about Texas. So, when all else failed, or when funds were short, a kid could always thumb his way home, to a game, or to another college for a date with a girl. The college printed thousands of *Thank You* cards to present to generous drivers.

For Fish there was no escaping until the Thanksgiving holiday. On this, the first weekend he was not required to stay on campus, Fish Fred Clark highwayed it back home to Dallas. He was relieved to have a couple of days' reprieve from Pisshead abuse and to find a friendly ear. As he lamented his mistreatment—the insults, the errands, the exercises, the whippings—his mother demanded more details and a look at his bruised, blistered buttocks. She promptly yanked Fred out of A&M and enrolled him at SMU.

Buryl and his teammates quickly discovered that they were treated differently from other students. Jock-Fish were excused from many of the demands and physical abuses inflicted by the everyday Pisshead population. They were instead strapped ("whipped," in Aggie-speak), and sometimes protected, by their own jock upperclassmen. Euel "Pappy" Wesson and Bill Buchanan, both fifth-year seniors and graduate assistant coaches, were self-appointed dispensers of justice, and to the Fish players, they seemed possessed by their positions of authority. They could swing mean paddles. These instruments of rectitude had been created from half- to three-quarter inch thick wood, with a handle on one end and holes on the other. The holes were drilled at the strategic points of impact and were intended to produce blisters over black and blue bruises. The fact that all Fish athletes wore blue butts beneath their jock straps brought a sense of pride to these sadistic seniors. Fish players often wondered if they might have fared better with the regular Pissheads.

Athletes did receive special benefits from certain College Station establishments. At Loupot Book Store, football players simply had to introduce themselves and inform the proprietor that they were on the team. "Old Army Lou" (Loupot) always responded the same way: "Get what you need," he would say; "it's on my tab. Good luck this week." Of course Lou knew the older players by name—they didn't have to introduce themselves.

Teammates regularly gathered at the Northgate Drug Store soda fountain. Dr. Lipscomb, the proprietor, never charged players for food. The Northgate also had another strong draw: beautiful young Joan Massengale, the soda jerk. Sodas, malts and shakes, banana splits, and grilled cheese sandwiches were standard fare. Players grabbed quick snacks between classes and, when time permitted, sat at the counter talking about the last game, the next game, professors, courses, girls, and other college interests. Athletes enjoyed similar gratuitous treatment at theaters, cafés, and other establishments.

Preseason workouts were rugged for freshmen. Intense drills and scrimmages between the first- and second-team Fish made for nicks and bruises and very sore muscles. Meanwhile, walk-on James Wiley practiced with the Fish third-stringers against the varsity team. This was tough duty; the scout team took a daily pounding and a huge dose of harassment from the varsity players across the line of scrimmage. During one of these hot afternoon practices, Wiley was cold-cocked by All-Southwest Conference guard Felix Buchek. From high in his coaching observation tower, Head Coach Norton shouted encouragement: "Good hit, Buchek!"

Meanwhile, Wiley lay numbed and motionless on the hard ground. Fish Coach Lil Dimmit hustled onto the field and kneeled over him. "Fish, you'd better learn how to p-p-p-play football, or you're g-g-gonna get hurt."

Wiley replied dryly from flat on his back, "I think I'm hurt now."

The trainer looked into his eyes, felt around his neck and shoulders, then proclaimed, "I think you'll be fine." Teammates helped Wiley stand and walk woozily to the sideline.

In the first Fish game, against Allen Academy, Buryl Baty was, according to the Aggie yearbook, *The Longhorn*, a "standout, throwing a touchdown pass that helped pave the way to the first Fish victory."[1] Every player on the roster saw action, and the Fish naturally assumed that this playing time was aimed at allowing them to "show their stuff." But they later learned that participating in a single play in a real game rendered a player ineligible for transfer to another football program, effectively ensuring that he would not part company with A&M.

Buryl distinguished himself again when the Aggie freshman team defeated Fort Hood's 628th Destroyer Battalion team. The *College Station News* reported on October 22 that "Baty completed 15 out of 20 pass attempts, three of them for touchdowns." The *News* went on to call him "a sensational passing ace" and reported that "the A&M coaching staff is quite amazed at his ingenious hurling accuracy, as well as his poise, coolness, and efficiency." The article went on to quote Coach Lil Dimmit, who called Baty "possibly the best passing quarterback prospect in years at A&M" and compared him to TCU's Davey O'Brien—who, the article pointed out, had been awarded the Heisman Trophy in 1938.

In their third game, the Fish beat the Rice "Slimes" while a frustrated Baty stood gingerly on the sideline on his once again injured ankle. The upcoming season finale was against the University of Texas' freshman team, the Shorthorns. During the week of preparation for the game, the Fish began to realize firsthand the depth of A&M's hatred for "t.u.," as the university in Austin was dubbed by Aggies. The Fish fell to the Shorthorns, but this disappointing finish nevertheless completed the season with a respectable 3–1 record. Baty again rode the bench, injured and discouraged. But all the adhesive tape in Texas could not have held his ankle in place.

The Aggies led an all-male existence and were naturally starved for opportunities to meet girls. Fortunately, the A&M administration regularly arranged for trainloads and busloads of female students from the Texas State College for Women to be brought in to College Station on varsity home-game weekends. Cadets vacated entire dormitory floors to accommodate these visitors, and dances were scheduled for both Friday and Saturday nights. These were very exciting weekends on campus. And the visitors cleaned their borrowed dorm rooms before returning to Denton, relieving a few Fish of maid duty for a day.

The sight of these girls only made Buryl think more longingly of Bo. He couldn't wait to see her again, and they stayed in touch through frequent letters and occasional long-distance telephone conversations. But dorm rooms didn't have phones, and he had to walk across campus to place a call from a pay phone in the YMCA (which served as A&M's student union until 1954). When Bo was not at home, Buryl would have to leave a message, then go back to his room to wait for her return call. Incoming calls went through the A&M switchboard operator, who scribbled the message on a piece of paper and then sent the note via bike courier. Cadets were excited when the courier appeared in their hallway and immediately disappointed to hear the knock on someone else's door. When the messenger finally arrived at his room, Buryl would hurry down the stairs and back across campus. After again waiting in line for his turn, he inserted his dimes into the slot. "Paris, Texas, Hutchinson residence, please," he would tell the operator.

Bo's younger sister always raced to answer the phone before anyone else. After Buryl chatted briefly with her, he would finally hear Bo's voice across the wires. But with Jeannie and perhaps the party line listening on Bo's end, and a line of students waiting for the phone on Buryl's, and with shyness tongue-tying them both, and the expensive long-distance minutes adding up fast, the sweethearts' conversations usually fell short of what they wanted to say and ended too soon.

. . .

Buryl's close friend James Jackson, who was attending Paris Junior College, described a military recruiter's comments there: "If you're eighteen, do not register for next semester, because you *will* be drafted," the officer had declared. In fact, a similar message was delivered on every campus across America. And most boys were anxious to enlist. They were afraid that they might miss the war—that it might end before they had a chance to fight.

Of course, many Aggies' careers were interrupted. Coach Norton lamented to friends, "If graduation doesn't get 'em, the draft will." Buryl realized that this would be his last semester, at least for now. After completing midterm exams, he packed everything he owned into his two suitcases and caught a ride home. Good Lord willing, he would return to College Station. But it wouldn't be soon.

• • •

Buryl was back in Paris the morning after finals. He was moving slowly that day. He hoped to stretch out and relax for a while—as much as he could with Uncle Sam beckoning a long, bony finger at him. This was the first day in a long time that he had been able to rest. He lounged at the kitchen table while his mother clattered comfortably with the dishes.

A racket at the front door sent June scuttling in its direction and then flying back through the house screaming, "Mama! Mama!" When Bobbie reached the living room, the plant manager from the vinegar works was hovering in the doorway, his face troubled. Both white-knuckled hands were gripping his hat.

"There's been an accident. Mr. Baty has been injured," he said.

Burton had been inspecting a large vat filled with apple vinegar at the Speas plant where he worked. Suddenly he had heard a creaking sound, followed by a loud, popping crack. Before he knew it, the heavy vat had tilted as the eight-by-eight supporting timber gave way. Burton saw it coming and was able to jump aside, but his arm was trapped under the debris.

On Sunday morning there would be an article in the *Paris News* about the incident:

December 20, 1942

ARM AMPUTATED AFTER ACCIDENT AT PLANT

R. B. Baty, 148 S. 32nd St., Gregory-Robinson-Speas Co. employee, suffered injury Friday to his right arm which necessitated its amputation at the Sanitarium of Paris.

His arm was crushed by a tank on which he was working at the vinegar plant, 318 Church St.

His son, Buryl Baty, former Paris High School football player, has just arrived home from Texas A&M college for the holidays.

Burton was devastated, and fearful about what lay ahead for him. But he was also comforted by his family. Still groggy from surgery, he mumbled to Buryl, "I'm glad you're here, son." Buryl put his hand on his father's left shoulder. His mother sat at the other side of the bed, her face still damp and splotchy.

Back at the house that evening, after the rest of the family had gone to bed, Buryl sank into a chair, exhausted and stricken. The unopened afternoon paper, which he had scooped up off the porch as he and his mother had returned from the hospital, lay on the table beside him. He unfolded it to the sports page, and his eye fell on an article that a few years later would have hit very close to home.

Paris News, December 18, 1942
QUARTERBACKS PRESENT CHOCOLATE BOWL TONIGHT
Gophers Slight Favorites over Denton Negroes . . .
   Gibbons Gophers play host to Denton's Dragons for the sixth annual Chocolate Bowl Negro football classic at 8:30 Friday night at Noyes Stadium.
   A brisk advance ticket sale and Friday's fine football weather caused officers of the sponsoring Quarterback's Club to forecast one of the season's biggest crowds for the post-season tilt. Negroes will occupy the east stands; whites the west stands.

· · ·

Shortly after the New Year, Buryl went to the armed forces recruiting office to join the fight.

11 Dark Clouds

1943

Buryl attempted to enlist in the Naval Air Corps but was declared ineligible due to his bad shoulder, bad ankle, and color blindness. His determination to serve, however, was unabated, and he joined the US Army Corps of Engineers. On March 1, he reported to Fort Walters in Mineral Wells, Texas.

"Buryl went to the Army today," Bo lamented to her diary. "I hated to see him go." On March 3 she added, "Talked to Buryl today. I wish I could see him." On March 7, "Talked to Buryl again this morning. Wish I knew where he's going." On March 8, "Buryl is at Ft. Sill, Oklahoma." In early June, at Buryl's insistence, Bo planned a visit to Ft. Sill. "*I can hardly wait!*" she wrote. The visit, when it finally took place, seemed much too short.

On June 29, Private Baty was transferred to Stillwater, Oklahoma, and then, later, to Conway, Arkansas. As he trained, the Allies were making headway on the other side of the Atlantic. In May, Rommel's German Army in Africa surrendered to Patton in Tunisia. In July, the Allies entered Sicily, and the battle for Italy and the rest of Europe began. Buryl was anxious to do his part.

Buryl progressed through a series of destinations. In Arkansas, he received orders for his next and final training stop before deployment. However, his destination was not disclosed until several hours into the trip. His mouth dropped. "Camp Maxey? Are you sure?"

Buryl was very familiar with Camp Maxey. It was only ten miles north of his hometown, and Bo. He had watched the camp's buildup. Named after a former Confederate general and later US senator from Paris, Samuel Bell Maxey, it was a reactivated site for advanced engineering and infantry training, and it served as an internment center for German prisoners of war, some of whom were deployed to build the Lake Texoma dam. Thousands of soldiers had unloaded at the Paris train depot and been driven in convoy trucks past Bo's front porch, en route to their new barracks.

There Buryl and his fellow combat engineers had repeated basic training before being schooled in the construction of Bailey and pontoon bridges, which they practiced building across the Red River. They also learned how to plant and remove land mines and booby traps, how to build and repair roads and other structures, and how to engage in combat. During regular five- and twenty-five-mile hikes through the rural countryside, the men drilled on tactical maneuvers, shooting, and hand-to-hand combat techniques and survival skills. This training would be essential for their missions, they were told, because engineers were experiencing heavy casualties in both theaters. Buryl received a promotion after completing the training, and Sergeant Baty and his unit then mentored the next batch of engineers.

Soldiers swelled attendance at Friday-night football games, and Saturday nights in downtown Paris seemed like New Year's Eve on Times Square. Countless GIs swarmed to the active town center, which was a magnet to the young people of Paris. Parents warned daughters again and again, "It won't look right for you to be with an older soldier."

During his weekend leaves, Buryl checked on Bo's little sisters like a big brother. He would say, "Don't go with any of these soldiers. Promise me you won't." Meanwhile, Bo and Buryl enjoyed every minute of their time together. They double-dated, went to games and picture shows, and sometimes just sat on the front porch.

One evening Buryl seemed quiet, nervous. Finally, he cleared his throat and blurted out, "Bo, I've been thinking. You know I've had my eye on you, and only you, since the first grade." He paused and swallowed, then continued, "And I can't imagine being with anyone but you." Another short silence left Bo hanging. "Bo, will you marry me?"

With tears welling in her eyes, Bo said, "Yes, I will marry you, Buryl."

A simple wedding ceremony was performed at the First Methodist Church on September 30, 1944. James Jackson was best man and Alta, Bo's older sister, was maid of honor. Mr. Hutchinson gave the bride away and seemed proud to do so. Hutchinson and Baty relatives attended, and this was the first time that many had met each other. Burton enthusiastically shook hands, using his left hand, with every person there. Buryl's fourteen-year-old brother, Al, was thrilled when Bo greeted him so warmly. He was also excited to meet another soldier, a friend of Buryl's, Cpl. Sam Corenswet, who spoke with a funny New Orleans accent. The *Paris News* chronicled the ceremony the next morning.

The newlyweds rented an apartment where Bo would live until Buryl returned from the service. Just a spare room on the first floor of an old Victorian-style house, it had dark hardwood floors and tall windows that could be raised to capture a cool breeze. Bo's good taste and flair transformed the apartment into a comfortable and inviting home. Sandwiched between Buryl's military duties during the week and Bo's occasional Saturday work shift at the phone company, their weekends together flew by.

Buryl's inevitable deployment arrived all too soon, and before daylight on the crisp morning of November 30, 1944, they were forced to say their goodbyes. Buryl held Bo in his arms as hundreds of other soldiers boarded the train. "Bo," he whispered, "I'll think of you every day."

"I don't know if I can stand it here alone, worrying about you."

"I promise I'll come back to you. Wait for me."

"I don't want you to go," she wept, as Buryl wiped away the tears that streamed down her face.

"Honey, I'll get back as soon as I can."

"All aboard! Last call!" the conductor cried as a train whistle screeched.

Bo watched her husband run, gunnysack over his shoulder, up into the passenger car as it started to ease toward the brightening eastern sky. She waved sadly as the train gathered speed and, in no time, disappeared behind a thicket of trees on the horizon.

12 The War Years

1944–1946

For three days and nights the transport train made its way through Arkansas, Mississippi, Alabama, Georgia, South Carolina, North Carolina, Virginia, and Pennsylvania before arriving in New Jersey. After a short night's sleep, Buryl's unit rode the harbor ferry to New York City and boarded a converted Canadian passenger ship for a "tiresome two-week ocean crossing," according to his personal war journal.[1] Soldiers slept in hammocks and endured awful British food. The seas were rough, and several GIs, miserably sick, stayed below deck for the entire trip. The *Dominion Monarch* docked at Southampton on a cold, rainy December 22, 1944. Buryl's 1267th Combat Engineer Battalion supplanted another combat engineering battalion, whose ship deployed to France on Christmas Day and was sunk by a Nazi torpedo in the English Channel.

By this time, the drive to the heart of the Third Reich was well underway. After the D-Day invasion of Normandy, the Allies had swept across occupied France with amazing speed. The liberation of Paris had been completed in August. However, Allied forces were now facing a last-stand German counteroffensive at the Rhine. Reports filtered in of heavy infantry and combat engineering casualties.

Meanwhile, Buryl's combat engineering platoon trained in Gloucester, in "terribly cold" weather. Much of London lay in ruins, but the British spirit held strong. A final preparation exercise was conducted at midnight on the Thames, and Buryl and his comrades anxiously crossed the English Channel early the next morning to Le Havre, France. The port city was "a complete mass of ruins," Buryl wrote.

His company trucked methodically through the French countryside over damaged roads, first to Paris, then to Rheims, and then through Luxemburg toward Germany. Buryl noted that "some towns are especially beautiful and have not sustained much damage." In other villages, bombing had leveled almost every structure. Sergeant Baty's company, staged three weeks behind Patton's front battle lines and armed with bulldozers and dump trucks, repaired roads and bridges to facilitate Allied pursuit of the retreating Nazi forces. In some places, road damage was so massive that they were forced to transport supplies and materials by pack mule. The threat of rogue enemy sniper fire slowed their pace.

In Saarburg, the 1267th made camp in a deserted German garrison, a series of gray stone buildings surrounding a large courtyard. Members of the battalion soon discovered that a medieval castle nearby housed thousands of bottles of vintage champagne and schnapps. One of the drivers claimed that he had driven several jeeps full of these bottles up to the camp, and that the GIs had put the spirits to good use through the night. The following week they advanced to Trier on the Moselle River. There they constructed a prisoner-of-war camp to house captured German soldiers. At one point they helped a group of Italian refugees who had been detained by the Germans and severely mistreated. Speculation was rampant about the horrors they had likely endured.

Spring brought warmer days and colorful blooms to the rolling hills. Soon, it also brought news of the Nazi surrender. Sergeant Baty and other members of the 1267th were among the revelers during the Victory-in-Europe parade in the streets of Luxemburg. The town was immersed in celebration—there was eating, drinking, singing, and cheering in the streets. This was the week before Buryl's twenty-first birthday.

In his journal Buryl reflected that "the past two weeks have been both bright and sad. We lost our President and Commander in Chief Roosevelt. It was a great loss to our fighting men. On the bright side were the death of Hitler, and Mussolini." Soldiers soon learned details of the demobilization plan. "We can now seal our own mail," he wrote. "There is no more censoring of mail in the ETO." And finally, to Bo: "I can't wait to see you."

On June 4, Buryl's convoy headed south past a line of dragon's teeth into and through France. At the end of this four-day journey it arrived in Calais, near Marseille, France's main southern seaport. "When we were given typhoid shots and issued mosquito nets and repellant, we realized that it would be some time before we saw the good old USA," Buryl observed in the journal. The afternoon before they were to board the transport ship, the troops received a treat at a nearby amphitheater: a USO show featuring Mickey Rooney.

The next morning six thousand men were loaded into semitrailer trucks, sixty-five to a truck, and driven to the port. Carrying full field packs, they waited and sweated in the summer sun for four hours.

They finally boarded the USS *General John Pope* super-transport ship and sailed westward at 5 p.m. on June 23. No one knew what was in store, except that meals would be served twice a day, at 9:30 a.m. and at 5:30 p.m. Two days out, the ship passed through the Straits of Gibraltar. Buryl wrote in his journal, "Our first day in the Atlantic was warm, and the sea was calm. Schools of porpoise swam alongside the ship, arching their bodies out of the water; then there were great numbers of flying fish. They surprised me, for they fly quite a distance before diving into a wave. It was so peaceful that it was hard to think of war."

Time passed slowly. Many days, with a stiff breeze in his face, Buryl stood on the deck and gazed out over the sea. He found himself thinking of Bo and recalling their dates to Lake Crook Park. He longed for those days with his sweetheart: picnicking, talking, and laughing with friends in the shade of huge oak and pecan trees until the evening's breeze cooled the air. Then, as crickets sang and bullfrogs croaked and Benny Goodman's swing music blared from the jukebox, they had danced on the clubhouse balcony that extended over the water. These evenings tended to pass quickly until, inevitably, Bo would say, "It's time to go. Daddy wants me home before dark thirty." Buryl had heard these exact words a thousand times.

Waves crashed against the ship's bow below. Buryl's thoughts jumped to the day he had left Camp Maxey and Paris. He visualized Bo crying and waving as his transport train chugged eastward away from the depot. That image of her was burned into his mind.

Meanwhile, back home, Bo was trying to stay busy. She enrolled in Paris Junior College and worked part-time as a telephone operator. "How fitting for someone who so enjoys talking on the phone!" her sisters joked. But it was hard for her to think about anything but Buryl. Every day she watched and listened for news about the troops. The days passed slowly. She wrote often, and wondered if her letters were being delivered. She waited and worried.

And occasionally she fretted about things closer to home. For example, she noticed sodas and shakes charged on her end-of-the-month drugstore statements. An inquiry of the soda jerk quickly identified the source of the suspicious charges: her little sister Jean. Jeannie had never seen Bo so furious.

But no distraction could keep Bo's mind off her soldier husband for long. "I think about Buryl all the time," she told her friends. When a small bundle of his correspondence arrived from overseas, she rushed to open the envelopes. She read each letter again and again. With one letter he included a photo inscribed "I love you" on the back, and "I'm glad you married me." These words touched her and made her miss him even more. Her worry did not subside.

On board the *General John Pope,* a few soldiers playfully wagered on who would be first to spot "the Lady." But instead of the Statue of Liberty, their first sighting was of palm trees on the island of Puerto Rico. "So near and yet so far," Buryl wrote in his journal. On July 4th, they passed into and through locks that raised the boat into the Panama Canal. Tropical birds sang from trees on both densely forested sides of the passageway. Eventually, the ship was lowered to the level of the Pacific Ocean and docked in Balboa, Panama, to take on food and fuel. There Buryl wrote in his journal that soldiers were "marched off the ship to see a USO show, and to drink a coke." The next morning they had another surprise: "Mail from home waiting for us. It made everyone so happy. I received letters from my wife." Buryl's good friend Sgt. Sam Corenswet was the hero of the day; he received sixteen care packages. His mother had religiously mailed one of these boxes full of goodies each week, but the backlog had just now caught up with Sam. He and his GI buddies gorged on candy bars, peanuts, crackers, and stale homemade cookies.

Resuming its journey across the Pacific to a still unknown destination, the ship was pounded by rain and storms. "But at least it's cooler," Buryl wrote. The *John Pope* zigzagged along its course so that Japanese subs, plentiful in the Pacific, would have more difficulty locking in on it as a target. On the twenty-fifth day at sea, Buryl wrote, "Last night a soldier was operated on for a ruptured appendix. He passed away and was buried at sea." A couple of days later he wrote, "We had a terrible storm last night, and about 0100 this morning we were hit by something—about midship. It was dark on deck; the gun and ship crews were running around as if they were lost. Speculation is that we were rammed by a Japanese sub or hit by a torpedo, which turned out to be a dud. Anyway, lady luck was with us." The ship continued to zigzag westward, still under cloudy and rainy skies.

After thirty-one days at sea, Buryl noted that he was "getting very tired of this trip." On July 27, the vessel entered Manila Harbor, in the Philippines. "We're anchored about three miles out. Harbor in bad shape.

There are over 200 sunken ships and it's impossible to get any closer in." At six o'clock the next morning, the soldiers disembarked down long rope ladders. "We were taken ashore in landing craft and set foot on dry land for the first time in 34 days."

That afternoon the GIs crowded into sixteen coal cars on a Filipino train to Colombo. "The natives here are very poor," Buryl wrote, "but clean and polite. Their towns are very primitive. The Japs left nothing. I feel so sorry for the little children; they hang around our mess halls begging for a crust of bread." And ravenous rats attacked any food scraps. Sam Corenswet bunked next to Buryl and remembers joking with him about the sound of these vermin scurrying beneath their cots at night. At 4 p.m. on August 1 they once again crammed into a train, this time to head 150 miles north. The trip, Buryl recorded, was "very slow and tiresome." They reached San José at 4:30 a.m.

There the 1267th worked to make the strategic "National Road" passable. The primitive, narrow, winding dirt passage was critical for transporting equipment and flushing out remaining Japanese mountain hideouts. This was treacherous duty because the slightest mistake could send a bulldozer or transport truck tumbling hundreds of feet down a steep mountainside cliff.

"You can see the tracer bullets at night in the mountains where there are still Japs holding out," Buryl noted in the log. "It's impossible to get them out of their caves so we pour gasoline in on them and set it afire to burn them up or out. Once in a while a few give up. When they come down from the hills they are so weak they can hardly walk." On one sweltering hot evening, a couple of diminutive Filipino natives caused a commotion in the American camp by presenting the severed heads of two Japanese soldiers.

And then there was the weather. "Had a tropical storm today; it rains the hardest I have ever seen. Our clothes are all wet and muddy. The water ran through our tent like a river." On the next day: "We received mail, so everyone is in a good mood." But in one of these letters, Bo conveyed the news of her father's death. Buryl responded immediately with condolences that would take weeks to be delivered: "I wish I could be there to comfort you, Bo."

On August 8, Buryl's journal reported important news. "We have a new bomb; we used it against Japan today. Also, Russia declared war against Japan. With these developments, Japan shouldn't last long."

Then: "This is what we've all been waiting for. Tonight at 7:30 p.m. Philippine time, Japan gave up. We were all so happy. This will end my overseas diary. I have covered two thirds of the globe, now I am ready to go home. I'll soon be seeing you, Honey; till then good-night," Buryl wrote on August 10. However, contradictory news was announced the next day. "We are still sweating out the Japs' surrender terms. This sweating should go down in history. Our artillery here in the mountains has never let up. The orders are to fire ahead until the official order to cease fire is given. Gosh! This could go on forever."

And then, on August 15, 1945, Buryl wrote, "This morning at 0800 Manila time, the war is *officially over*. Most of our boys think they will be home for Christmas, or on their way home. Well this time I will close for good. Hope to be home soon."

Buryl and thousands of other soldiers waited months for ships to arrive for transport back to the US. They were ready to return to the lives they had left behind.

13 Homecoming

The soldiers had longed to return to their girls, their families, and their hometowns, and to regain the carefree innocence of their youth. And on the surface, home looked the same. But nothing was the same.

Staff Sergeant Baty arrived at the Paris, Texas, train depot on a cold, drizzly February day. After almost fifteen months apart, he and Bo were speechless when they first embraced. Tears streamed down Bo's cheeks as her fear and longing were suddenly replaced with relief and joy. Normally a self-controlled person, she was overwhelmed by the reunion. Buryl's deployment had forced her to bottle her emotions and nervous energy. Now her feelings poured out; she cried one moment and laughed, trembling, the next. Finally the couple could relax, enjoy each other's company, and live their lives together.

Buryl was delighted to reunite with his family, too. His father had received a modest compensation for his injury from the Speas Vinegar Company, and with it the family had bought a new home, the first that was really theirs. Burton's loss of his arm had been traumatic, but he had returned to near normalcy. He was still an easygoing, quiet, old-fashioned man. He walked to and from work and nurtured his "victory garden," just as before. He enjoyed his kids. He still made frequent treks to shop for grocery bargains. However, now unable to carry more than one grocery bag at a time, he would shop at one store and leave his bagged purchases by the door while he walked to the next store. There he also stashed his groceries near the entry before continuing to his next grocery stop. When his shopping was complete, he called a taxi to his current location and then swung by for his previous purchases before finally being delivered back home. When he was in town, Buryl acted as his father's driver.

Bobbie's life had also changed. She was now saddled with the heavy chores that her husband had previously performed. Simple tasks like nailing or screwing something in place were nearly impossible for Burton. Bobbie just tackled the chores herself. "No reason to complain or wait for someone else to do it," she replied to concerned questioners. She also assumed many of the disciplinary measures taken with the children, frequently ordering one of them to "go cut a switch!" However, Al and sister June remembered their mother's punishments as rather benign.

Meanwhile, the Hutchinson household's spirits were gradually improving, but the family still mourned the passing of Daddy Hutchinson. Buryl's renewed presence filled a small part of the void that his father-in-law had left.

Eventually, after the restorative break at home, it was time for Bo and Buryl to return to College Station.

The Spartan A&M campus looked pretty good to war veterans who swarmed back to the school. Enrollment exploded to more than nine thousand students, from about two thousand in '45. Roughly two-thirds of these were returning vets, ready to complete their education and secure good jobs. They also hoped to recapture the simplicity of their prewar days. However, they soon understood that they themselves had changed; they had left their innocence and their boyhood on Omaha Beach, at the Rhine River, and on the sands of Okinawa. Many experienced recurring nightmares and intermittent anxiety and paranoia. And some flunked out. It was a tough transition from battlefield to classroom.

Re-entering vets felt it absurd that two longstanding A&M policies, mandatory Corps participation and dorm residency requirements, be upheld. These were men who had fought and won a war.[1] They had no patience for adolescent nonsense or pretend soldiering. Outrage festered when their concerns were ignored, and an uprising brewed. Several hundred veterans protested, the president was terminated and replaced, and the unpopular policies were rescinded.

The Batys returned in the midst of these unprecedented changes and moved into the College View Apartments just south of the football stadium. This new married housing was merely converted old two-story military barrack buildings, eight apartments to a building, that rented for twenty-one dollars per month. The box-shaped buildings, even with fresh white paint, were not very attractive, inside or out. But the setting was unimportant to people who were simply happy to be together. And Buryl had dreams to pursue: completing his degree and playing football. Meanwhile, Bo got a job in the athletic ticket office.

Coach Homer Norton did not protest the return of married players, but he did prohibit single players from marrying. He isolated these unattached veterans in an athletic dormitory, with curfews, in order to minimize their drinking and partying and their trips to the Chicken Ranch in LaGrange, during the season.

In contrast, married players barbequed or went out to eat for entertainment. The Batys socialized with other married athlete couples, including Nancy and Sam Jenkins and Margaret and Herb Turley. They usually convened on Sunday afternoons; the girls cooked and talked in the kitchen while the three vets joked around in the yard and turned the manual five-gallon ice-cream maker. One lazy afternoon Sam Jenkins declared, "We're the luckiest guys in the world. We have everything to look forward to."

• • •

When dozens of faces, new and old, returned to his team, Coach Norton, a believer that "right will prevail," graciously honored all prewar scholarships. One hundred fifty players reported for the varsity team, both boys and vets. But many of the veterans were no longer adequately conditioned for the physical demands of the sport and had clearly lost their spark. Some had wives, all had new perspectives. Still, competition was intense for limited roster space. Norton faced a monumental task: identifying his best players and, concurrently, melding them into a successful team in a short period of time. Regardless, Buryl felt optimistic. "We've got a chance for a good season," he claimed.

The Aggies, along with most of college football, were transitioning to a "T" formation attack. A learning curve was required, especially for quarterbacks who now had to take the snap from under center and drop back to pass. These skills did not come easily. One afternoon Buryl and Bob Gary, a former walk-on center who had earned a starting position, stayed late to work on their ball exchange. After a few frustrating snaps, Bob suggested that he and Buryl switch places to provide each other with a firsthand feel for the other player's position. They tried it. "No, Buryl!" Bob shouted. "You're holding your legs apart like a girl! Hold 'em closer together and bend your knees before you snap the ball. Then you can fire out and hit somebody."

Buryl painfully snapped a few footballs before standing up straight. "I'll never play *that* position!" Little did he know that Bob Gary's counsel would come in handy a few years later.

The next afternoon, as Buryl and friends Odell Stautzenberger and

Warren Gilbert walked across campus and past a group of drilling cadets, they overheard a Pisshead barking at his at-attention Fish about fighting a war. Stautzenberger abruptly jumped in front of the young ROTC officer. "You pissant Pisshead, would you like me to show you what it's like to fight in a war?" he bawled.

The wide-eyed sophomore responded, "No, *sir!*" Buryl and Warren struggled to maintain straight faces. Word of this incident spread quickly, and Corps cadets agreed that it would be a good idea to stay out of Stautzenberger's path.

Younger players stood in awe of war veterans and their combat experiences. Warren Gilbert had commanded an artillery company charged with burning Japanese soldiers out of caves. Slight in stature, he served as student equipment manager for the football team, a position that suited him very well. Warren was known for one of the biggest smiles on campus.

Stautzenberger, or "Stautz," as his teammates called him, projected a more intimidating presence. He had a chiseled body, a rugged complexion, and fire in his eyes. This former marine commando had fought with the elite Carlson's Raiders in the Pacific hellholes of Bougainville, Guam, and Okinawa. "He killed more men with his hands than most soldiers did with guns!" cadets whispered. Several soldiers credited Stautz with saving their lives, and he was awarded a Bronze Star for his valor. One of those people was an old friend from San Antonio, Stautz's hometown. The soldier's legs had been blown off by mortar fire, and Stautz had carried him through enemy fire to safety. When later visiting his friend in the hospital, he found the young man very depressed. "I'm a cripple. What do I have to live for?" the vet lamented from his hospital bed.

A scowl darkened Stautz's face. "I didn't risk my life for you to feel sorry for yourself," he snapped. "Get up and get going!" The prodding— or something—apparently worked. The former GI subsequently earned his law degree and became a district attorney in San Antonio.

Football season finally kicked off. As a backup quarterback for the first five games of a 2–3 start, Buryl entered the sixth game of the 1946 season as what the *Bryan Eagle* called a "new and much needed passer" and threw two touchdown passes to secure a 17–0 victory over Baylor. His old friend and former Paris teammate, Ollie Jack, played linebacker for the Bears, and it seemed odd to be across the line of scrimmage from him, especially since Ollie and his wife were staying over for the night.

Friends Bettie and James Jackson also drove down from Paris to watch the game and stay the night. Buryl suggested that James join him in the locker room after the game. "After I clean up, we'll meet Ollie and the girls and all go over to our house." James enjoyed the euphoria in the victorious locker room. Half-dressed players laughed and talked loudly and exchanged hearty congratulations. Equipment managers picked up abandoned jocks and socks and jerseys from the concrete floor, while shoulder-pads, helmets, and shoes were stuffed into each player's locker. White tape flew in all directions as it was ripped from ankles, shoulders, wrists, and knees. Several older men in suits milled around with the Aggie players, shaking hands.

The season continued. After a loss to Arkansas, the Aggies took on SMU. "Baty's beautiful passing led to a 14–0 victory over the Mustangs," according to A&M's yearbook, *The Longhorn*. The season closed with disappointing losses to the eventual champion, the Rice Owls, and to the Bobby Layne- and Tom Landry-led Texas Longhorns, on Thanksgiving Day.

Always the optimist, Coach Norton complimented his team on their effort and heart, and encouraged them about their possibilities in the next year.

· · ·

After a weekend in Dallas to see his parents and his girlfriend, Buryl's friend Bob Gary hated to get back in the car for College Station. But it was time to go; his roommate was honking in front of the house. After the four-hour drive, they walked up the steps to their dark dorm room. Bob turned the handle to open the door and flipped on the light. Two large eyes stared back at him. "Oh, my God!" Gary gasped. There stood a yearling calf in its feces, which had been trampled throughout the room. Urine had streamed into every corner and seeped deeply into the floors. The smell all but knocked the two roommates over as they slammed the door and staggered back.

Bob Gary screamed, "I want every Fish on this floor out in the hallway, now!" Fish stuck their heads out of their rooms and peered down the hall. "Line up here in front of my room, right now!" Gary yelled again. "*Now!*" Freshmen clad only in boxers or briefs scurried down the hall and stood in a line at military attention.

Next, they cleaned. It was a long, miserable night. Monday was especially rough as everyone involved had to struggle to stay awake. And the stench lingered for weeks.

Another something lingered as well. All Fish on that floor, in that dorm, and across campus reveled as word spread of this glorious prank. Fish were inspired to new heights of ingenuity, and upperclassmen thought twice about the intensity of their subsequent hazing. The balance of power and respect had turned slightly in favor of the Fish. And they would laugh about it for the rest of their lives.

14 A New Season

A lot needed to be accomplished to build a successful season. The Aggies seized a head start at the Kerrville Boys' Camp for the two weeks preceding two-a-days. Players coached the young campers, while they themselves also went through rigorous conditioning drills with their own coaches' direction. Veteran quarterbacks Hallmark and Baty were out early every day, according to Fish Homer Johnson, taking snaps and passing the ball and generally working out the cobwebs.

Two-a-day practices were intense. During one early scrimmage, fullback Dan King, an acclaimed combat paratrooper, burst through the line carrying the pigskin. After stepping through the small passage, he ducked his head to ram into Stautzenberger, and they both fell to the ground. The immediate and war-conditioned instinct of both men was to retaliate. They fought fiercely, as though their lives were at stake. Coach Norton just watched from his coaching tower. Teammates Bob Gary and Buryl Baty finally wedged the two apart. Afterwards, conciliatory logic proved fruitless. Both Stautz and King fumed, and their hostilities culminated in bitter words and frequent fights during subsequent practice sessions. The coaches ultimately decided that the distraction could not continue, and one day, Dan King was gone.

Several times a week the varsity practiced against the freshman team. Charlie Royalty, a 150-pound halfback from Freeport, remembers being pounded in the scrimmages. He and his fellow Fish players were intimidated every time they walked to the varsity field.

After a season-opening victory, the Aggies looked forward to playing Texas Tech in a neutral location, San Antonio. The Aggies stayed in a first-class hotel on the river near the Alamo and were hosted in grand fashion. Local Aggie alums seemed to compete over who could give the most to the better players on the team, and ten- and twenty-dollar handshakes were plentiful.[1] These road trips were always rewarding for players.

On Saturday morning before the San Antonio game, still in their standard suit-and-tie travel attire, the Aggies were strolling onto and around the sunken stadium's precisely striped grass field when they heard a sudden, loud racket and turned to determine its source. It was Odell Stautzenberger—chasing a uniformed policeman. The officer topped the stadium steps and scurried through the parking lot. Stautz stopped to watch him awhile before lumbering back down to the field to rejoin his teammates.

Bob Gary, holding his hands out in a puzzled gesture, asked, "What was that about, Stautz?"

"Oh, last summer I had a little trouble in a honky-tonk here in San Antone. It wasn't my fault—some idiot picked a fight with me." Stautz paused as he wiped sweat from his forehead. "Well, I punched him and broke his jaw. But before I could get out of there, I got hauled down to the station. And three cops mugged me while I was handcuffed," he said indignantly. "Then today, I saw that patrolman—one of the guys who beat me up. And he saw me. He took off runnin' like a scalded cat."

"Stautz, I'm glad you're on *our* team," Buryl howled. A hard laugh relieved the Aggies' pregame butterflies.

Stautz was known for his insatiable appetite for excitement; his friends claimed that he always had his own way with a good time. He was driven by adrenaline, for which football games and practices served as outlets. The dull months between seasons, however, left voids that he filled with creative and sometimes reckless activities, such as barroom fights. Stautz was also on record as not being fond of quarterbacks. However, he had acknowledged that Baty was "okay." The two were as different as night and day. Stautz was passionate, mercurial, and "in-your-face"; Baty was intense, but quiet and steady. Still, somehow, they shared a good chemistry.

The Aggies headed to the locker room to be taped and to suit up for the game, and many players found money in their helmets. After a victory over the Border Conference's Red Raiders, they walked proudly. The next afternoon at the field house, star players, as usual, found more bills in their lockers.

The team subsequently fell to the nationally ranked Oklahoma Sooners (with a young Darrell Royal), to LSU, led by Y. A. Tittle, and to Coach Dutch Meyer's TCU team. Quarterbacks Hallmark, Cashion, Holmig, and Baty all saw time on the field.

That following week during practice, Stautz and Herb Turley, former teammates at San Antonio Jefferson High School, lined up across from each other in a light scrimmage. Before Herb knew it, his nose was bleeding profusely, thanks to one of Stautz's punches. People learned to stay out of Stautzenberger's way.

But Stautz took care of his teammates off the field. For example, he dated an English-department secretary and repeatedly convinced her to change his friends' grades in the official records. Never a football player flunked English. He also protected Fish players on occasion. For example, when a Pisshead was overly zealous with one of the freshman players, Stautz would show up at the sophomore's dorm room door and bark, "Pisshead, we'll take care of our own!"

"Yes, sir!" answered the shrinking sophomores.

The upcoming Baylor game extended a decades-old rivalry, and the Corps traveled en mass to the Waco contest. Before the trip they were cautioned to be "on guard." History warranted the alert because this church school seemed to have it in for the Aggies. In fact, a cadet had been smacked on the back of his head with a two-by-four in a 1926 halftime brawl; the Aggie died the next morning, and the Baylor aggressor was never identified.

The 1948 *Longhorn* (the A&M yearbook) credited Baty's 9-of-18 passing performance with "sparking A&M's win over Baylor." Ollie Jack played well for the Bears, as underclassman Hayden Fry watched from the sidelines. They were coached by head man Bob Woodruff and a fine young assistant, Frank Broyles.

Baty's passing was also credited with salvaging a 21–21 tie with Arkansas. This moral victory was followed by a loss to Doak Walker's SMU squad. Next up was Rice Institute. A&M fans read in the *Houston Chronicle* on November 12 how Rice's defense "drilled against the expected Aggie aerial attack, with Vernon Glass, an all-state back from Corpus Christi, doubling for Aggie passer Buryl Baty." The *Chronicle* also reported the Aggies' rage that while A&M cadet officers were guarding the Rice campus in Houston against vandalism in a "friendly relations" pact between the two schools, the Aggie campus was getting a dose of blue-painted "*Yea, Rice!*" and other slogans.

On Friday's bus trip to Houston, cadet yell leaders hooted and hollered in an attempt to get the team fired up. Players did eventually become energized when they arrived at the Rice campus and a group of coeds followed them from their bus to the campus hotel. The Aggies were not accustomed to seeing girls on campus and were especially thrilled for the girls to be stalking them. Of course, Houston's A&M alumni congregated around the team's hotel to rub shoulders with the players. In the pre-game locker room, cash was handed out by a teammate whose father, himself a former Aggie player, had provided the big stack of bills.

A sizeable fan base hoped to see their inconsistent Aggies upset the defending champions at Rice Stadium, but the Owls prevailed. In the locker room afterwards, Coach Norton puffed on his Chesterfield cigarette before speaking. "Stand tall, men. Adversity makes us stronger." He was quick to say things like this.

So far, the season had been a disappointment. However, if the Aggies could somehow win the final game against Texas, their campaign would be deemed a success. The rivalry between A&M and t.u. had begun in 1894 in the first intercollegiate game played in the state. The first Thanksgiving Day game against the Texas "Varsity" was played in 1900. By that time, football fever had taken hold in the Aggie psyche.

But the football rivalry touched only the surface of the tension between these two institutions. Founding UT administrators and legislators had pushed for the elimination of A&M or, at the very least, the annexation of A&M under the younger UT system. They had reasoned that every dollar going to A&M was one dollar less for the University of Texas. Perhaps A&M president Sul Ross's greatest contributions were his successful battles against these factions and his solidification of A&M as an up-and-coming institute of higher learning. Ross did not, however, diminish the tea-sippers' arrogant condescension toward Texas A&M, nor the Aggies' deep-rooted loathing for everything orange.

Seasons were made or lost on the outcome of this contest. It was the biggest game of the year, and tickets for good seats were always in high demand—and players generally sold them for healthy profits. A student manager facilitated these transactions and discreetly distributed the cash in plain envelopes.

This t.u. game started off like trench warfare. Bob Gary was matched against a tough nose guard by the name of "Trimble." Most of Trimble's right hand was missing; he had only a thumb, and this thumb persisted in scratching or poking the Aggie center in and around his eyes on almost every play. Gary was certain that the poking was intentional. Early in the second quarter, he caught the attention of referee Ebb Curtis, who was standing behind the Aggie's huddle. "Mr. Curtis, that noseguard keeps scratching and poking me in the eye. I need a little help here, or I'll be blind by the end of the day."

The referee raised his head up to peer past the Aggie huddle and toward the UT defense, then turned back to look straight at the Aggie captain. "This is an important game, Bob. Don't tell me you're gonna let a one-handed man push you around."

"No, sir." In the huddle, however, Gary appealed to the guard standing next to him. "Can you help me with that noseguard, Stautz?"

"Bob, have you seen the guy in front of me? I need some help myself!" Stautz growled.

Quarterback Baty quickly took control of the conversation in the huddle. "OK, men. We're gonna take care of that boy. The call is 30 Dive, right up the middle, on one. And Stautz, you help Bob out."

"Ready," began the quarterback's call. Then, the offense yelled "Break!" in unison as they clapped and lined up in three-point stances at the line of scrimmage. Baty yelled forcefully and rhythmically over the roar of the crowd, "*Down! Set! Hut!*" At the snap of the ball Stautz pinched into the middle toward the Longhorn noseguard. The play gained only two yards, but afterwards, Trimble lay pancaked and motionless under the Aggie line. He seemed much less aggressive for the remainder of the game. However, the Aggies came up short. Quarterback Bobby Layne's passing, Tom Landry's punting and running, Max Bumgardner's fine line work, and a successful Statue of Liberty play led t.u. to victory.

But despite the discouraging loss, the Aggie spirit remained strong. Throughout the up-and-down season the Fightin' Texas Aggie band, drums beating and horns blaring, had played proudly and marched precisely at every halftime. Cadets had stood and cheered at the top of their lungs for the full four quarters of all ten games. And for those not able to attend in person, the voice of Texas Aggies' radio announcer Bill Stern exuded hope and excitement.

But the season's results didn't sit well with disgruntled alums, Coach Norton resigned, and it wasn't long before rumors spread across campus, and the state, that his contract had been bought out. Norton had been respected for his toughness, his creativity, his knowledge of the game, and his successes. He had approached coaching as a noble profession. He never swore, and he felt that one of the finest things a coach does is develop character. He was a good man and a good coach. Norton was heartbroken to leave, but he did so with the respect of players and opposing coaches. The team was saddened and left for the holidays feeling empty.

While players hated for the season to end as it did, the free time would allow for extra coursework and more social activities. Until spring training the next March, the guys were on their own. Bo and Buryl looked forward to weekend trips home, socializing with other couples, and being together.

Late in the spring, the NFL held its annual draft of college players. Aggie Monte Moncrief was drafted at pick #62. Taken 166th was Buryl Baty, by the Detroit Lions. Eighteen picks later, at #184, the Giants chose Tom Landry. And later, additional Aggie teammates Odell Stautzenberger (#247) and Bob Tullis (#266) were claimed. Other noteworthy players chosen by professional football clubs were Ara Parseghian from Miami (of Ohio), Hardy Brown from Tulsa, and Dewitt Coulter from Army (both from Ft. Worth Masonic Home). Buryl and Bo were thrilled about his being picked, and they could weigh their options many times before they had to make a decision—after Buryl's senior year of college eligibility.

Back in College Station, a new era was dawning. A new football coach would be at the helm.

15 Last Chance—Gig 'em, Aggies!

FALL 1948

Assistant Harry Stiteler was promoted to head coach. He had been very successful in high school, winning state championships both in Corpus Christi, where he had been Coach Raymond Berry's successor, and in Waco. A former Aggie quarterback, Stiteler was known as being imaginative and offensively minded. With blond hair and pale blue eyes, he stood out in a crowd, even though he was the shortest man on the field. But what he lacked in size, he made up in confidence and intensity. Of course, Buryl had established rapport with the coach as a result of their mutual association with Coach Berry.

"Little Harry," as the press called him, inspired his new Aggie team by saying, "You have to play this game with *heart!*" In private, players and fans voiced concerns about whether Stiteler and his new assistant coaches, straight out of high school programs, were up to the task of coaching in the Southwest Conference. And returning players retained their loyalty to Coach Norton, of course; they would be wary of any new coach. But they wanted to win a championship and hoped that Stiteler would be successful. The coach quickly made another positive impression by recruiting perhaps the strongest A&M freshman class since Buryl's '42 Fish team. Many of these new players drove new cars to campus in the fall.

These incoming freshmen were obliged to practice on the scout team against the varsity. The seasoned upperclassmen took out their frustrations on the newcomers regularly and enjoyed doing so. In addition to inflicting physical pain on the lowly Fish, certain varsity players— All-Southwest Conference lineman Odell Stautzenberger in particular— enjoyed harassing the wide-eyed kids. "You can do better than that, Fish Touchdown!" he barked at heralded freshman halfback Glenn Lippman. And then, scathingly: "I thought you were the best player in Texas!"

Charlie Royalty, the only starting sophomore on this varsity team, enjoyed being on the other side of the line of scrimmage for a change, practicing with the varsity instead of against them as he had the previous year. He especially appreciated the fact that Stautzenberger now had his back, so he was spared the lineman's violent hits and verbal abuse. Stautz even joked around with him occasionally.

Despite early optimism, the season began as a lesson in futility. After several close and discouraging losses, the Aggies' record stood at 0–7. The bounces had not gone their way. And Buryl had struggled with his knocked-down shoulder and bad ankle. He anguished silently with extended time on the bench.

In spite of the team's mounting losses, Stiteler remained a positive influence. He was knowledgeable about football and was a fiery speaker; his team was always inspired when it walked out onto the field. Quick to compliment a good play, he was a players' coach.

The Cotton Bowl served as the venue for the eighth contest of the season against SMU. The defending conference champion Mustangs were led by Doak Walker and a strong supporting cast. Walker, who had been an All-American as a sophomore, was well on his way to repeating the honor in this, his junior year, and enjoyed frequent mention for the Heisman Trophy. He was a great open-field runner, passer, receiver, kick-returner, punter, and defender. About the only thing Doak didn't do was the team's laundry, and if he had, he would have done a good job of it. The Mustangs were well coached by Matty Bell and assistant Rusty Russell, the former Fort Worth Masonic Home coach. Folks didn't expect much from the Aggies, and bookies rated this mighty SMU team as heavy favorites.

This would be a big weekend. Since the 1920s, about the time that the name "Aggies" replaced the earlier labels of "Cadets" and "Farmers," official Corps trips had been regular affairs. In alternate years, cadets hitchhiked or travelled in chartered trains and buses to games in Austin, Houston, Dallas, and Fort Worth. There, Aggie yell practice was held the night before the game, and the Aggie Corps and the Fightin' Aggie Band paraded through the streets toward the stadium on game day. Cadets always brimmed with excitement over the Dallas trip. In addition to enjoying a conference football game, they had an excuse to meet pretty girls and to party. Hundreds of blind dates were arranged with SMU and other local coeds for the game and a Saturday night dance, after which cadets loaded onto their trains for the midnight journey back to College Station.

As usual, the team checked into the downtown Baker Hotel on Akard

Street late on Friday morning. That afternoon, during their free time, the players walked the streets of downtown Dallas. Student manager Warren Gilbert had informed them that certain establishments were especially friendly to Aggie players. Reynolds Penland, the men's store, was one such place. A star player simply informed the salesman who he was, and a new suit would be provided at no charge. Of course, Aggie alums reimbursed the store.

The entire athletic department—staff, players, and coaches—along with school administrators, alums, and parents, showed up for the Friday evening team supper, a traditional prelude to the Saturday afternoon game. The gathering provided for plenty of mingling. Prominent exes who underwrote the event included J. L. Huffines, the auto dealer, Field Scovell of Southland Life, Tyree Bell of Austin Road Company, Julius Schepps and Jacob Metzger of Schepps Dairy, and others. Aggie alums always looked forward to rolling out the red carpet and rubbing shoulders with players, coaches, parents, and each other.

After the dinner concluded, alums made rounds on the team's floor—knocking on doors, shaking hands, passing out ten-dollar bills. Later, Cadets staged their traditional midnight yell practice outside the Baker. Of course, this was past the players' curfew and they were supposed to be asleep, but most participated through open windows in their rooms before hitting the sack.

Following a seven-thirty wake-up call and a pregame breakfast, the Aggies gathered outside the hotel. Suitcases were loaded into the bus's underbelly by student equipment managers. Players resembled soldiers preparing for battle—they were solemn and quiet, and their nervous energy intensified as they rode quietly toward the Cotton Bowl. Once there they would have their ankles, wrists, and knees taped, put on the pads, review strategies with position coaches, and relax for a few minutes before warm-ups. But first, the players walked out onto the field. Fans had not yet begun to arrive, and only the sounds of workmen preparing for the game broke the morning's silence. The guys mingled quietly, thinking about the day ahead.

As game time approached, an excited overflow crowd bustled toward their seats. It was a crisp fall day, a perfect day for football. Occasional billowy white clouds floated through the powder-blue November sky.

From only ninety minutes away, many Parisians drove in to see their hometown boy Buryl, not to mention SMU's Walker, take the field. Buryl's personal fan club was in attendance. Bo and her siblings, her brothers-in-law, Buryl's father Burton, and Coach Berry and his son Raymond Emmett joined another fifty-three thousand plus fans to crowd the stadium. Aggie faithful traditionally outnumbered SMU's fans at Dallas games. This day seemed no different, despite the dismal Aggie record and the Mustangs' spectacular team.

Just before escorting the Ags down toward the chalked field of play, Coach Stiteler spoke to the team. "Men, this is a great day for football. Games like today are why we play the game. This is what we live for, so let's go get 'em!" Claps and whoops and "Gig 'em, Aggies!" yells came from the fired-up players as their metal cleats clattered down the concrete ramp.

The Aggies wore white jerseys with block maroon numerals, light gray pants, maroon helmets with white stripes, and no face masks. From polished black high-top cleats, white stockings were pulled up to the knees. White-clad male yell leaders and the collie mascot Reveille II led the team onto the field. Corpsmen and fans stood to welcome their team as the Aggie fight song blared from the band's horns.

Coach Berry turned to Buryl's family and yelled over the crowd noise, "I love college football!" Folks within earshot nodded in earnest agreement. Then Coach leaned toward Bo and whispered, "I just hope Buryl is able to play." Naturally, he anticipated that Buryl's persistent ankle injury might again sideline him.

"He thinks he'll be okay," Bo said. "They're giving him a pain shot and a special tape job."

Coach Berry's eyebrows rose with Bo's comment. He knew that Buryl was tough and played with pain. But this was different. He could do irreparable damage to a "deadened" ankle. He knew that Buryl was aware of the downsides of such injections. But he said nothing to Bo.

At that moment, enthusiastic cheerleaders in red and blue uniforms led the Mustangs into the stadium. The team wore bright red jerseys accentuated by white numerals and helmets, white pants, blue stockings, and black high-top shoes. After the captains' coin toss at the center of the field, each band played its school's alma mater while rival fans stood in respectful silence, fedoras and military Cadet caps in hand. The SMU band played "The Star-Spangled Banner," and then, finally, it was game time.

Almost everyone in the stadium anticipated a one-sided SMU victory, and the game certainly started that way. Two early touchdown drives engineered by Doak Walker resulted in a 14–0 A&M deficit. The Aggie offense had been stymied, and momentum flowed significantly in SMU's direction. About the only positive Aggie development to this point in the game was the fact that Stautz had knocked Gil Johnson, one of the Ponies' better passers, out of the game. In response to several unproductive Aggie offensive series, Coach Berry lamented to Burton, "The coach is shuttling in plays. He needs to let Buryl run this game, let him call his own plays!" Burton enjoyed Berry's insights and was in agreement that Buryl could walk on water.

With the clock running out in the second quarter, Walker again guided his team toward pay dirt. A score would effectively put the game away before halftime. Doak rolled out and threw a tight spiral toward the end zone. Suddenly, at the last possible instant, safety Buryl Baty snatched the pass out of the air before it reached receiver Paul Page's hands and returned it all the way out to the SMU forty-six-yard line. Aggie fans finally had something to cheer about. A&M had dodged a decisive bullet.

"Nobody ran in a play this time," Coach Berry pointed out as the Aggie huddle assembled.

Now on offense, quarterback Baty called the signal and completed a thirty-nine-yard pass to Charley Wright at the SMU seven. The Aggies punched in a touchdown as the final seconds clicked from the scoreboard clock. After the successful point-after attempt, A&M had narrowed the deficit to 7–14. Aggie fans sent up an enormous roar that echoed clear across the deserted state fairgrounds. This was the first real sign of life that the Aggies had shown. And the momentum turned.

Uniformed cadets loved touchdowns for more reasons than one. By Corps tradition, they were entitled to kiss their dates (no matter how well they knew them) each time their team scored. Fathers of these coeds were no doubt comforted by the fact that this Aggie team had been floundering in a low-scoring streak. Certainly, a few blind dates were surprised, but ultimately most probably consented in the name of tradition. Several thousand kisses were exchanged before arm-in-arm Aggies swayed and sang, "Saw varsity's horns off, saw varsity's horns off, saw varsity's horns off . . . short!"

The dynamic voices of Bill Stern and Kern Tips boomed from radios all across the southwest. As the visiting team proceeded up the Cotton Bowl ramp to their halftime locker room, Coach Stiteler caught up with his quarterback and slapped him on the shoulder. "Good job, Buryl Baty!"

The Fightin' Texas Aggie Band marched onto the field for its precision halftime performance, and the crowd responded with a standing ovation. Bo's sister Glenda was awed and shouted with excitement. The smaller Mustang band's performance followed, and fans rose to their feet when the teams returned from their locker rooms to start the second half.

Each team suffered an unproductive possession before Baty again took control of the game on his second offensive series. Working from his own thirty-five-yard line, he completed a long pass; the ball flew almost fifty yards through the air to Charley Wright at the SMU 14. Another completion to Wright went to the eight-yard line before the Aggies drove the ball across the goal. The score was suddenly tied, 14–14. Game on! The Aggie band played and the fans went wild, screaming like all get-out after another traditional kiss.

I played, officiated and watched a lot of Southwest Conference football, and I never saw a better pure passer than Buryl Baty.—Barney Welch

In the stands, Coach Berry rested easier. "That's better. Buryl's calling the plays now. A smart quarterback has a better feel for the game than a coach on the sideline."

Unfortunately for the Aggies, it was now Doak Walker's turn to show his mettle. He returned the ensuing kickoff fifty-eight yards to the Aggie thirty-seven. From there, he willed his team to a touchdown by passing or running the ball on every play. Doak was a coach's son, so his great natural ability was augmented by exceptional fundamental techniques in all facets of the game. On this occasion, however, he missed the point-after attempt, making the score 20–14 in SMU's favor. Would this score be a backbreaker for the Aggies?

After SMU's kickoff, the game was again in Baty's hands. On the first play of the series, halfback Bob Goode raced down the field and cut sharply to the inside against tight coverage. He caught Baty's bullet for a big gain, but was judged to have pushed off of the defender. The pass interference call brought the ball back with a disheartening penalty. This put the Aggies deep in their own territory and a long way from where they needed to go. A collective Aggie "ooh" could be heard all the way over to the idle roller coaster. This game was beginning to feel like a roller coaster.

Back in the huddle, a deflated Cadet offense heard a calm but forceful signal caller: "Bob, I want you to run the same route, but this time, fake inside and break out on a zig to the flag. I'll hit you there. OK, guys, let's go get 'em. Drag-Z right on two. Ready, *break!*" Baty took the snap from center and dropped back to pass. As he saw Goode turn inside, he looked left and pump-faked the ball to ensure that the defender bit on the fake. It worked beautifully as Goode reversed back to the outside, wide open, and ran under a perfect Baty spiral for a huge gain. First and ten in SMU territory! Aggie fans were again on their toes, bouncing up and down and cheering at the top of their lungs. The Aggie offense rushed up to form a new huddle. Another spiral zipped toward pay dirt. However, Bob Folsom, the future Dallas mayor, intercepted Baty's pass at the SMU ten-yard line, killing the drive.

A&M's defense held Walker and SMU out of the end zone for the rest of the game. But Baty's offense was not finished. Late in the fourth quarter, consecutive completions to Copeland, Hillhouse, Goff, and Copeland put the A&M offense at SMU's twenty-two-yard line. The stage was now set for an improbable come-from-behind upset. The seconds were quickly ticking away. As fifty-three thousand tense spectators stood and cheered, Baty took the snap from the center and launched a bullet to his open receiver—and victory! But at exactly the last instant, Doak Walker came from nowhere to tip the pass out of the receiver's hands and into the hands of fellow Mustang, Paul Page. The clock ticked down as SMU fans chanted in unison, "Five, four, three, two, one!" It had been a great game, but it was one more heartbreaking loss for the Aggies. The teams and the fans streamed out onto the center of the field.

Doak and Buryl congratulated several people as they sought each other out in the crowd at midfield. SMU's Coach Matty Bell walked past and said, "Good game, Baty." Buryl nodded his thanks.

"Great game, Walker," Buryl said as the two finally shook hands. "You're a great player. Good luck the rest of the way."

"Thanks, Baty. You gave us everything we could handle today. Heck of a game!" Walker replied.

As soon as the two stars disengaged, the redheaded, bespectacled Coach Rusty Russell, who had coached Masonic Home against Buryl's Paris High team in the playoffs eight years earlier, stood in front of Buryl, smiling broadly. "You've had a good career, Buryl, and you were terrific today."

"Thanks, Coach. Congratulations on the win," Buryl replied, still engaged in a firm handshake.

Coach Russell's words were kind, but the bitter taste of the loss remained. Buryl worked his way back up the ramp, among a number of teammates, to the visitors' locker room. There, in disgust, Stautz kicked his locker and slammed his helmet violently on the concrete floor. This had become a common occurrence over the course of eight straight losses.

By that time, quite a few boosters were already milling around, talking with and congratulating players, shaking their hands. "We almost beat Doak Walker!" they bellowed.

Buryl showered and dressed hurriedly to greet his family and friends outside the locker room. Bo hugged him excitedly, and his father extended his left hand to shake. Coach Berry chimed in. "Y'all didn't lose; the clock just ran out on you."

Buryl, still fired up, nodded. "Yeah, Coach, we should have won that game."

The next morning's headline read, "Baty Passes Scare Ponies as Walker Prevents SMU Defeat." The *Dallas Morning News* article by Felix McKnight reported the consensus of the press box (consisting of press and rival SWC coaches) that the Aggies had delivered the highly touted SMU Mustangs their toughest contest of the season. The *Dallas Times Herald* reported that "Baty's pinpoint passing befuddled SMU" and named Buryl as the Southwest Conference Passer of the Week. Perhaps this would set the stage for better things to come. Starting A&M players found more sealed envelopes in their lockers the next afternoon.

The next week, Buryl's ankle was painfully sore after having played the game with the deadening injection. He hoped it would feel better before Saturday, but for now, he could only ice and rest it. During practice, the Fish scout team noticed that their varsity opponents didn't seem quite as surly as in weeks past. Their spirits seemed, on the contrary, more upbeat. Afterwards, alums made rounds with the varsity players in the locker room, or in Baty's case, the training room, shaking hands.

The battle-worn Aggies' next opponent was the tough Rice Owls. During the second quarter, Odell Stautzenberger cold-cocked a Rice defensive lineman with an uppercut to the nose, and an official's time-out allowed trainers to help the disoriented player stagger from the field. Still, at the end of the day, the Aggies suffered a convincing defeat.

The final and most important Aggie contest of the year, any year, was all that remained. Along with it went one of the most revered Aggie traditions: the bonfire and midnight yell practice held on Wednesday night before the annual Thanksgiving Day game. Since the first bonfire in the '20s, cadets, with Fish doing most of the heavy work, had labored for weeks in preparation. They gathered lumber and logs and stacked them dozens of feet high. When ignited, the huge fire would be visible for miles while thousands of students and alums participated in a spirited pep rally. For the weeks leading up to the event, this growing pile of kindling received around-the-clock protection by Fish guards. "Tea-sippers" (t.u. alums and students) were notorious for attempts to sabotage the tradition. In fact, in '47 they had attempted to drop a makeshift firebomb on the woodpile from a Piper Cub airplane before being chased away by cadet .22 rifle fire.[1] Tea-sippers argued that such retaliatory actions were warranted, as their Longhorn mascot had been repeatedly stolen and branded, painted, and otherwise mutilated by Aggies over the years. In fact, Aggie lore has it that the mascot's name, Bevo, was creatively engineered as a result of a villainous Aggie prank.

A&M had never avoided defeat in Memorial Stadium. To add to their woes, Baty, identified by the *Bryan Eagle* as "the great passer on whom A&M's hopes were pinned," was not expected to play due to his ankle injury.

Still, sixty-eight thousand enthusiastic fans, the largest crowd to ever witness a UT-A&M game, filled the stadium on this brisk clear Thanksgiving Day. Aggies flocked to Austin. Busted lips and black eyes were not uncommon in the Corps section, because uniformed cadets were frequently mugged in the hours leading up to the game by groups of fired-up t.u. students and fans.

Blaring bands and screaming fans greeted the two teams as they ran single file onto the field. Bevo, t.u.'s horned bovine mascot, stood sedately in the south end zone. "The Eyes of Texas are Upon You" echoed loudly as t.u. faithful sang at the top of their mighty lungs. The in-your-face song grated on the nerves of every Aggie and alum, and its rendition intimidated more than a few visiting players.

The Ags wore simple dark maroon jerseys with white numerals, white football pants, maroon stockings, and maroon helmets. "They look great!" pumped-up Aggie fans exclaimed. The proud Longhorns wearing white jerseys, white helmets, orange pants, and orange stockings, looked to Aggie fans like a bunch of tropical fruits.

After warm-ups, each team retreated to its locker room for a few preparatory minutes before the game. Nervous Aggie players dealt with pregame jitters in different ways. Some sat alone in stony silence, others jawed to anyone who would listen. Weak ankles were re-taped. Some players discussed assignments on certain plays or defensive schemes. A few heaved their guts out. The thick tension was interrupted as Coach Stiteler spoke loudly: "Aggies, listen up!" The room turned dead silent.

"This game today, against this Texas team, is the reason we all came to Texas A&M. And you seniors, this will be your last college game. You'll remember this day for the rest of your lives, so make it a good one. We're here to *win* this game! Let's go!" The players responded with loud claps and shouts of "Let's get 'em!" and "Gig 'em, Aggies!" They were raring to go as they ran out onto the field.

Baty sat injured on the sideline bench. The Aggies were ineffective in the first half, reaching midfield only once, and Texas led at halftime, 7–0. This margin held until early in the fourth quarter when Aggie Ralph Daniel intercepted a pass at the Longhorn twenty-three-yard line. As the Aggies pushed the ball across the goal line to tie the game, 7–7, the Fightin' Texas Aggie Band blared . . .

Hullabaloo Caneck! Caneck!
Hullabaloo Caneck! Caneck!
Goodbye to Texas University
So long to the orange and the whi-i-ite
Good luck to the good old Texas Aggies
They are the ones who show the real old fight . . .

"Beat the hell outta t.u.!" screamed thousands of Aggies at the conclusion of the resounding tune.

The teams exchanged punts. The Aggies, attempting to mount a scoring drive, put the ball in the air. However, an errant pass fell into the hands of t.u.'s Tom Landry to end the drive. The Longhorns took advantage of this opportunity, scoring with only three minutes and fifty seconds left in the fourth quarter to surge ahead, 14–7.

As orange-clad players and fans celebrated, the Aggie faithful surely felt their day was done. This was beginning to look like a familiar and disappointing finish. A&M had been stymied by the Longhorns all game long. Even Bill Stern's normally excited radio voice revealed a twinge of pessimism over the airwaves. It would have been easy for the maroon-and-white to write the game off as another close loss, and call it a year.

On the sideline, Coach Stiteler knew that a spark was needed. He turned to look on his sideline bench. His eyes immediately met those of Buryl Baty, who had positioned himself next to the coach. "How's your ankle?" Stiteler asked.

"I can take us to a score, Coach," Baty replied.

"How's your ankle?"

"I can go, Coach. I don't need to run."

"Okay, show us what you've got left in the tank, old man."

Baty jogged out to the referee and checked into the game. He fielded and returned the Texas kickoff to the A&M twenty-eight-yard line, but was noticeably limping when he climbed from beneath the pile. As he lined up at quarterback, the well-coached Texas team knew to anticipate a pass play. Meanwhile, to a man the Aggie team rose from the bench and stood excitedly on the sideline. They'd seen Baty's passing antics before, and they knew that anything could happen. The game rode on this series.

With 3:10 left on the clock, sophomore halfback Charlie Royalty lined up wide on the left side and end Charlie Wright lined up on the right, while Baty stood in the shotgun formation. The ball was snapped, and Baty dropped back a couple of steps. Royalty raced straight down the field, then cut toward the middle to cross his pattern with Wright's.

Baty eluded a tackler and launched a towering spiral. Fifty yards downfield, Royalty extended his open hands as the football approached. However, at the last possible second, the Texas defensive back dove and tipped the ball into the air. Wright, running nearby, reacted immediately to catch the pigskin and bolted untouched toward the Promised Land.

"*Touchdown . . . Aggies!*" screamed radio announcer Stern. "Charlie Wright caught Buryl Baty's pass and out-raced the Longhorns seventy-two yards to the end zone!"

Aggie fans cheered wildly as t.u. fans stood silent, dazed. As the energized Aggie offense reassembled for the extra-point attempt, an alum yelled from the stands, "If the kicker makes this extra point, I'll pay him twenty-five bucks!"

"Hell, I'll buy his kicking shoe if he makes it!" another Aggie fan responded. After Herb Turley's successful extra point, the score was tied, 14–14.

UT's following offensive series was unsuccessful, and they punted. The Aggies regained possession in Texas territory with plenty of time to advance downfield again. However, Stiteler yelled, "Run out the clock!" In the huddle, players asked, "What's he thinking? We can win this game outright!" But the coach insisted. When the final gun sounded, the winless Aggies had broken the Memorial Stadium jinx and knocked the mighty Longhorns out of a tie for the SWC championship. A&M fans jumped and cheered as the teams left the field.

The postgame locker room buzzed. While not a championship or even a victory, the game had represented the best showing of the year on the greatest stage: Memorial Stadium. Coach Stiteler spoke a few words of praise, answered by players' cheers and clapping. Alums crowded the room, laughing and shaking hands. In the meantime, each senior made his way around to every teammate to bid farewell.

"Stautz, it was an honor to be on the field with you. Good luck," Buryl said as their grip tightened. Buryl had always felt a connection with this man—a respect for his passion and even for his reckless abandon. In a way, Buryl's wild side had lived vicariously through Stautz. And Buryl knew that behind his rough and gruff exterior, the guy was nothing but heart.

"Good luck to you, too, Buryl," Stautz answered. "You pulled us out of the fire today." He paused. "I'm ready to hurry up and graduate, but let's stay in touch."

After showering and donning street clothes, Buryl emerged from the locker room to find his family waiting outside. Dozens of lingering fans cheered and applauded as they recognized him. "Way to go, Baty! Yea, Aggies!"

Buryl first embraced Bo. This was a bittersweet moment. He had just played his final collegiate game. He then turned to the rest of his friends and family.

"We could've won that game," he muttered. "Stiteler was trying to save his job." Buryl was also perplexed that so many Aggies appeared so happy, as if the game had resulted in a victory. His family recognized this competitive spirit; they had seen it before.

A&M had finished the season 0–9–1. The next day, the *Dallas Morning News* called the game "the greatest performance of the '48 season;

the Aggies battled the highly favored Longhorns to an astonishing 14–14 tie." The touchdown that saved the day for the Aggies was the stuff of legends; the A&M yearbook ran a headline that read, "A&M Breaks Austin Jinx, 'Beats' t.u. 14–14."

I can still see the touchdown unfold in my mind. It was a great day, and as far as we were concerned, we'd won the game. It was a moral victory to us.—
Alton Bailey

This game ended Buryl's college career on a high note. He had attended A&M with plans to win championships. That goal had not been realized, but he could not have been prouder to be an Aggie. He had loved playing the game and he loved his teammates. "We had so much potential. I wish we'd won a few more games," he lamented at that evening's Thanksgiving supper table.

After the season, Bo and Buryl returned frequently to Paris. They always enjoyed socializing with old friends. Buryl also looked forward to visiting with Coach Berry on these trips home. Berry could talk endlessly about the game he loved, or a particular play that he liked. "The Sweep is a great play," he would claim. "The key is for the ballcarrier to run as fast as he can. I once watched a young coach yell at his blocker to hold his block longer. I told him he was 'jumping on the wrong boy. The ballcarrier has to run faster to get to the hole when it opens.' They can always run faster. You gotta push 'em hard every day," he said. Buryl's memory immediately flashed back to the countless times he'd heard Coach Berry yell out, "Run, son, run!" and "Run faster!" Buryl grinned and nodded.

"Coach, you have the perfect job," he told his mentor.

• • •

Buryl needed to make a final decision. The Detroit Lions had drafted him to play pro ball after his junior year. He had also established himself as a leader and was in demand as a coach. He had debated the options in his mind for the past several months. Was he ready to move on to the pros? Or had the war changed his priorities? What about his recurring injuries? Coach Berry had advised him to follow his instinct. Buryl, in the end, had had enough.

Bo encouraged him. "You love playing football. It doesn't have to be forever; we can come back anytime we want."

"No, I've made all the touchdowns I'm gonna make. I want to work with kids," he responded. "And to win a state championship." He knew what he needed to do. At age twenty-five, Buryl hung up his cleats, on his own terms.

Soon an announcement appeared in the press:

Luling News Boy, June 15, 1949.
BURYL BATY WILL COACH THE LULING EAGLES
Buryl Baty, ex-serviceman and outstanding football player for A&M College, has been employed to coach the Eagle eleven next season. He will complete his master's degree at A&M before moving with his wife to Luling in July.

Mr. Baty has a congenial personality, and the Athletic Association and School Board are congratulating themselves on their good fortune in being able to employ a man with such an outstanding gridiron experience. He's a Texas boy, a graduate of the Paris High School, and as a football player with A&M, he was reputed to be one of the outstanding passers of the Southwest Conference.

Luling was not far from College Station. But life would be a long way from what Bo and Buryl had been accustomed to.

Buryl Baty, circa 1942. (Family photo)

Buryl, Coach Raymond Berry, and Lowry Inzer after the Sherman victory, 1940. (Courtesy of Skipper Steely, *The Raymond Berry Years*)

Football Queens

Bettie Jo Hutchinson
Betty Cross

Although both are named Betty, one is a stunning brunette and the other is a dazzling blonde. These two girls are known to both students and teachers for their charming personalities. During their four years in Paris High School, they have both been very active in extracurricular activities, taking part in numerous club activities and being recipients of several other honors bestowed on them by their classmates. They both justly deserve the honor given them by the football squad.

Football queens Bettie Jo ("Bo") Hutchinson and Betty Cross Abbett, 1942. (Courtesy of Paris High School yearbook—*The Owl*)

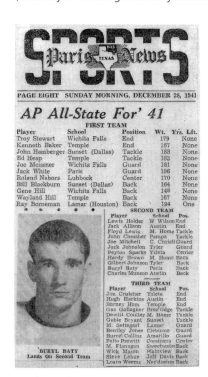

Buryl on All-State team, 1941. (Courtesy of the *Paris News*)

Buryl Baty Freshman Passing Sensation, Amazes Coaches With His Accurate Tossing

A facsimile of Davey O'Brien—that's the name given to Buryl Baty, sensational passing ace of the Aggie freshman team who has coaches quite amazed at his ingenious hurling accuracy.

Baty, former Paris High school star, has looked like a million dollars both passing and running in the two games played by the Fish. He's looked so good in this passing game that Coach Lil Dimmitt prompted to say that the tall, lanky freshman is the best prospective aerial star to hit Aggieland in many a year. And don't forget, Lil was taking into account such tossers as Walemon Price, Marion Pugh, Derace Moser and Leo Daniels!

One thing I like about Buryl. He's cool, methodical and knows exactly where he's throwing the ball. He's the kind of a boy who will never whimper or fret because his teammates failed to block for him properly. Only the other day, while carrying the offense against the varsity team, Baty was spilled continually to the ground on his pass attempts and not once did he complain or utter a word.

Yessir, there's a boy that'll set this conference on fire someday and give Coach Homer Norton a truly great passing ace. He has everything desired of a football player—poise, coolness and efficiency.

If you really want to see some passing skill, then trot out to Kyle Field Thursday, November 12 when the Aggie Fish play the Rice Slimes and watch Buryl Baty toss that pigskin! He'll really amaze you.

In praise of "a boy that'll set this conference on fire." (Courtesy of *Bryan-College Station Eagle,* Fall 1942)

Above is the star-studded Texas Aggie freshman backfield which is expected to deal misery to the Rice Slimes this afternoon. Left to right are Marion Flanagan, David Daily, Gus White and Buryl Baty.

Bo and Buryl before European deployment, 1944. (Family photo)

Buryl's squad in England, 1944. (Photo by Buryl Baty)

Trier in ruins, 1945. (Photo by Buryl Baty)

Victory in Europe Day parade in Luxemburg, with dummy of Hitler, May 1945. (Photo by Buryl Baty)

Luzon, Philippines camp, Baty's squad HQ, 1945. (Photo by Buryl Baty)

Aggie QB Buryl Baty passing near Kyle Field, 1947. (Courtesy of Texas A&M Yearbook—*The Longhorn*)

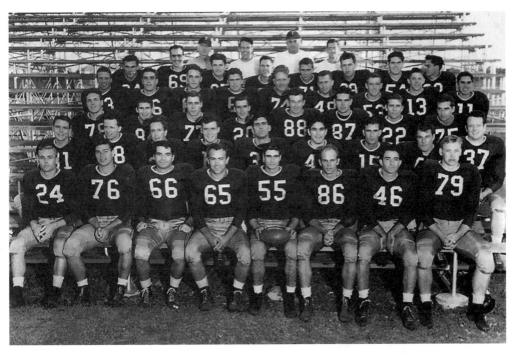

Aggie team picture, 1948. Buryl Baty is in second row, third from right, no. 15. Odell Stautzenberger to Buryl's left. (Courtesy of Texas A&M Yearbook—*Aggieland,* 1949)

November 6, 1948, Texas A&M vs. SMU game program.

PASSER OF THE WEEK

Buryl Baty, A&M's pin-point passer, almost upset the Southern Methodist apple cart Saturday with a brilliant aerial show. Buryl tossed 33 times, completing 16 for 224 of the 238 Cadet air yards. (Dallas Times Herald, November 7, 1948)

Drawing by Bill McClanahan. (Courtesy of the *Dallas Times Herald*)

Aggie Bonfire and midnight yell practice, before the 1948 Thanksgiving game at t.u. (Courtesy of Texas A&M Yearbook—*Aggieland,* 1949)

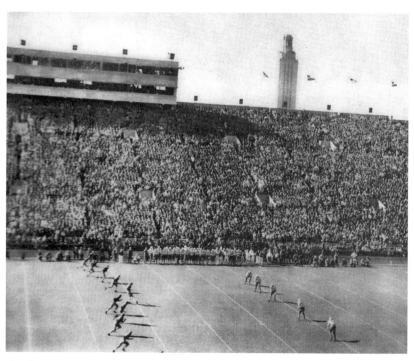

Thanksgiving Day, 1948. Texas game at Memorial Stadium, Austin. "The tower did not shine as bright as t.u. students had hoped." (Courtesy of Texas A&M Yearbook—*Aggieland*)

16 A Calling

Luling was a beautiful little town in the heart of south Texas, fifty miles due south of Austin. Founded in 1874, it had originally been a rowdy center for cattle drivers on the Chisholm Trail. These cowboys' contempt for the law contributed to Luling's reputation as the toughest town in Texas. After the great cattle drives ended in the late 1880s, the community quieted down and cotton ruled the economy. Luling gained some degree of commercial prominence when it was designated as a railroad stop between Houston and San Antonio, and in 1928 oil discoveries brought economic prosperity.

This seemed a comfortable fit for Bo, with a familiar small-town feel. Luling sported a well kept downtown with shops, a drugstore, a theater, and cafés. There was an impressive new Petroleum Building near the train depot, and oil pumpjacks were scattered across the town and countryside. The Batys rented a well-maintained old house with a wide front porch, in a pleasant neighborhood with manicured lawns and big trees. Bo's sister Glenda spent her vacation helping them move. As they settled in, high school football players stopped by the house to introduce themselves. They couldn't wait to welcome Coach Baty to town.

Luling's teams had been consistently weak, and they were routinely and soundly beaten by rivals San Marcos, Seguin, New Braunfels, and Lockhart. More than a few townspeople complained that the new hire had no coaching experience, but Luling's players were excited about him. Rumor had it that he had set a record for the longest TD pass in Aggie history. They were not disappointed when they met him.

Over the next few days, Coach Baty made a few visits himself, one of which was with Ralph Smith, a returning senior letterman for the coming season, who lived out amid sprawling cotton fields and the oil patch where his father worked for the Mobil Oil Company. Ralph was surprised on that hot August afternoon to hear the cracking sound of tires rolling down the gravel driveway. The car door swung open, and out stepped a tall man with dark hair.

Baty extended his hand and introduced himself. "I've heard about you," he said, "and I'm looking forward to working with you. We should have a good team this year. You'll be there Monday, right?" Ralph was flattered that the coach would come all that way. No coach had ever come to his house before.

From the first day, players were impressed with Coach Baty's knowledge of the game, his attention to detail, his emphasis on discipline, and his confidence. He seemed relatively quiet, but he had a strong presence and his voice was a powerful baritone. He quickly earned the respect of the team's members—with a few exceptions.

During the first week of school, the new coach entered his packed third-period study hall. As he passed a small group of his new players, Jimmy Earl Brown deadpanned to his nearby friends, in a low, deep voice, "Hello, Buryl." Jimmy Earl was reportedly a very good fullback and a popular kid. Surrounding teammates quietly snickered under their breath, confident that Jimmy Earl's defiance was their private joke. They were wrong.

That afternoon, Coach Baty pulled Jimmy Earl aside. "Jim, do you want to play football this year?"

"Yes, sir."

"Look me in the eye when I'm talking to you."

"Yes, sir."

"I know I don't need to tell you why we're having this discussion. If you want to play football, you will run fifty laps, starting right now. If you don't run or if you stop before you've finished all fifty, you won't be on this team. Do you understand?"

"Yes, sir."

Jimmy Earl took off around the practice field for his first of fifty. Every player took notice. This new guy commanded, and demanded, respect. He didn't take any nonsense.

The new coach applied everything he had learned from his own coaches and his playing experiences, including fundamental, motivational, and conditioning techniques. And most important, he required good grades. This all seemed natural, as he emphasized principles that he had heard a thousand times. It was all programmed into him.

From the first days of practice, a number of grown men gathered around the field to watch the team's drills and check out the new coach. This seemed to be a promising sign that the parents supported the team.

Inevitably, a few of these men found their way into the coaching office to introduce themselves as fathers of certain players. They were very friendly and chatted about the heat, the coach's Aggie career, the team's prospects. Before long, dads were politicking: "My boy Bobby was the best quarterback" or "My boy Joey scored the most touchdowns last year." The coach's office eventually emptied as the locker room cleared out. The boys and their fathers had finally gone home for supper. Coach Baty sat alone with the returning assistant coach, Kenneth McGee.

"Is that normal behavior around here, Ken?" the new head coach asked.

McGee rolled his eyes. "Yep, it's been going on for years."

The following day, many of the same men again clustered around Coach Baty as he walked from the practice field and into his office. One conversation led to another, and again the discussion moved to their respective sons' abilities and exploits.

"Gentlemen, I'm sorry to interrupt you, but we can't have this. I'm the coach, and I will have to determine who plays and how much. You're all welcome at practice anytime, and I'm happy to talk about other things. But these discussions are not fair to the boys, your sons included. And from this point on—the coaches' office is offlimits to parents."

I remember the conversation like it was yesterday. The office was right next to the locker room and we heard every word. We were impressed that he'd talk to them that way and glad he said what he said. We didn't want the dads to influence how much we got to play.—Charles Bullock

Early September practices were hot and tough, tougher than the Eagles had ever been through before. They practiced hard and ran countless conditioning laps and sprints. With every repetition, the coaches would reiterate that the team had to be in better shape than their opponents. "It will give you an edge in the fourth quarter," they promised.

I remember thinking I was gonna die. Coach Baty taught me that if I kept on going I wouldn't die. "Never quit, keep on going!" he'd say. He made men of us.—Jerry Patillo

Paris friends James and Bettie Jackson drove down to visit the Batys for a weekend, and they all enjoyed catching up on old times. Buryl invited James, one of his old teammates at Paris High, to one of the team's practices, and James was delighted to watch a lively session, one that reminded him of Coach Berry's routine. After a very well organized, two-hour practice working on individual and team skills, the boys ran wind sprints and headed for cold showers in the locker room. But not all the players went inside. A sizeable group of enthusiastic boys gathered around Coach Baty for some voluntary work—and fun. First, they had a punting competition. No one punted farther than the mentor. Next they held similar competitions in passing and catching the ball. Charles Bullock loved the private tutoring. Coach Baty taught him advanced quarterbacking techniques, and they discussed game plans: how to take advantage of the opposing team with play selection and sequence, how to call a smart game. Everyone seemed to be learning and having fun. It was obvious that the players liked being with their young coach.

We looked forward to every practice. He inspired us.—Charles Bullock

After practice James marveled, "Buryl, I'm amazed at how well you work with those boys."

"Simple," Buryl said. "First, I love those kids. And second, they'll play a whole lot better if we make it fun."

Later, as the couples sat down to their home-cooked supper, James commented, "Bo, it looked like the coach was having more fun than the kids on the practice field today."

"I'm not surprised," she said. "I don't think I've ever seen him this happy."

As the season got underway, the fun intensified. First the Eagles put away a strong South San (San Antonio) squad. This was the first team that Coach Baty had ever seen consisting of all Mexican kids. The next morning, all the good people of Luling turned first to the newspaper story about their own team:

Luling News Boy
SMITHVILLE AT LULING
By Jedge Winkle

At long last a mighty cheer goes up for Coach Buryl Baty, an old Aggie from Texas A&M. Coach Baty, us watching him with anxious eyes, sprung the combination and lo-and-behold the lock to the "tomb" was mastered. We can get back into the groove of whooping it up in Luling once more. . . .

Crowds of interested spectators have been watching workouts during the pre-season and are pretty well impressed with what they've seen. Fans can now get behind the Eagles with confidence and watch a bunch of boys come to life. . . .

Three victories will do it; then comes San Marcos, the first important collision between these old feudists. Buryl Baty wakes up to find himself the most popular coach in South Texas, bar none. . . . The fans can flock in Friday night with a new twinkle in their eyes. He is it—folks—take our word for it—and stand with him to the last toot of the whistle.

And victory was indeed in their future. The Eagles snuffed Smithville 32–0 and then beat Bastrop 31–0, with quarterback Bullock completing seventeen of eighteen passes and several TDs. Strong rival San Marcos was next to fall, 14–6. Luling's boys had not beaten San Marcos in years. The town was going crazy; their team was 4–0 and undaunted. The main topic of conversation, and often the only topic of conversation, was how their Eagles had rolled over the first four opponents. The school, the entire town, was on a high, bursting with pride.

But how would they hold up against the next opponent, the powerful New Braunfels Unicorns? New Braunfels had always been a Goliath-like opponent to Luling. Locals just wanted to win for a change. This Unicorn team, however, presented a major challenge; they had just beaten Yoakum, 62–7. "I can't wait for Friday night to get here!" echoed on the streets, in business establishments, in halls and in classrooms.

That week, practices were intense and spirited, and Friday night arrived quickly. The Eagles started out with a fast-paced spread offense, passing the ball on every play. New Braunfels seemed to be confused and in a state of chaos. Few substitutions were allowed, by rule, so New Braunfels tried dropping defensive linemen back to cover all the Luling receivers. Luling played a great first quarter and was very much in the game until halftime. However, New Braunfels adjusted their approach in the second half to slow the Eagles down. Superior talent and depth took over, and Coach Baty's team suffered their first painful loss of the season.

During the season, a variety of challenges confronted Coach Baty's authority and stamina. In one case, a player had earned his way into the coach's doghouse and was ordered to take a certain number of laps. As the boy's enthusiasm for his punishment rapidly dwindled, he heard a loud, clear voice: "You will run those laps or you will not play in the game this week. We'll count every one of 'em or you won't play." The kid picked up the pace immediately. In another instance, the entire starting line sat on the bench for the first quarter of a game as punishment for loafing at practice. When a player had to serve a detention for getting into trouble during school, he was, without exception, met with a hard swat or two from Coach Baty's paddle, administered on the goal line with the player in a three-point stance. Immediately after receiving the painful licks, the player was required to sprint to the fifty-yard line and back.

As the play caller, quarterback Bullock occasionally got himself into a different form of trouble. By rule, plays could not be called or signaled from the sidelines. Coach Baty was infuriated by frequent and risky Bullock attempts to "go for it"—to try to move the chains on fourth down. His fussing abated, however, when fourth-down attempts were successful.

After amassing a to-date 5–2 record, the Eagles made a miserable showing in the first half of the Seguin game. Down 0–14 at the break, the dejected team trudged into the locker room to regroup. There, anxiety filled the air. How would Coach react? Coach Baty always seemed to have something motivational to say, but after this dreadful performance, he would surely chew them out for what they all knew was sloppy work. "What will he say?" Time passed, and passed, with no appearance by their leader.

After fourteen minutes had inched by, Coach Baty suddenly appeared, and a hush fell on the room. After a few long seconds he spoke. "You look real pretty in your dresses tonight."

Silence . . .

"OK, girls, powder your noses; it's time to go out and play."

He turned around, pulled open the heavy gray metal door, and walked toward the field with assistant Coach McGee a half step behind. The team sat stunned, embarrassed for a few seconds, then followed angrily.

The Eagles brought a different tempo from the halftime locker room. Luling switched to a no-huddle spread offense. Momentum turned, and the complexion of the game changed. The Eagles scored three touchdowns in the fourth quarter to win 21–14. Another victory!

Coach Baty always knew what to say. I'll never forget that talk as long as I live.—Jerry Patillo

We never complained again about conditioning drills in practice after that fourth quarter comeback. We appreciated the results of our efforts.
—Ralph Smith

After another victory, the record stood at 7–2. In addition to Bastrop and Seguin, the Eagles had rolled over Yoakum (where the ragged, cocklebur-filled football field was not mowed; it had been grazed—and defecated upon—by sheep), San Marcos, Smithville, South San, and the Texas School for the Deaf "Silents." But the Lockhart Lions were the prize, and they were up next. Luling had not beaten Lockhart, its most hated rival, in years.

Early in the week, Coach Baty spoke to his players: "Men, as you know, Lockhart is a tough team. And believe me—they know you're a tough team. In fact, they're practicing extra-hard right now to try and beat you." A moment of silence passed. "You can beat Lockhart. And there's something you can do to make sure of that. Do you want to know what that is?"

"Yes, sir!" all replied loudly.

"OK, this is strictly voluntary; I want it to be you kids that do it. You'll increase your chances to beat Lockhart by running four extra laps after practice every night this week. That's almost an extra mile a day. It'll help you in the fourth quarter, when we're gonna win the game." Each night after practice, every player enthusiastically ran his voluntary laps.

Friday finally arrived. A short school day awaited the team. After a fourth-period pep rally in the gym and an early lunch, the team was excused from afternoon classes for some free time before the trip to Lockhart. Nervous players donned their uniforms, then stuffed shoulder pads, helmets, and game cleats into duffle bags. Fifteen short miles to the north, their team bus pulled through a gate and toward the visitors' locker room.

Lockhart fans were already lined up to watch the Eagles arrive. "You boys better hold on to your jock straps!" one surly old fellow jeered as Luling's players filed past. The sound of a practicing band's drums in the distance served to help rattle the Eagles' nerves.

Inside the locker room, the players rested and waited. After a time,

Coach Baty summoned them to "gather up!" He knew they had a severe case of the pregame jitters, and he wanted to calm them.

"Men, we've prepared all week, all season, for this game. And most of Luling has driven up here to see you win. You're ready. You're better prepared, better conditioned, and a better team than Lockhart." Coach Baty paused. "The only thing that matters is how well you play. If you play just like you practiced this week, you'll win. That's all you have to do. Can you do that?"

"Yes, sir!"

"Ok, let's go do what we came here to do."

They jogged slowly out into the sharp November air and the quickly filling stadium. As the Eagles worked their way to the visiting sideline, the team captains ran ahead for the coin toss. It was as if the bright stadium lights had lured in the entire town. Every person in the packed stadium stood quietly for the national anthem, the pregame prayer, and school songs. Then, with bands dueling and cheerleaders jumping and the air thick with anticipation, the opening kickoff burst into the cold breeze.

The Eagles led 6–0 after two quarters. In the halftime locker room, Coach Baty encouraged his team. "What did we tell you? You played a great first half, and you're going to play a great second half. We're going to start by scoring another touchdown in the third quarter. Got it?" All agreed.

Both teams moved the ball successfully to begin the quarter. Luling converted a turnover into a touchdown, then drove for another score and a commanding 19–0 lead. Lockhart, however, answered with two scores to narrow the margin to a too-close-for-comfort 19–14 score. And there was still time left on the clock.

Eagle fans, players, and coaches began to sweat. Lockhart had wrestled away momentum, and Luling's now small scoreboard advantage was in jeopardy. The Eagles needed to move the ball and eat up the clock. The home team knew in their hearts that they could stop these Luling kids, just like in years past.

The largest crowd of the season stood tensely and yelled at the top of their lungs, but not a player on the field noticed the roar.

After the ensuing kickoff, a couple of straight-ahead plays earned an Eagle first down. The clock ticked. Children in the standing crowd maneuvered on their tiptoes to catch glimpses of the action. Three conservative plays resulted in another first down. Then a pass on third and long earned another. Bullock, Williams, and Ohlendorf drove the football down the home team's throat. They were threatening inside Lockhart's twenty-yard line as Luling fans loudly mimicked the clock: "Five—four—three—two—one. *Yea!*"

Luling players and fans swarmed the field. They hugged each other, their parents, and their girlfriends. The band played the fight song again and again. The bus ride home seemed to last mere seconds. Townspeople celebrated and mingled in the square into the wee hours and honked their horns up and down the drag.

Luling's Eagles finished the season at eight wins and just two losses, the best record in years. The icing on the cake was the victory over Lockhart. The team was the talk of the proud town. They had finished second in district to undefeated New Braunfels, but a "Wait 'til next year!" sentiment prevailed.

The postseason football banquet was scheduled. Several players hung out at Coach Baty's house the Saturday afternoon of the event. The kids obviously felt right at home. Sitting on the comfortable front porch, they relived the just-finished season. Midafternoon, several of the team mothers stopped by. After chatting for a few minutes, they insisted on taking Bo for a drive as they continued their visit. As they passed Mr. Hoskins' Ford dealership on the town's square, the small talk was interrupted. "Bo, look at that car. Isn't that the most beautiful car you've ever seen?"

"Well, it looks like a nice car," Bo said, "but I don't like that color."

That evening at the banquet, Head Coach Baty handed out accolades to his team for their glorious season. He then surrendered the microphone to the president of the Booster Club, who announced a "special presentation." Every person in the room turned to look at Coach Baty and his wife. The Batys were thrilled as keys to a brand new black Ford sedan were presented to them. A long standing ovation followed—a gesture of appreciation and respect. Of course, Bo was embarrassed and quickly retracted her earlier comment; she liked the color after all.

In March of 1950, Bo sent a note to her sister Alta. It read,

Dear sisters, brothers-in-law & aunts,
    Guess you'll all be surprised to death. The date is September and we are really thrilled (especially Buryl—you'd think no one

else had ever had an addition before.) We are fine. Must go now
and hope you all don't mind us sending a community notice.
      Lots of Love,
      "Bo"

The Batys had wanted a baby for some time. Bo had even suggested the possibility of adoption, but Buryl would not hear of it. "No, if God wants us to have a baby, we'll have one." They were both thrilled about starting a family. "Bo, this is great! We're in a great place and we're gonna have a baby. We are on top of the world!" Buryl paced the kitchen floor. He was too excited to sit.

• • •

Baty's reputation had grown rapidly as one of the top young coaches in South Texas. He answered calls about several potential coaching jobs, including one in nearby Conroe. Another inquiry came in from the athletic director in El Paso. Buryl listened, and consulted with Coach Berry for advice. "Buryl, to my knowledge no all-Mexican team has ever won the state football championship. It may be a long shot, but if anybody can do it, you can."

The Batys discussed the move. "This is a promotion—a bigger school. They have good athletes. They just won state in baseball. We can do it, too," Buryl reasoned. "And we have friends out there; we can find a house in the same neighborhood."

"But it's so far from home," Bo argued. "Mother is alone now, and she'll need us someday. I want her to know our children, and for them to know her." Now that she was pregnant, the importance of family ties grew for Bo. She fidgeted, rubbing her forefinger back and forth over her thumb. "I'll never stand in your way. But I want to move back closer to home in the not-too-distant future. Promise me that."

"I promise," Buryl agreed.

Coach Baty now faced one of the hardest tasks he had ever encountered—telling the kids, his next year's team, of his decision. He called a team meeting. "Men, I have news for you," he began, "news that's very hard for me to deliver. I've accepted an offer to become the head coach at a larger school in El Paso, Texas. This is difficult because I am very fond of you all. And I know you'll be confused about what it means." He paused.

"This is an opportunity for growth for me and my family. Don't think for a minute that it's not painful for me to leave you, and to leave Luling. We'll miss you. But don't let it hurt your team. You're good players, and you know that now. I'm confident that you'll make Luling proud. I wish you the best of luck. Don't hesitate to look me up anytime."

Long faces left the locker room that afternoon.

Before leaving town, Buryl returned the new Ford he had been given. "I just don't feel right about keeping this car if I'm not going to be here," he explained to Mr. Hoskins, the booster who had orchestrated the generous gift in the first place.

He was an honorable man.—Larry Hoskins, Luling player and Mr. Hoskin's son

A headline in the *El Paso Herald-Post* announced Bowie High School's new hire:

June 15, 1950
BATY GETS COACH JOB AT BOWIE
Buryl Baty, 26-year-old graduate of Texas A. and M. College has been appointed head football coach of Bowie High School, H. E. Charles, director of personnel for El Paso public schools, announced today.

Baty . . . will move to El Paso this month. He is married but has no children.

Baty played quarterback for the Aggies three years. He also quarterbacked Paris High School grid squad.

He was head coach at Luling High School in 1949. His team won eight and lost two. Baty replaces Buck Gibbs at Bowie. He came to El Paso Saturday and was pleased with the Bowie High setup. He returned his signed contract to Charles this morning.

He will be assisted at Bowie by Jim Bowden, Fred Rosas, Vic Clark and Gerald Simmang.

Coach Baty knew this was the right move. But he could not have imagined what the future would hold.

17 A Different World

Bo hadn't realized how far away and how different this place would be. One night, during the heat of a blistering Texas summer, with Buryl at the wheel, the couple had driven eleven hours through flat, desert-like terrain. With all the windows rolled down for ventilation (automobiles were not air-conditioned in 1950), it was a hot, loud, harrowing trip. Bo, six months pregnant, was exhausted. "I apologize, Bo. I should've flown you out later," Buryl lamented.

In the westernmost tip of the state, at the intersection of Texas, New Mexico, and old Mexico, El Paso is a natural mountain pass on the Rio Grande River and has been settled for thousands of years. The Mescalero Apaches roamed the region before Spanish explorers and conquistadors first established it as a base for the New Mexico territory in the mid 1600s. It is surrounded by the Chihuahuan Desert, with several high-desert peaks towering nearby. This was a barren place: hilly, dry, and sandy.

El Paso was considered a part of New Mexico until 1848, when the Republic of Texas sought the territory out as a condition of its statehood. This was also about the time that a US Calvary post, Ft. Bliss, was established. The present state boundary was drawn by the US Senate in 1850, largely ignoring history and topography. El Paso's population in 1950 consisted of about 131,000 citizens, 20 percent of whom were of Hispanic descent. Ciudad Juarez, El Paso's sister city, lies just across the river separating the United States from Mexico.

Bo surely had second thoughts about the move. But there was no turning back now.

The arrival of these new residents was announced in the local papers. On July 11, the *El Paso Herald-Post* ran an article by Bob Ingram:

As I Was Saying
COACHES WORK, DREAM
    Keeping a Watch on El Paso coaches this summer: . . .

Clarence Jarvis, El Paso High Basket coach, is working for the maintenance department of the public schools. So is Buryl Baty, new head grid coach for Bowie. As they wield paint brushes, they plot winning court and gridiron plays. Coaches can dream of winning teams, can't they?

That was followed the next day by another article in the same paper, this one by Ramon F. Sanchez:

BATY, NEW BOWIE COACH, IS AIR-MINDED

Opposing District 4-AA teams can look for plenty of passes from Bowie High School come football season. Buryl Baty, new Bowie head coach, is air-minded.

Baty's 1949 squad at Luling High School averaged 15 passes per game in winning eight of its 10 tilts. "Give me a good quarterback and you'll see plenty of pass-throwing," Baty said. . . .

Baty likes his game rugged, but clean. "I'll emphasize that to the boys all the way," he said. . . .

Baty graduated from A. and M. in 1948. Luling is his only teaching experience. He holds a bachelor of arts degree in physical education and a masters degree in education. . . .

He will work in the maintenance department of the public school until he takes over his coaching post Aug. 1. He plans to attend coaches' school at Austin in August.

He is married and his wife, Betty, is expecting in August. They have been married six years.

After painting schoolrooms and locker rooms for half the hot summer, Coach Baty was ready for some football. The coaching staff had huddled daily to plan practices and prepare for the coming season. They had inquired around the neighborhood and watched sandlot games, looking for athletes. Promising prospects were encouraged to try out for the team. As Coach Berry had told Buryl, "Good athletes won't do you any good sittin' in the stands."

Bowie High School is on the south side of town, in the Segundo Barrio, then and now the poorest section of El Paso. From the campus, Mexican flags flying in Juarez are clearly visible, just across the Rio Grande and a short walk away. Bowie had been founded in 1927 as a segregated school, and its student body reflected the neighborhood demographics, 100 percent Hispanic. Segundo Barrio, known as the Second Ward to Anglos, was full of athletically inclined youngsters. There was usually a football or baseball game in progress on one of its bare, flat, sandy lots. Such Latino sub-neighborhoods were also very territorial. Boys attempting to join a game uninvited were frequently chased away by rocks hurtling in their direction.

Despite its abundance of aspiring athletes, the Bowie High School football team had perennially been dominated by larger and richer El Paso high school teams and had finished 2–7 in '49. The Bowie Bears had achieved little success, and, worse, had little expectation of achieving any. The 1949 coach had been a huge improvement over his predecessor, a heavy drinker who had treated the players like "a bunch of dirty Mexicans," according to senior players Tony Lara and Alfonso Burciaga. But the new man had seemed tired, and was frequently unable to get enough kids at practice to conduct a scrimmage. He had retired quietly after only one season.

In late August of 1950, a tall, dark-haired Anglo man knocked on one of the neighborhood doors. "Hi, Fernando. I'm Buryl Baty. I'm your new football coach. We're having a team meeting on Friday morning for the guys who want to play. Will you talk it up and get everybody there?" Fernando was flattered and agreed to try. Later that morning, Tony Lara was approached by the same man on a sidewalk in the barrio. Tony acknowledged that he had been on the squad and warned Baty that the football team was not very good. He too promised to spread the word about the team meeting. Fernando and Tony quickly made their way around the unpaved streets to run-down adobe shacks and tenement apartments, telling their teammates and friends about the team meeting. Word traveled fast.

About sixty tattered teenaged boys showed up that first day of September. Four coaches enthusiastically shook hands with every kid who walked through the door. This warm welcome captured the boys' attention. They also noticed another change. The locker room had been thoroughly cleaned and a new coat of paint applied. Of course, the room's clean smell would diminish as the season progressed, to be replaced by the pungent odor of sweaty bodies and unwashed practice jerseys, socks, and jocks. Still, if only for today, the locker room's condition symbolized a fresh start for the team.

The recent freshening did nothing, of course, to soften the locker-room sounds. Smooth concrete floors and cinderblock walls bounced the echoes of loud voices, slamming lockers, and clattering cleats around the room. But the racket would soon just be background noise, almost unnoticeable, even comforting. During the course of the upcoming season, this room would house the boys' laughter and joy, their pain and disappointment.

A short, stocky man with carrot-red hair whistled shrilly to break the boys' banter. Coach Simmang waited for silence before booming, "I want to introduce you to our new head coach, Buryl Baty. Coach Baty built a winning team last year in Luling, Texas. Before that he played quarterback for the Texas Aggies. He is now here to build a winning team at Bowie, and he's going to say a few words."

The boys watched intently. What they saw was a tall, muscular man, neatly combed, wearing a starched white short-sleeved shirt, khaki pants, and polished shoes. His carriage was confident and authoritative. His voice, when he thanked Coach Simmang, was a baritone.

"Hello, men," Coach Baty began in his Southern drawl. "Of course, our coaches all played college ball and all have coached before. So there's plenty of experience on this staff." A pause set the stage for what he was about to say.

"We're happy to see you all here. I understand that we have some good athletes in this room, and that's a start. We now have to become a good *team*. And here's how we're going to do it. First of all, there are two ways to practice and play football: the right way and the wrong way. From this day forward, we will practice and play the right way. We'll work hard, harder than you've ever worked before. We will play with heart. We will win games and we will have fun doing it. Football is a lot like life. When you work hard and you do it right, good things happen.

"In addition, you'll go to school and make your grades, or you will *not* play football." Several boys squirmed. "You will be good citizens, respectful and respectable. There'll be no cursing. And no alcohol. If I hear of anyone drinking, he is automatically off the team. There's no room for that here. Do you hear me?" Players nodded in the affirmative. "These are the same things that will make you successful in your lives. And by the way, I'll be involved in your lives on and off the field. If you're not willing to follow these rules, don't even check equipment out this morning. Any questions?"

The room was silent.

He looked big and strong. He told us what he wanted from us, and showed concern for us. We were totally impressed. We had so much respect for him from that first day.—Alfonso Burciaga

At first I thought, "Here we go with another group of flunkies." But he changed my mind that day.—Tony Lara

Coach Baty continued: "I have two more things to say before you form your lines to get your equipment, so please listen up. First, we are very fortunate. The school board has provided new gear for us. Here are our new jerseys." He and Coach Simmang held up both royal blue and white game jerseys. "Aren't they great?"

"Yes, sir." "¡*Órale*!" the boys chorused. This was exciting.

"And these helmets—look at 'em!" Baty said, holding a dark blue plastic helmet out above his head. "These are the best that money can buy." He paused.

"Now, I want everyone to understand what I'm about to say. This year, we will *not* lock the gear up like they have in the past." A few seconds passed before he continued. "And here's the important part; if equipment disappears for any reason, we will not play football."

There was a shocked silence.

"Does everybody understand?"

Nods and "yes sirs" followed. The weight of the coach's statement began to sink in.

The players did not, however, know the background of the pact their new coach had just made with them. Until this season, the meager equipment room had contained only used, worn-out gear, and a depleted supply of it at that. The previous season, in fact, Edmundo Rodriguez had been forced to wait until someone quit before he could suit up for the junior varsity squad. Otherwise, there was no uniform for him. The El Paso School Board had authorized replacing damaged or worn-out equipment, but not replacing a school's entire athletic wardrobe. Considering Bowie's shoddy gear, Baty had requested an exception to the policy. He had first appealed to the principal, Mr. Pollitt, who had brought him to Bowie. Pollitt had explained, "Only the school board has that authority. And I have to tell you that I'm doubtful that they'll agree to your request. Heck, I have trouble getting new textbooks approved. But if you're determined to fight for it, I'll get you an audience at the next meeting."

In front of the governing body, Coach Baty had spoken confidently about his objective: coaching football and teaching his boys to be men. He urged the board to endorse the purchase of the equipment. Surprisingly, they did.

Afterwards, the athletic director had approached Baty. "Coach, you'll need to lock up that gear, or these Mexicans will steal you blind," he warned. Something about this advice riled the new head coach, and he did not accept it. Instead, in one short statement, Coach Baty had established the foundation for his relationship with his team. The players would be trusted, and they would be held accountable.

> We used to take stuff home with us . . . steal stuff. But not after he told us that.—Joe Cordova

> He gave us the opportunity to do the right thing. It made an immediate impact.—Tony Lara

The kids excitedly dressed out in their new shorts, t-shirts, and helmets for a tiring practice. After a long, tough second practice on that sweltering afternoon, exhausted players were not sure how much they liked this new coach after all.

During the coming days, Coach Baty visited players' homes and met their parents. These families lived in tiny stucco and brick shacks with flat, leaky roofs, or in crowded tenement apartments with communal toilets. They cooked tortillas and warmed their homes with wood-burning stoves, and many had no running water inside; they retrieved water from outdoor faucets. Articles of tattered clothing hung on clotheslines stretched across open spaces. Stray cats and dogs roamed the unpaved, gravel streets. Compared to the rich sections of town, compared to almost anywhere, the Segundo Barrio was a ghetto. Amid this deprivation, however, beautiful and lively kids filled the neighborhood with continuous energy.

These people, and generations before them, had lived in poverty and expected to continue living in it. They had little regard for education. Many of the students' and players' parents had not finished school themselves and now toiled in menial jobs. Some kids, like the Maldonado brothers, had no parents and lived with relatives or friends. Outside the barrio, they were treated with condescension.

One of the families Baty visited was the Cordovas. Six boys and their mother lived in a two-room apartment. One of the older sons was Joe, a letterman, who would be a senior this season. "Joe, it'll take some time, but we'll have a good team by the end of the year. And Bobby," he said to Joe's younger brother, "we'll bring you up from the junior high field after practices. I'll teach you how to pass and kick, and you can help us win championships when you get to the varsity." After this visit, the brothers were bursting with anticipation.

Players' families were astonished. No coach, or teacher, had ever called on them in their homes before. The language barrier complicated a few visits, but it was usually easily managed by one or more English-speaking family members. The coach was warm and confident. He asked the parents about their lives and their kids. He described his expectations of their sons and his emphasis on education, discipline, and good behavior. Parents realized that their sons were in good, strong hands. This was a man they trusted.

The dry summer's heat had produced a hard-packed practice field with parched, patchy grass. The coaches had watered the field continuously during the late summer, but large bare sections of sandy red dirt persisted. Weathered goalposts stood at each end of the field, and several huge cottonwood trees clustered just beyond the southernmost end zone.

Two-a-days ran for one week, with a practice early each morning, then again late in the afternoon. When classes started, the boys practiced once daily after school until the first game, one week later. These were intense practices, organized and strenuous. Drills emphasized fundamental blocking, tackling, passing, catching, and recovering fumbles. The team scrimmaged daily. Players had to run conditioning laps and sprints during and after every practice and punishment laps for not hustling or for breaking the rules. This was tough football. The boys had never been pushed this hard. These new coaches knew what it would take to win. A lot would have to be accomplished before the first game, and time was scarce. All the while, the hot sun beat down mercilessly, draining the boys' energy. They ached; their muscles were both stiff and sore from fatigue. It hurt to get out of bed each morning.

"After this, you'll be able to do anything." Baty said.

Coach Baty's new code of discipline extended well beyond the football field, and he did not let his players forget it. "I expect you to go to every class—on time—make good grades, act like gentlemen, and to speak English at school. These are the things you have to do to earn a diploma and to succeed after graduation."[1]

Some players resisted. Not much had been expected of them previously, and this new order—the tough practices and the off-the-field expectations—took their toll. Some boys quit. Some were kicked off the team. But Baty's high standards motivated most of them to step up the pace.

Practices also became very interesting, on another level. The coaches mentored on the mental aspects of the game: preparation, strategy, and confidence. Bowie players experienced something new—"chalk talks." With boys sitting around him in fourth-period homeroom, Baty stood at the blackboard, chalk in hand, diagramming offensive plays, defensive positioning, and individual assignments. The X's and O's of football took shape right there in front of them. They now had to think. What was chalked on the blackboard they practiced that afternoon on the field. "I want you to listen. I don't like to repeat myself," Baty would say. "You all need to learn your plays because it's important that you accomplish your assignments. A play will *fail* if only *one player* blows his assignment. This is called 'accountability,' because you've *got to do it*. This also prepares you for your future as adults. Remember—accountability."

> Before, we weren't used to the mental preparation. Now we thought about football from the moment we woke up.—Bobby Cordova

Despite his claim to the contrary, Coach Baty did like to repeat himself on certain favorite topics. "To win, you have to think—and when you think, you can beat anybody." And after a short pause, he would continue: "Just like in life, you need to think to succeed. Never forget that."

Nevertheless, there was a lot of information to absorb in a short period of time.

Everything the team worked on was designed for the upcoming game. Skull sessions and practices were tailored to counter the next opponent's strengths and tendencies. The game plan also included a few special plays, plays intended to take advantage of the opponents' weaknesses and to score a touchdown early in the game.

"The way you practice is the way you play," Baty said, again and again. "There's no substitute for preparation, and with good preparation you can beat anybody. That's true in football, and that's true in life." Coach Baty imposed his will on his players, and they improved by the day. However, sparks of brilliance were offset by boneheaded mistakes. Beautiful touchdown runs were followed by penalties, missed assignments, or dropped passes.

Baty was supported by three young assistants: Jerry Simmang, Jim Bowden, and Fred Rosas. Coach Simmang, his orange hair combed to the side and his pale skin burned by the sun, coached the line. When a player blundered, Simmang stared the culprit down; his fierce glare meant "You are in deep, deep trouble."

Coach Bowden, a recent star quarterback and graduate of Texas Western, coached the backfield. Jim was smart and direct; he called it like he saw it. He was tall, dark, and handsome, as most quarterbacks think they are.

Rosas was the B-team coach. After serving in the US Navy and playing football at Texas Western, he had returned to coach at his high school alma mater. He was so youthful-looking that he might have been mistaken for one of the kids. "You have to play for *you*," Rosas repeatedly told his players. "You can't play football because your girlfriend wants you to play. You have to want to play in your own heart." When he said it he would clinch his fist over his own chest. It was obvious that he loved football. Waiting for him at home that fall season of 1950, Fred's wife Mary Louise was pregnant with their first child.

> Tony Franco frequently mimicked Coach Rosas by joking, "You can't play for your girlfriend! You have to want it in your heart!" We laughed 'til it hurt to laugh anymore.—Leo Munoz

One promising player was sophomore Edmundo Rodriguez. "Rod," as Coach Baty had nicknamed him, had decided to attend Bowie instead of his closer neighborhood school, El Paso High. Bowie somehow appealed to him in spite of the two bus connections necessary to get there every morning. He wanted to join the Bowie band, but his uncles insisted that he play football instead. Rod, a quiet, thoughtful boy, agreed to try out for the team, reasoning that he could play in the band after he got cut from football. But he never got cut. He had decent size, played center and linebacker, and it turned out that he had a mean streak. His presence at Bowie was an instance of good luck for the team.

Coach Baty knew that his success was influenced by the talent on the field, and he had already begun to identify elementary and junior high players for his feeder system. A number of these kids eagerly came up to the varsity field after their own practices for one-on-one skill development. And for some fun.

Meanwhile, Bo was very uncomfortable. She was expecting any day. She was lonely, and restless for Buryl to come home. One afternoon she called his office, promising him a mysterious surprise from Paris. As she had anticipated, her husband's curiosity got him home a little earlier than usual that night. He carefully unfolded and read the *Paris News* clipping about Coach Berry, his record, and his better teams. Buryl, along with other standout players, was prominently mentioned. The feature article took Buryl down memory lane. Berry's impact on his life had been huge.

But Buryl's attention quickly jumped to more immediate issues when Bo asked about his own team. He answered, "We have a ways to go."

And the first test was just around the corner.

18 Finally, a Real Game

The Bears were bruised, nicked, and tired to the bone, but they improved considerably during the short preseason. They could feel it. After two grueling weeks of practice, they were ready to hit *another* team for a change. The players were optimistic that with all their hard work they would win their first game.

However, the Carlsbad Cavemen had other plans. During the first two quarters the Carlsbad visitors dominated offensively and defensively. With the Bears down 0–20 at halftime, Coaches Bowden and Simmang pointed out their squad's mistakes, and Coach Baty emphasized what the team had done well.

In the second half, the Bears' defense held Carlsbad and the offense moved the ball more effectively. However, as the clock ticked the last seconds of the game, the final score still reflected the halftime deficit. Afterwards, dejected players waited. Sitting quietly in the locker room, they had time to question the loss: "With all our hard work, why did we lose? Was it us? Was it the coaches? Was all this work for nothing?"

Senior Joe Cordova always dreaded this part of the game. He had been here before—many times. In the past, this was the point when coaches had ranted about how miserably the team had played. Joe had always left these postgame critiques feeling belittled and worthless. He was prepared for more of the same.

Finally, Coach Baty led his assistants into the locker room, and called out, "Attention, men!"

"You played a solid second half. Carlsbad[1] is a great team, and you played them toe-to-toe in the last two quarters. Congratulations! You made a lot of progress here tonight. Now you know that you can play with a good team if you play well for four quarters. And you learned something that's important, to never give up. Good game!" All the coaches then circulated through the room, congratulating and shaking every player's hand.

The mood shifted immediately. The boys were visibly relieved and suddenly felt good about their effort. Of course, the coaching staff knew their progress had been largely against Carlsbad's reserves. But the team's positive psyche was what mattered most. The season was still young and more strong opponents would follow. And if Coach Baty didn't have the team's attention before this night, he surely did going forward.

The following Monday the *Herald-Post*'s cub reporter Ramon Sanchez wrote, "The Bruins' defeat on Friday didn't disappoint Coach Buryl Baty a great deal. Carlsbad had too good a club for the Bears."

Players noticed the young Sanchez talking with Coach Baty at quite a few of their practices. Ramon was a slight, good-looking man, Hispanic, fresh out of college. He was youthful enough to pass for a Bowie student except for his white shirt and thin black tie. He was a man with a huge smile and a cheerful personality, and he had quickly developed a chemistry with Coach Baty. Shortly after they met, Baty asked Ramon if he could call him Ray. "Sure," said Sanchez.

A couple of days later, Baty called the *Herald-Post* sports department and asked for Ray. Nobody there knew who "Ray" was until Baty explained whom he was talking about. Fellow *Herald-Post* employees also began to call Ramon Ray, and a few games into the season his published articles began to credit "Ray" Sanchez instead of "Ramon."

Practices the following week were long and physical. Significant flaws, shoddy blocking and tackling, fumbled balls, dropped passes—all pinpointed work that needed to be done, but a short week of practice limited the opportunity. Most of the team ran sprint after sprint and lap after lap after every practice, while a couple of boys hid and rested behind the nearby cottonwood trees.

According to Coach Rosas's scouting report, the Douglas (Arizona) Bulldogs sported a razzle-dazzle offense with plenty of reverses, passes, and hand-offs. Rosas also indicated that Douglas had several "Negroes" on their team. This news aroused the Bowie players' curiosity. At Thursday night's game they watched the field and the visitors' sideline closely, but couldn't spot anybody with especially dark skin.

Three hundred twenty rushing yards carried Bowie High, as La Bowie prevailed for its first victory, 13–6. Loud laughter, and relief, filled the locker room. The boys were feeling much-needed gratification for all their hard work. Coaches happily shook hands with every player. "The game was more lop-sided than the score," according to the *El Paso Times*.

Still, the boys wondered about the Negro players who had been so conspicuous in their absence. They soon learned that these Bulldog team members had been left behind in Arizona due to a rule prohibiting their playing in Texas. This was confusing. "Why?" the Bears asked.

The next day, Friday, September 22, the new baby arrived. Bo lay in her hospital bed, totally fatigued but very happy. Buryl stood, holding his new son proudly. The boy was given family names: Robert, which was both Buryl and his father Burton's first name, and Gaines, his grandmother Opal Hutchinson's maiden name. He would go by "Gaines." Over the coming months and years, Buryl would seem especially observant of the boy's right arm. "He looks like a future Aggie quarterback to me!" the father declared.

Several family members and friends visited the proud parents and their new son in the hospital. This show of support warmed Bo's heart, a heart already overflowing with love for the two men in her life. Bo's sister Elaine, knowing how alone and overwhelmed Bo must surely feel, also travelled to help the new mother out. Her presence, especially considering Buryl's long work hours, helped to make Bo's first few days of motherhood much happier and more manageable.

The week's practices had been sloppy. "Let's go, boys! You play like you practice. We need to concentrate. We're up against a good team this week!" Baty urged them. Newfound confidence had bred lapses in the players' concentration—they missed assignments, fumbled hand-offs, and dropped passes. Amid this chaos, several new plays were added to the Bears' repertoire. The passing game, highlighting solid quarterback Alfonso Burciaga, was probably the Bears' best hope.

Big, strong, fast, and athletic were words that only began to describe the undefeated Big Spring Steers. The visiting Bears were outclassed by them, 21–0. Again, Baty's postgame critique was direct but positive. "You're getting better. Keep working hard. You'll be glad you did."

While a little more slowly than Baty had hoped, the Bears were improving. "The seeds of success have to be planted," he reminded himself.

The team boarded for a long bus drive back to El Paso, and the players' chatter soon faded as they drifted off to sleep. Coach Baty, however, didn't sleep. He was steaming. First, his team had been beaten soundly on the field. Second, he had been insulted by Big Spring's coaches, who had not forwarded promised scouting information to him. And to top it off, his team had been treated with disrespect in Big Spring. This surprised and disturbed him, but he didn't know exactly what to do about it.

A front-page article in the *Herald-Post* captured Buryl's attention on September 29. Loyola University had forfeited a game with Texas Western "because of restrictions against Negroes playing on Kidd Field, home gridiron of Texas Western." Black players were prevented by Texas law from playing on the home fields of any state colleges.

The account troubled Buryl. For days and weeks he pondered the report about the game cancellation. Loyola's forfeiture, based upon principle alone, seemed a very steep price to pay.

He wondered what he might do in a similar situation.

Monday began another week of tough practices, and Coach Baty upped the number of wind sprints. "If he makes us run one more sprint, I'm gonna quit," Alfonso Burciaga remembered saying to himself. Sure enough, the whistle blew for another agonizing race down the field. Alfonso thought to himself, "Okay, but if he blows it one *more* time, I'm gonna quit!" The whistle blew again. The pattern kept repeating itself: Alfonso panted, Baty blew the whistle, and Alfonso sprinted.

Eventually the sprints ended, and Coach Baty praised the team for working so hard. "This will help you win a game that you wouldn't have won otherwise," he assured them.

We were in great shape, better than at any other time in our lives.
—Alfonso Burciaga

A good week of practice was not quite enough to topple unbeaten Galena Park, which travelled in from Houston. But the Bears played respectably, losing 33–28 in a thriller. Quarterback Burciaga played well, and his intensity and competitiveness commanded respect from his teammates.

Coach Baty addressed his players: "We can learn a lot in a defeat like this," he said. "We need to get up off the ground, and go at it again—just like in life. This was a very good team, and we played 'em tough. We're learning what we have to do to compete. We'll get there. We'll learn how to win these games. Just keep your heads up!" The coaching staff reminded each other of this as well.

The next game was one the Bears had looked forward to for some time. A chartered plane would transport them to Austin to take on the mighty Stephen F. Austin Maroons, last year's second-place finisher in the state playoffs. The twenty-four squad members were instructed to "dress like champions," with clean shirts and ties, and jackets or letter sweaters.

The morning of the flight, the student body prepared the team in style, with a spirited pep rally. Cheerleaders, in their bright blue tops and ankle-length white skirts, pumped inspiration into both players and students as they cheered and led the crowd in singing the fight song. Dressed-up players fidgeted nervously on the gymnasium floor as they glanced up into the stands at faculty and fellow students. Lacking suitcases, when they finally boarded the bus for the airport many carried paper grocery sacks containing their extra clothes and other belongings.

At the airport, the players were herded into a corner next to the ticket line for a surprise. There, the coaching staff introduced their wives to the boys for the first time. The women were attractive, neatly dressed, and seemed to carry themselves confidently. After short introductions and warm handshakes, Joe Cordova whispered to a couple of teammates, "I feel 'related' to these ladies." Alfonso Burciaga added, "Mrs. Simmang: WOW!" They then boarded for the first flight of their lives.

Coach Baty had been warned by Coach Nemo Herrera about discrimination in the state capital. At last year's state playoffs, Herrera had been unable to find a hotel that would accommodate his baseball team, and they had slept on cots in a room under the UT stadium. Coach Baty ensured that hotel accommodations and meal reservations were confirmed.

The early portion of the trip did not go well for the visiting Bears. First, they were routed by a championship-caliber team. Then, they didn't fare well off the field, either—two cafés turned them away. "Didn't we have reservations here?" Joe Cordova asked under his breath as from inside the bus he watched his coach arguing with the café manager. The boys hadn't really thought much about incidents such as this before. They had been turned away in this manner all their lives and were surprised by Coach Baty's heated response.

Coach Baty was very upset. The man told him, "We don't serve Mexicans."
—Tony Carmona

Before this, we were used to staying at dirty roadside motels. This was the first long trip with Coach Baty, and we stayed in nice hotels and ate as much good food as we wanted. It was amazing compared to what we'd been used to.
—Alfonso Burciaga

On Saturday morning, after a big breakfast of bacon, eggs, pancakes, milk, and orange juice, the Bears were bussed to the nearby UT campus to watch the Texas Longhorns play the North Carolina Tar Heels. Bowie's boys were in awe of the huge crowd, the UT band, and the sea of burnt orange. Only North Carolina's powder-blue uniforms broke the orange color code. The coaches urged the kids to watch carefully: "Those are the same plays we run."

On that night's return flight to El Paso, the boys squeezed toward the side windows, marveling at the distant lights passing below.

In the next Friday morning's *Herald-Post*, Southsiders read Ray Sanchez's account of the game: "Bowie Coach Buryl Baty has one of the best guards in the district in Joe Cordova. But he's too tough for his own good. 'Against Austin (Texas) last week he was our roughest defensive player,' Baty said. 'But we had to bench him. He hit an opposing man so hard he knocked himself out.'" Joe Cordova had put everything he had into this game, and he was proud to read Coach Baty's comments. The other players also took notice.

Over Bo's home-cooked Sunday lunch, Buryl seemed preoccupied, bothered. "I've thought about it, and I think I've figured it out," he explained. "At first I felt sorry for the boys, then mad that anyone would treat my kids that way. But it also seemed like it was directed at me. And it was; I'm part of the team. I must say that I had never realized how demeaning it feels to be discriminated against. Now I know."

The next contest was also a long way from home, way up in the Texas Panhandle, where Bowie sought its second win of the season. After a flight to the Amarillo airport, the team bussed to Plainview, just under an hour's drive to the south. There they stopped at a roadside diner and waited while the coaches went inside. Eventually the coaches stepped back up into the bus. Baty seemed angry as he explained, "They're full and can't serve us for two hours."

A more accommodating restaurant was found just down the road, but it closed to the public once the Bears walked through the door. Customers pulled into the parking lot were turned away, in spite of the fact that there were still empty tables available.

During the game, Plainview's undefeated team gave their smaller Bowie opponents a lesson on how to run the T-formation. Mistakes also contributed to the defeat, as Bowie fumbled several times on both ends of the field. The Bears now stood, demoralized, at one win and four losses.

With all this adversity, the boys' psyche was on the verge of spiraling downward. Push the wrong buttons and the team could be "lost" for the season. Coach Baty chose his words carefully. "The outcome of this game is not as important as how you played. You are an improved team from our first games. You are tackling better, blocking better, and moving the ball on offense. If not for a few mistakes, we had a chance to make a game of this one. Keep working hard, and we'll appreciate our successes that much more."

Baty understood about losing streaks. Sometimes the ball bounces the wrong way and you lose a close one. Sometimes you get routed. It's discouraging, disheartening. It's embarrassing. Every team, and every boy on it, wants to believe they can win. But deep down, this team had to wonder about its ability, about the coaches' competence, and if all the hard work was worth it. It is very difficult for a team with a losing tradition to believe they can win, and then to know how to do it. They wanted to believe their coach, who kept preaching and prodding, but it was increasingly difficult to do so.

Before leaving the room, he added, "It's important to remember that nothing that's happened up to now matters one bit. Every game before now was just a practice game, and we're starting a new season of district play, right now." He let that view of things sink in, and then, after a pause, he continued, "Every team we've played so far is better than the teams we'll play in our district. These tough teams have prepared us for what's ahead. We have an excellent chance to win this next game. We're very close to being a good team. Keep working. You can do it!"

Coach Baty then reminded himself: "Keep working, *we* can do it."

As Rod Rodriguez walked from the field toward the team bus he spoke for a few minutes with his parents, who had also been turned away from a restaurant; the proprietor had pointed to the sign at the front entrance: "We reserve the right to refuse service to anyone. NO Mexicans!"

. . .

That Sunday morning's newspapers carried a shocking story, one that hit Bowie High School hard. Tragedy had struck four Bowie students and one alum who had been driving home from the Plainview game. At seven o'clock in the morning they had been on the road all night and were within twelve miles of home when the driver, the older boy, fell asleep at the wheel. The car crossed the dividing line and was plunging down the wrong side of the roadway when it collided with a truck. The truck driver survived. All four students and the driver were killed.

Word spread quickly. Five classmates and friends were gone. Forever. Their vacant school desks served as eerie reminders of their fate. It was hard to imagine that these kids were never to be seen again, never to be in class, at lunch, at mass, at games. Fellow students were confused and grief-stricken. Teary-eyed high schoolers asked, "How could this happen? Why? Why them?" For many, this was their first experience with death. It was a somber week at La Bowie.

Despite the mourning, the Bears had to prepare for the El Paso High Tigers. With ten players out due to injuries, the Bears' much-needed scrimmage was called off and replaced with light drills in an attempt to prevent additional injuries. However, these setbacks didn't stop Coach Baty from mentoring his quarterbacks about play-calling strategy. Rules dictated that only a player on the field could call plays, and with no assistance. Referees' flags would fly if the coach was caught helping with play selection during a game. Quarterbacks, therefore, had to be mentally prepared by the coach's prodding: "On the first possession, run the exact sequence of plays we've practiced this week. Continue this progression of plays to put them to sleep; then you'll call Fake 42 Trap, 7 Pass. And we'll take it to the end zone. You got it?"

"Yes, sir," quarterbacks Burciaga and Martinez assured him.

The offensive huddle was one of Coach Baty's all-time favorite places and afforded countless opportunities to teach the game. During practices, the head coach frequently knelt in its center to remind players of assignments and success tips, and to provide some measure of inspiration. Here, he expected discipline and strict business. And here, only coaches and quarterbacks were allowed to speak. "No horseplay!" he growled over and over. This set a good example for Burciaga, the leader of the offense. Early in one afternoon's practice, Coach Baty bent over with his hands on his knees in the middle of the huddle, explaining the next play. As he did so, his t-shirt rode up and exposed a patch of hair on his lower back.

David Canales could not resist an impulse. He reached out and plucked a hair from Coach Baty's backside. Poorly suppressed giggles followed. The coach, on the other hand, was not amused.

"Who did that?" he asked sharply.

Everyone got serious, very fast. Canales thought to himself, "Oh, no, what have I done?" He was a regular joker, but had he gone too far?

"Who did it?"

No one responded.

"Okay, the whole team will run laps until you tell me who did it."

More silence.

"Take off! Start running!"

And off they went. Lap after lap after lap brought no pointed fingers. The players ran until their tongues hung out. After running too many laps to count, Canales felt bad for causing his teammates such pain. "Coach, it was me. I did it," he confessed.

"Alright, everybody come over here. Boys, you wouldn't have had to run if you'd told me who did it."

"But, Coach, we're not squealers," answered Joe Cordova as he bent over, gasping for air. The drills resumed while Canales ran a few more laps. Later, as the coaches walked in from the practice field, they privately rejoiced in how the boys were becoming a team, protecting each other, and being accountable.

Home and intracity games were played at one of El Paso's two high school stadiums, McKee and Jones, both over three miles away from the Southside campus. Most Bowie fans walked the distance to and from every game. This week, thousands paraded to see the clash against a major district rival.

With crowd noise and marching band music coming from outside the locker room, the Bears listened intently as the Segundo Barrio's Father Rham led them in prayer. Then Coach Baty spoke. "Men, we are a much better team than we were two months ago. And as I've said, nothing that's happened up to now matters one bit. Our season begins *tonight,* and you are well prepared. Give it your best, from start to finish, and we'll win the game!"

The boys bolted onto the field to cheering fans.

That night, October 7, Bowie strutted into the district limelight by winning one that counted. Fourteen thousand fans watched Bowie's stunning 13–6 upset of El Paso High. After preparing for a likely Bowie passing attack, EPHS had seen Bowie High run the ball right down their throats.

The postgame locker room was alive with energy. Players laughed, whooped it up, and shook hands. They had beaten a strong crosstown rival. What went unspoken was the relief that everyone felt. They had broken the losing streak.

On the way back to the Southside, the team bus stopped for ice cream cones. As players and coaches savored the treat, Coach Baty conceded, "This is not good for us, but it's a reward for your hard work and for winning." Lots of "mmms" were heard from mouths full of ice cream. "This weekend," he added, "keep your noses clean and go to church."

The Bears' newfound confidence was uplifting. Later that night, most of the players met at a local café. Heroics were relived and everyone shared a sense of camaraderie and brotherhood. They had overcome a lot for this great victory.

After a weekend of celebration, the boys were abruptly thrust back into reality—and with it, classes. Players had to show their grade reports to Coach Baty. Any player who had a failing grade would *not* play in the next game, no matter who he was or what his level of talent. These same boys also had to deal with Coach Baty's paddle—the "board of education."

"You can make it on the outside, but first you need an education. I don't want to have any dropouts on this team. I want you all to finish high school, to earn that piece of paper, and go to college." It was a point on which he never wavered.

It seemed to the players that this was the first time a coach, or even a teacher, had taken a personal interest in them. Coach Baty treated them with respect, but he held them accountable on and off the field. He was tough, but his team felt secure and protected. The team was like a family: working together, competing together, joking together, and now winning together. In their minds, it was "us" against the world.

They were all excellent coaches, but Coach Baty was our leader.—Joe Cordova

Meanwhile, far West Texas was challenging for Buryl's young wife. Almost eight hundred miles from Paris, El Paso seemed lost and desolate. To Bo it felt like the end of the world. The life of a coach's wife was lonely to begin with, considering her husband's long working hours and frequent travel. Bo's sister Elaine, who had come to help with the new baby, had returned home to her own children. Bo was left with the routine of taking care of a house and an infant and making a home for a husband who was often absent from it. Still, she did her best not to complain.

Her loneliness was eased on the few evenings that Buryl was home. She also enjoyed a few good friends, including women from an active church community and several wives in the El Paso coaching ranks. Local restaurants fed the couple's rapidly developing affinity for Mexican cuisine. They played bridge and dominoes. And Bo attended all the home ball games and a number of school functions. The Batys adapted, and they felt the community's warmth, which helped these East Texans feel as if El Paso were *almost* home.

• • •

Local Austin High School loomed as the next test. This was always more than just a game between two city rivals; it was a grudge battle of cultures. Austin High was located in the rich, white section of town. Its residents riled those from the Segundo Barrio with condescension and discrimination, on and off the field. The Panthers had regularly routed Bowie and were heavily favored to do so again this Friday night. The Southsiders' prospects seemed bleak.

Significantly cooler weather fostered a high-spirited week of practice. Newspapers hyped the contest, describing how Austin's Panthers drilled from scouting reports of previous Bowie games, and how Bowie's Burciaga "pitched 'strikes' in a rough scrimmage." However, receivers, with cold, numb fingers, "had trouble holding on to Burciaga's passes."

Finally the kickoff drew near. After Father Rham's pregame prayer asking for player safety and good sportsmanship, Coach Baty spoke to the team. "Austin High is good," he said, "but you can beat them. Did you see those people who walked all this way, sitting out there in the cold? They're from the Southside, and they came here to see you win. So, let's go *win!*"

On this very cold November night, the Bears fought Austin's Panthers to a tie game, 7–7. Both teams walked off the field confused, not knowing how to feel. Nobody had won. Unfortunately for the Bears, Austin High had accumulated more penetrations and would be considered the victor should the two teams finish the season tied for the district championship. From his high school playing days, Coach Baty was all too familiar with penetration rules.

In the postgame locker room, Baty addressed the team. "You played a good game. We led in all statistical categories but one: penetrations. I guarantee you that Austin High feels very lucky right now, and they would *not* want to play us again. I want every person in this room to walk out of here proud, because we're still undefeated in our district."

La Bowie walked tall that week. The buildup for the next game was intense. The Ysleta Indians were a strong and balanced team and heavily favored. The Bears had shown flashes of brilliance at times during the season but had been inconsistent. Their practices featured heavy contact drills and work on their potent aerial game. They also worked on recovering fumbles and the art of holding on to the pigskin, since four lost balls had cost them a victory last week. In fact, two of the penetrations that gave Austin its victory margin had been the result of Bowie fumbles deep in its own territory. "At least this week we'll be prepared to recover our own if we can't learn to hold onto the ball," Baty told newspaper reporters.

Shockingly, the Bears were still in the race for the championship. Of course, the players couldn't help themselves; they had to read every word of their press clippings that week. Reporter Ray Sanchez showed up again at their practices. Pregame jitters, usually reserved for the day of the game, began midweek. While they projected confidence, the boys were actually scared to death. This "undefeated" stuff was uncharted territory for them.

As always, the team reported in at the Bowie field house three hours before the kickoff for taping and dressing. They then boarded the bus for the drive across town to the stadium, where they relaxed before game time. More activity hummed around the stadium than usual, as homecoming festivities required earlier preparation. Loud voices and laughter could be heard from outside the locker room. The cheerleaders, wearing bright blue tops with "Bears" in white script across the front under their warmest jackets, had arrived well in advance to hang hand-painted banners and streamers in the stadium. The marching bands soon arrived, and the rhythm of practicing drums and the blare of random horns intensified the excitement. This extra energy, of course, fueled the boys' anxiety as they tried to relax.

Coach Baty sensed that the team might be wound too tightly and in need of some calming down. He waited until they had finished putting on their cleats, shoulder pads, and helmets. Then, just before time to run out on the field, in his deep, confident tone, he said, "Men, you are so well prepared that you only have to think about one thing: the play you're about to run. You've run it dozens of times in practice. Just give it your best. Then, only think about the next play, and give it your best. Don't think about anything else." His calm confidence continued. "If you just do what I say, you'll come out ahead."

This tilt was as rough as they come. Vicious tackling highlighted the action, and the thrilling contest went down to the last thirty seconds. Helped by a pair of blocked punts, the underdog Bears squeaked past Ysleta's Indians 8–7.

In yet another jubilant locker room, a shrill whistle and loud voice interrupted the buzz. "Men, celebrate this victory tonight. And tomorrow, I want you to visit Arturo in the hospital—his collarbone is broken and he's not happy about missing the rest of the season. Then, I want you to focus on beating Jefferson High on Thanksgiving Day. It's now the most important game we play all year. We're undefeated in district play. Let's keep it going." The boys were so excited that they had trouble falling asleep that night.

Coach Baty visited Arturo Lightbourn's hospital room every day until he was released.

El Pasoans read that week's sports page in the *Herald-Post* with great interest:

November 22, 1950
MORE BOWIE PASSES IN TURKEY TILT
    Key injuries, prime ingredients for football upsets, still reared their ugly heads today as the heavily favored Bowie Bears went through final drills for tomorrow's Thanksgiving Day clash with Thomas Jefferson at 2:30 p. m. in R. R. Jones Stadium.
    Missing from the final Bear workout were no less than three varsity linemen all officially ruled out of tomorrow's game. The result was a sieve-like defense which a hustling reserve unit tore to shreds in the hour-long heavy contact drill.
    Coach Buryl Baty, visibly worried over the loss of tackles Carlos Duarte and Armando Rodriguez, along with end Arturo Lightbourn who doubles as tackle on defense, said he only could hope the replacements would stop the lightening-fast Silver Fox backs.

On Thanksgiving Day, Bowie's Bears defeated Jefferson 20–7. The postgame locker room rang with celebration. With a district record of three wins, no losses and one tie, Bowie stood at the top of the standings, above also-victorious Austin High.

Interrupting the joyous chaos, Coach Baty asked the Bears to "gather up."

"I have good news and bad news," he said. "First, the disappointing news: Austin High will be the representative of our district in the state playoffs. Austin's two ties were officially recorded as victories based on the penetration rule. What that means is that our 3–0–1 win-loss-tie record is trumped by Austin's 2–0–2.

"Now, the good news. I want to congratulate you. You played a great game, and you are district co-champions! You can hold your heads high. We're *co-champions* from now on.

"You turned this season around with hard work and a never-quit attitude. Lots of teams would've quit after some of our early games, but you kept fighting and getting better. Now, you're champions! Graduating seniors, you'll remember this experience for as long as you live. If you make the same commitments in life that you have for this team, you will be successful adults."

More grins and congratulations followed. The coaches moved around the room, shaking every player's hand.

"I've never felt this good," Joe Cordova repeated again and again. "We did it!"

The Bears had learned how to work hard, how to play as a team, how to keep fighting, and how to win.

And Bowie fans had filled the stadium. Crowd energy had been invigorating. Not only did most students attend, but for the first time parents were there, too, supporting their kids and their friends' kids. They were inspired by the new fight in the Bears. Now, people talked about La Bowie.

Citizens from other neighborhoods, who generally looked down their noses at these Southsiders, were aghast. "Those Meskins are acting up," was the popular Anglo sentiment, "playing tough all of a sudden. Their new young coach must be pretty good." In light of the co-championship, Coach Baty was named "District Coach of the Year," the first-ever such award for a Bowie football coach. And Joe Cordova, Alfonso Burciaga, Carlos Duarte, Joe Turrieta, and Arturo Lightbourn were named to the All-District team.

Graduation, however, would strip Bowie of its entire first string. Not a single starter would return in '51. Coach Rosas's B-Team would need to provide young talent for next year's varsity.

Meanwhile, Bo's homesickness gnawed at her. She had never been away for so long. She never complained, but Buryl sensed it. One day he said, "I have an early birthday present for you: plane tickets home." Bo could hardly wait for the two weeks to pass.

On her birthday, Bo and Gaines boarded a flight to Dallas. Sisters Alta and Jeannie picked them up at Love Field. They stayed over that night and drove on to Paris the next day. Bo showed off her new baby to her mother and her siblings and best friends and was overjoyed to be home at last. Buryl followed in the car after school let out for the Christmas holidays. He also enjoyed being home, and he did his share of visiting and hunting. The couple drove back to El Paso together on New Year's Day, 1951.

Buryl was always anxious for updates on his beloved Aggies, either through the news or from friends still connected with the A&M football program.

He, like Aggies everywhere, had chuckled over a news story that had made the rounds that fall. It appeared in the *El Paso Herald-Post* on October 20:

Texas Aggies are Blamed
TEXAS FINDS WILD OATS SOWN ON FOOTBALL FIELD
    Austin—University of Texas officials pondered the problem to-day of removing wild oats, neatly sown in the form of a burgeon-ing "A and M," smack in the middle of the turf of the Longhorns stadium.
    Action by the Longhorns' archrivals from College Station was discovered late yesterday as Assistant Coach H. C. (Buddy) Gil-strap directed a crew covering the field with canvas to protect the playing surface from rain.
    Authorities tried a vacuum cleaner, hopeful that the machine would soak up the oats. But that failed. Rain and watering had rooted the seeds.
    It was estimated that raiding Aggies had used as much as 40 bushels of oats to do the job.
    Unofficial reports were that the group completed their foray

last Saturday while a large portion of the Longhorn student body was at Dallas watching the SMU-Texas game. . . .

The Aggies had improved dramatically in 1950, to a 7–4 record and a victory over Georgia in the Presidential Cup, their best record in years. Coach Stiteler seemed to be making considerable progress with the program. However, whispers about the coach trickled from College Station. Stiteler had been beaten up badly, presumably by young men known to him, but he had refused to reveal his attackers' identities in his conflicting accounts. Within a few days, Stiteler resigned as A&M's head coach, for reasons that were never clear to the public.

At the January Bowie Bear Football Banquet, Joe Cordova and Carlos Duarte were honored as team captains for the previous season. Twenty-four players were awarded official letters, as Coach Baty revisited the successful season in gratifying detail. It felt good to say the word "co-champions."

In the back of the coach's mind, however, lingered worrisome knowledge. Next year, they would have to start over. The cupboard would be bare.

19 Rebuilding

1951

Seventy-plus kids showed up for the first day of spring training, reflecting the enthusiasm that last year's success had created. No one doubted the potential of these new players, but they were young and inexperienced. The lessons learned in the 1950 season, about consistency, composure, and winning, would leave campus with the now-departing seniors. Every position would be occupied by a rookie.

Spring practices would provide time to assess and grow the incoming talent. By Texas Interscholastic League rules, spring training now began on January 30 and was allowed to run for exactly one month. The Bears' first few practices were dedicated to fundamentals—blocking, tackling, ball handling ("Tuck that ball!"), recovering fumbles, running into the hole ("Full speed!"). These lessons would all have to be taught again. Later, more team drills were integrated into the sessions.

"How hard we work right now, in spring training, will determine how we fare next season," the coaches preached. "We're preparing to win against the big boys: the Carlsbads, Austin Highs, and Big Springs. They'd better look out for us! With good preparation you can win on the field, just like in life."

"The seeds of a championship are planted now," Coach Baty said, knowing that it might be two years before the fruits of their labor could be harvested.

It didn't take long for the young players to recognize the idiosyncrasies of their coaches. For example, Coach Simmang was quiet, but tough— very tough. He was built like a rock and frequently challenged his linemen by demonstrating proper tackles and blocks at full speed, without a helmet or pads. He would hit and be hit by uniformed and helmeted linemen and never flinch. He worked the kids hard, he pushed them. He commanded his players' attention and earned their respect. Jerry and Coach Baty seemed to genuinely like and respect each other. Sometimes Baty would rib Coach Simmang, who would get red and embarrassed.

Coach Baty floated during practice between position drills to observe and to ensure that proper techniques were emphasized. He had a keen eye for technique. When he recognized something that a player could do better, he would step in and correct the issue immediately. "I don't have to see a good tackle . . . I can hear it!" he frequently yelled.[1] To the running backs he would shout, "Run faster, backs! Run faster!"

He was unwavering. He was impeccable and precise in the techniques he taught. He expected near perfection and minimal mistakes. This disciplined approach fostered precise execution in games.—Bobby Cordova

In early scrimmages, a troublesome leak appeared as defensive linemen repeatedly broke through the middle of the offensive line to throw offensive plays into chaos. Coach Baty quickly recognized the problem. Juan "Baca" Mendoza, a center, was being knocked flat on his back after snapping the ball.

"Baca," he began, pulling the center aside, "you're getting knocked on your butt. Do you want to know how you can fix it?"

"Yes, sir," answered Baca.

Coach Baty rechanneled what his old center at A&M, Bob Gary, had taught him. "Okay, here's the problem. You've got your legs spread out too far, like a girl. From now on, hold your legs closer together, bend your knees, get your balance, and then snap the ball—just as you fire out to block!" The leak was immediately plugged. Baca found new confidence, and his teammates could count on him.

The entire team was undersized. First-string quarterback Jesse Martinez, for example, stood 5'6" and weighed 125 pounds and was protected by linemen of 165 or 170 pounds at most. To compensate for Jesse's short stature, linemen were taught to block their assignments "*low*—at the knees" on pass plays so it would be harder for tall defenders to block Jesse's view of his receivers or knock down his passes.

By the end of spring drills, these kids looked pretty good at times. But then, there were the other times. Inconsistency and mistakes would probably haunt them until the hard lessons of experience sank in.

At the end of the school year, Coach Jim Bowden delivered disappointing news. He had resigned to take over his family's cotton farm in the nearby valley. His absence would be felt next year: a year of rebuilding. Rosas was promoted to varsity backfield coach.

The summer flew by, and as football season neared, predictions began. An article by Ray Sanchez ran in the *El Paso Herald-Post* and stated Bowie's case plainly:

September 7, 1951

BURYL BATY IN ROLE OF BUILDING COACH

If he can't have a winning football team, Bowie High Coach Buryl Baty claims, a coach develops character.

"So I guess I'll be developing plenty of character this season," the Bears' mentor, now in his second year at the Southside school says.

That about sums up the Grizzlies' chances in the District 2-AAAA grid warfare this season.

Bowie was the hardest hit of all the local schools by graduation. The Bears, who didn't lose a game in district play last season, lost every regular and have only three returning lettermen. . . .

Baty will be building for '52. . . .

No coach in the district gives the Southsiders much of a chance this season.

For the second consecutive season opener, New Mexico's reigning state champion Carlsbad High routed the "Baby Bears," as Ray Sanchez labeled them. The next opponent, the Douglas (Arizona) Bulldogs, proved to be more manageable. A well-devised game plan and more consistent execution proved to be a winning combination as Bowie posted victory number one.

Looming on the horizon were the Big Spring Steers, who had embarrassed a more experienced Bowie team last year. The coaching staff worked well into Sunday evening to develop a game plan from archived notes and paper napkins—upon which creative plays had been drawn during countless breakfasts and coffees. Fresh on their minds was the fact that Big Spring's coach had neglected to send scouting information in advance of last year's game. In the face of predictions that "at least a two- or three-touchdown loss" was imminent, Bowie's coaches resolved to ensure that Big Spring would respect them going forward.

Other, less wholesome things than football were going on among teenagers in El Paso, including at Bowie High:

El Paso Herald-Post, September 27, 1951
SCHOOLS TACKLE GANG PROBLEM; PLAN CONFERENCE
Dr. Mortimer Brown, city school superintendent, said today he
will discuss with high school principals what steps can be taken to
curb "gangsterism" among teenage youths.

His statement was prompted by the reported armed kidnap-
ping of a 17-year-old Bowie High School student as he walked
near the school Tuesday, and reported beatings of two other
youths at Jefferson High School yesterday. . . .

"They never give us trouble on the school premises," [Principal
Frank Pollitt] said. "Even boys who become involved in such activities are well behaved when in school. . . ."

Police have received reports of other attacks on Bowie High
students by members of the 7-X gang. Seven known members of
the "rat pack" were rounded up last week and lectured by Bowie
High instructors and City detectives.

It is reported that a vigilant and involved Coach Baty was one of the
major reasons that these gang members were well behaved in school.
And he minimized their influence on his players—he was determined to
keep them on the right side of the street.

In Big Spring, home of the fearsome Steers, the local paper acknowledged the Bears' speed and their famous coach. But the article didn't
seem to give Bowie much of a chance:

Big Spring Daily Herald, September 28, 1951
STEERS TACKLE BOWIE BEARS IN EL PASO AT 9 THIS
EVENING
Still seeking that elusive first win of the season, the Big Spring
Steers open the Texas Interscholastic League's program for the
week in a game tonight in El Paso.

The Longhorns' opposition will be formed by the pesky Bowie
Bears, and, for once, the locals will enter the game as favorites. . . .

Big Spring will field a much heavier line than the Bears but the
home club may be lightning fast and hard to hold. Too, the Bruins
are due to be air-minded. They're being taught by one of the best
Southwest conference aerialists in history, Buryl Baty, who was at
Texas A&M some years back.

The Big Springers flattened the Bears by three touchdowns last year.

Since that time, the Bowie team has been hit hard by graduation. Every Bowie player who started the game a year ago has departed the campus and Baty had only four lettermen greeting him when he opened fall drills last month.

If the Longhorns play complacently and let their guard down, there's a good chance an aroused Bowie team can make them regret it. There's no reason, though, why the Steers shouldn't hustle like all get out and pull out all stops in efforts to win.

But back in El Paso, reporting in the next morning's *Herald-Post* under the headline "Speedy Bowie Eleven Romps over Big Spring," Ray Sanchez clearly enjoyed telling the rest of the story:

El Paso Herald-Post, September 28, 1951
BEARS BECOME LOOP MENACE
Speedy Bowie Eleven Romps over Big Spring
. . . Look who's popped up as a district contender.
Bowie High's Grizzlies, rated rock bottom last by the four opposing coaches in pre-season dope, hopped into the 2-AAAA limelight by crushing heavily favored Big Spring, usually a Texas toughie, 39–25, last night at R. R. Jones Stadium.
The some 4000 shocked fans who sat in on the spectacle couldn't believe their eyes as the Southsiders, displaying the speediest all-around backfield seen here this season, ran their bigger visitors ragged. . . .
"I was very well pleased with our running," Baty said. . . .
Baty had instructed his charges to take to the air before the scrap, but was surprised to see his speedsters running all over the field when the tussle started. The Bears piled up 336 yards rushing to 162 for their foes. . . .

After the game, Coach Baty had praised his players. "Remember what we talked about last spring—beating the big boys? Well, you just beat 'em. This was a good team you played tonight, but you just proved you're a better one."

Students and faculty members wore smiles to school the next Monday, and every player felt like a hero. Wow! What a victory! This game put a spark into everybody's eyes, and the future looked great. Or, could this be the present? Were the Bears for real? Other El Paso coaches took notice. Ysleta Coach Roger McAdams and Austin High's Red Harris were very impressed with the Bruins. "Good offense," both said. And Harris added, "But still a little green."

This Bowie team was, in fact, still young, and very fragile. The coaches knew that they needed to protect the delicate balance between improving and maintaining confidence. The next opponent would not allow much margin for error.

Twenty-seven excited players, including many first-time flyers, flew to Houston to battle Galena Park on Friday night. Only a few fans sat in the visitors' bleachers: a couple of sets of Bowie parents and Galena Park High's only Hispanic student. The intimidated Bears were handed a big loss. They were also eaten alive by a relentless attack from mosquitoes. Afterwards, the coaches reminded the boys, "You're learning this year, you're learning how to be good sports, to avoid mistakes, and to win."

The following afternoon, the Bears attended a Rice Institute football game. "You can go to college if you work hard." Many did. "And those are the same plays we run," the coaches reminded this year's players.

After a win the following week over Cathedral, Bowie's win-loss record stood at 3–2. Perhaps this season would be better than expected? The answer would come soon, as district play began the following week.

The next week's *Herald-Post* ran an article datelined Des Moines, Iowa, that caught Buryl's attention:

DRAKE CHARGES NEGRO STAR SLUGGED BY OKLA.
AGGIES, OCTOBER 22, 1951
Des Moines.—Drake teammates of Johnny Bright will tell university athletic officials today that the sensational Negro football star suffered a fractured jaw Saturday because Oklahoma A. and M. was "out to get him." . . .
Bright, leading ground-gainer in the history of college football, was forced out of the Aggie game after only 10 plays.
He said he was hit on the jaw in the first two plays and teammates named Okahoma A. and M. Guard Wilbanks Smith as the man who used his fists.
Doctors said the triple-threat halfback may be able to see lim-

ited action against Iowa State this Saturday if his jaw can be protected. . . .

Drake Coach Warren Gaer said news pictures of the game showed Smith twice landing blows on Bright's jaw after he already had gotten off a pass.

Discrimination and gratuitous acts of hostility against people of color were coming to light in the postwar era.

. . .

Each of the next three district opponents, El Paso High, Austin High, and Ysleta High, would be heavily favored over the Bears. Austin High's Coach Red Harris, however, told reporter Ray Sanchez, "We can't afford to relax or Bowie will beat us."

Meanwhile, in an attempt to correct the previous week's sloppiness, Coach Baty added new wrinkles to his passing drill. Every receiver who dropped a pass was ordered to take an immediate lap around the practice field. "Watch the ball all the way into your hands," he reminded each pass dropper, "then wrap it up!" Quarterbacks also ran laps when they were off target on three passes in a row. In the same vein, backs were tutored and drilled on their fumbling problem, one that could kill their chances against a good team.

After practice, a slew of kids stayed out for extra work, and quite a few younger players ran over from the adjoining B-team and junior high fields. Backs, receivers, and kickers were instructed on proper techniques for their respective specialties. Young quarterbacks Jesse Martinez, a junior, Bobby Cordova, a sophomore, and Sal Garcia, a freshman, got a big slice of Coach Baty's attention. Their potential was obvious and with refinement and some experience they would each develop into very good leaders. Over time, a strong pipeline of young talent at every position would ensure consistent success—the seeds of which were being planted.

We had a great time at those sessions. Coach Baty would talk to us, joke with us, and teach us. It was fun.—Ed Camacho

All three crosstown rivals beat Bowie's "Baby" Bears handily. Of course, everybody was discouraged. The glorious victories of earlier weeks seemed long ago. This was a point at which fortitude had to prevail. Despite swelling doubts, the players still hung on every word Coach Baty uttered.

"Keep your chins up! Football is like life, and life is tough sometimes. We're going to persevere. What Bowie fans are gonna learn is that we never give up—never quit fighting. I'm proud of you for that. We're a young team, but we're learning and getting better every day. Walk out of here with pride, and let's practice and play our hearts out to win our last game. That's the only thing we'll think about."

Bo encouraged Buryl at the supper table the following week. "Rebuilding takes time," she said. Buryl took a deep breath and nodded in agreement. Then the coach's coach added, "I'm proud of you."

A 41–12 victory over Jefferson raised the record to four wins and five losses. The early flashes of brilliance had been offset by youthful mistakes and lapses of discipline. This win, however, ended the season on a positive note.

As his own season had wound down, Buryl followed the national news about his sport. On November 22 the *Herald-Post* reported what must have been a rankling turn in the Johnny Bright story:

MV NOT TO TAKE ACTION AGAINST AGGIE PLAYER
The Missouri Valley Conference has announced it will take no "disciplinary action" against the Oklahoma A. and M. lineman who broke the jaw of Drake's ace halfback, Johnny Bright.

Presidents and athletic representatives of conference teams said after a meeting yesterday that under the present constitution "the conference has no authority to take disciplinary action against an individual player."

Bright, the nation's ground-gainer king, was injured Oct. 20 in the Drake-Oklahoma A. and M. game, won by the Aggies. Drake officials charged that guard Wilbanks Smith of the Aggies smacked Bright in the jaw deliberately early in the game.

Smith said he did it unintentionally.

It was not a perfect world in El Paso, either. The Segundo Barrio had been plagued by the 7-X, the Lucky 13, the OK9, and El Pujito gangs. Some of these boys were in Coach Baty's classes, and he made it a point between classes to engage those who were not. They were all intimidated by him, because he laid down the rules and he allowed no nonsense. His expectations and punishments were applied firmly and equally to all. He challenged gang members just as he did his athletes, and he talked to them about their lives. Coach Baty frequently asked his players to "Go find Elia and Armando and Tomato. Tell them to come talk with me. They won't bother you," he explained to his players, "because you're too strong."

"Armando," he would say, "you can go places with your life. You can be somebody. But you gotta stay away from the bad influences, and you know who I'm talking about. You have to stay away from drugs and alcohol. Work hard in school to graduate. Get that piece of paper, so you can get a good job and make some good money. Do you hear what I'm telling you, son?"

A few of these kids heard his message and went on to graduate. Still, his words fell on many deaf ears. Accountability was not a concept embraced by most of these boys. They wished Mr. Baty would leave the school and the neighborhood.

It was a blessing that Ruth and Bob King, natives of hometown Paris, lived next door to the Batys. The couples entertained each other and went out to eat together, and their sons, Kyle and Gaines, played together almost daily. Bo and Ruth enjoyed each other's company thoroughly and talked on more days than not.

Ruth, Bo, and Buryl occasionally drove to Paris together for visits. They would leave immediately after school, and Buryl would drive for the entire twelve-hour trip. Ruth remembers Bo and the two small boys asleep in the back seat while she cut up lemons for Buryl. The sharp, tangy taste gave him a jolt and helped keep him awake.

Buryl knew how Bo yearned for her family back home, and he tried to arrange visits as often as possible. After one of their off-season trips to Paris, Bo decided that she and Gaines should extend their visit, while Buryl drove back by himself.

Alone and lonely in the empty El Paso house, Buryl called Bo every night. Days seemed to drag on, and he had no idea how long it would be before she returned. Late one afternoon after school, he pulled his car into the driveway and saw Ruth in her front yard next door. "How's Bob?" he asked her. Ruth, eight months pregnant with her second child, sighed that her husband was out of town on business. She seemed to be missing her husband and her best friend Bo.

Buryl blurted out, "You look like you could use a movie." Ruth agreed.

Later that night, as always when they were apart, Buryl called Bo. He told her about his day and mentioned that he and Ruth had gone to the movie together. "Bob was out of town and she seemed lonely," he explained.

Alarmed by this news, Bo quickly arranged a ride from Paris to Love Field and flew back to El Paso the next day, cutting her trip short by at least a week. Buryl was glad to have her back with him.

Ruth maintains to this day that Buryl's hidden agenda was to get Bo back to El Paso sooner.

Just before Christmas, the coaches drove around to loading docks and farms to arrange holiday and summer jobs for their boys. They sought out strenuous work that required loading fifty- and hundred-pound blocks of ice, heavy bales of hay, appliances, or furniture. This improved the players' strength, kept them out of trouble, and augmented jobs they already had, such as Francisco Avila's shoeshining enterprise in the street next to the church. The extra money also helped the players' families.

One Sunday after church, the phone rang. It was Ralph Smith, a former Luling player, saying that he was in El Paso. Ralph and two Navy buddies were hitchhiking from basic training in California back home. "I just called to say hi," he said.

"Ralph, you stay right there. I'm on my way to get you." Within a few minutes, the coach pulled up to the young men. "Hop in. Let me get y'all out of town so you can make some time," he insisted. The three soldiers loaded into the car. Ralph and Coach Baty talked about the military, the good old days in Luling, and about beating Lockhart to finish the '49 season. Time flew, and before they knew it they were over a hundred miles east of El Paso. Coach Baty dropped them off at a gas station where they could no doubt hitch a ride in short order.

> He made me feel really good—like I was important to him and that he cared about how and what I was doing. And, he went way out of his way to take us so far.—Ralph Smith

"Watch the Bears in '52" was the theme of the annual football banquet held in the school cafeteria immediately following the holidays. The Southsiders would have nineteen lettermen returning next fall, including all but four starters. Bright blue "B" football letters, mounted on handsome white sweaters, were awarded to twenty-six players and two managers.

Of course, the coaches wanted every athlete possible to participate in spring drills. One afternoon Coach Baty strolled through the gym past a few B-team basketball players who were shooting hoops before practice. One of the boys asked him about spring training. Coach Baty responded with, "It starts next week—are you coming out?"

All of a sudden he heard a loud voice. "Coach, get out of my gym!" It was Coach Nemo Herrera, the varsity basketball coach, staring angrily at him from the end of the basketball court.

The hint of a smile appeared on Coach Baty's face. He said softly, "I'll see you boys—I think Nemo's mad." He casually continued his stroll out the gymnasium door.

Coach Herrera shouted the boys over to him. He was indignant that Coach Baty might be poaching his athletes. "I'll get to the point, boys. If I ever see any one of you talking with Coach Baty in my gym again, you will be off the team, and furthermore, I will blackball you from basketball and baseball, because I am the coach. Do you understand what I just said—blackball? I'll blackball you!" The boys scowled. Tony Lujan, Bomba Gonzalez, and several other B-teamers promptly yanked their practice jerseys off over their heads and threw them on the floor before walking toward the locker room.

A few days later, Tony Franco showed up for the first day of spring training, imagining himself weaving through potential tacklers and running for touchdowns. But after an encouraging explanation by Coach Rosas, Tony ran over to practice with the lineman. Young Manny Morales, on the other hand, *would* be a star running back. Nicknamed "Mule Train" for his tough, determined, and powerful running style, Manny was short, stocky, and fast, and he liked to hit people on the football field. This aggression was highlighted during one spring scrimmage when Manny attempted to make a block. Despite a bad angle, he dove at the linebacker's knees anyway—clipping him. Linebacker Rod Rodriguez's knee painfully buckled under him. The knee swelled and stiffened. Fortunately, however, it improved over the next few days— almost back to normal.

As linebackers tend to do, Rodriguez remembered Manny's cheap block and nursed a grudge. During his first scrimmage back in action,

Rod delivered an elbow to the face, knocking out two of Manny's front teeth.

Manny, full of spirit and stubbornness, was perhaps the only player who didn't fear Coach Baty. And he frequently earned a spot in his coach's doghouse. For example, Baty examined every player's grade report weekly. For each unacceptable mark, a player received three swats, no questions asked. Manny almost never got past a grade report without at least a few licks. "Manny, I'm doing this because I want you to graduate," the coach would say.

In retrospect, the '51-'52 school year had been a tough one. But the Bears were tougher because of it. Last year's freshmen and sophomores now had more muscle and more experience. Coach Baty didn't mind repeating himself: "You're getting stronger, and you're getting better!"

20 This Should Be Our Year

1952

A small, frail, dark-complexioned boy followed a couple of players into the locker room. Coach Baty knew exactly who the boy was; he had seen him hanging around the second ward, the bakery, and even the high school campus. "Nell" was his nickname, short for Manuel. He was a slightly older, intellectually challenged boy from the barrio. He was unable to attend school, but he had a curiosity about him. He wanted desperately to be included in, or at least to witness, the activities of his neighbors. Nell could frequently be seen watching other boys play, fight, or just shoot the bull, usually observing their activities from a distance. Despite his presence at this gathering, he was not sure about its purpose. "Come on in, Nell," Coach Baty called.

Coach Baty provided all the inspiration at this first team meeting, and as usual, players grasped his expectations clearly. In closing, just before the squad was released to check out uniforms and gear, Coach Baty added, "And, Nell, you're welcome to join us as an honorary member of this team."

A huge smile stretched across Nell's face as players cheered him: "Yea, Nell!"

Last year had been one of preparation. This year La Bowie was very optimistic. However, devastating news kicked off the season. Two of the team's most talented players were ruled out—Manny Morales was declared ineligible and Robert Hood had health issues. Eleven additional players dropped off the team because of illness or the need to work after school.

One promising newcomer, David Holguin, announced that he would also quit the team because practices extended past the time for him to report for his downtown busboy job, a forty-five minute series of bus routes away. Coach Baty proposed a solution; David could leave practice at 5:30 p.m., foregoing post-practice sprints and laps, and *run* to work. David quickly figured out that his daily three-mile "sprint" was more strenuous than what he would have done on the practice field, but it allowed him to play football. His presence and talent would later contribute greatly to the team.

As expected, La Bowie lost the first game to another strong Carlsbad team but won in week two against Cathedral. The next week, heavily favored Pecos came to town. Ray Sanchez painted a picture of frustration in the next morning's paper. As he recounted the heartbreaking 27–26 defeat, he described Coach Baty as "stunned" by the loss. "I don't know if I'm alive yet," Baty was quoted as saying. "But I can't blame my boys. They played a good ball game and I'm proud of 'em."

Win or lose, the Bears were among El Paso's best-drawing high school teams. Devoted Bear fans came out in droves every time the squad played at home. Ray Sanchez's news article declared this phenomenon "amazing, to say the least."

Despite having only one win so far, Bowie coaches were optimistic after three strong showings. Senior quarterback Jesse Martinez's experience was paying off, and his backup, junior Bobby Cordova, was loaded with talent and coming on strong. Momentum was building.

In week four, the Bears endured a four-hundred-mile bus trip on Thursday for a Friday night game against the Snyder Tigers. That night, once again, a restaurant closed to the public in order to serve the team's supper. After finishing their late meal, the well-dressed boys filed out of the café, one by one. As the team's bus accelerated slowly up the dark street, its passengers could conclude only that Snyder was just a sleepy little town.

In a matter of minutes they pulled into the parking lot of a roadside motel. This long u-shaped building would serve as their home for the next two nights. After unloading gear from the underbelly of the bus, teammates congregated in the fresh air while the coach checked in at the office. It was a clear west Texas night, and the stars in the dark sky were brilliant. The players were given keys to their rooms.

"Men, I want everyone in bed with lights out in twenty minutes," Baty decreed. "We need the rest; tomorrow night's game is going to be a tough one."

Senior team leader Rod Rodriguez yawned. He knew as he carried his suitcase into his room that it wouldn't take him twenty minutes to fall asleep. The coaches walked from door to door, checking off each player from their list to ensure that they were all in their rooms with lights out. Apart from the loud rushing sound of an occasional passing car on the nearby highway, it was dead silent. Rodriguez quickly drifted off to sleep. But soon, a strange sound echoed in his mind.

"Tap . . . tap . . . tap."

"Tap . . . tap . . . tap."

Rod thought he was dreaming.

"TAP . . . TAP . . . TAP."

The tapping continued and grew louder. Rod opened his eyes. The sound was coming from outside the back window.

"TAP . . . TAP . . . TAP."

As Rod pulled the curtains apart, he and his three roommates could not believe their eyes.

"Open the window!" whispered a feminine voice from outside. Rod quickly raised the window, which was the only thing between him and a pair of very attractive Anglo girls.

"We're havin' a party, y'all come on!" whispered the giggly, ponytailed teenagers.

Normally a thoughtful, conservative kid, Rod did not have to be asked twice. After quickly throwing on his clothes, out the window he and his roommates jumped, lickety-split.

As it turned out, several windows must have been tapped upon, as quite a few Bears showed up at the gathering. Girls and boys danced, drank, talked, and laughed. Rod and his buddies had a grand time, partying into the wee hours. But Rod had a nagging feeling that Coach Baty was watching or waiting for him.

It was in the early morning hours when the last of the partying Bears scurried the few blocks back to the motel, squeezed through their still-open room windows, and slipped back under the covers.

> I don't know how those girls knew where we were, or which windows to knock on. The party was obviously well organized. I don't think it was just the kids who inspired it. There must have been some adults involved.
> —"Rod" Rodriguez

> Sometimes we got away with stuff.—"Rod" Rodriguez

In what seemed like a few short minutes, a loud knock came on the door and a coach's voice announced, "Time to wake up, boys! We leave for breakfast in fifteen minutes."

"It can't already be 7:30, can it?" Rod groaned. It was. A long day followed with a full schedule of activities: breakfast, skull sessions, a movie at the theater on the square, pregame meal, then taping and treatments for the game. No time for napping, unless it was done at the picture show.

When the boys arrived at the restaurant for their scheduled pregame meal, they heard the manager claiming that he didn't have enough food to feed them. After a heated discussion, the proprietor apparently gave way to Coach Baty's persistence, and the team was escorted through the rear door of the restaurant and into an isolated room in the back. After an unreasonable wait in an otherwise empty café, surly waitresses served them. It was clear that they were not welcome.

The day wore on. Finally, after taping and dressing out, the Bears climbed aboard the bus for the short trip to the football stadium. As they rounded the corner approaching the football field, they suddenly heard loud noises.

"Pop! Pop! Pop-Pop!"

It didn't take long to realize that Snyder fans were throwing rocks at the bus, and the barrage did not subside when the Bears arrived at the stadium. In fact, it escalated. Rusty, the Bears' red-headed bus driver, jumped from the vehicle, with his hands shielding him from flying rocks, and retreated to a safer location to get his bearings. Eventually he spotted a Stetson-clad, uniformed sheriff and hurried to seek assistance. The lawman casually watched as stones pelted the bus. "Can you help us?" Rusty pleaded.

Given the sheriff's decidedly indifferent reaction, Rusty made his appeal more forceful, pointing out that the bus was owned by the Carlsbad Caverns Bus Company, not the school or the team. He warned that the company would sue the city of Snyder and its school administrators to pay for damages. The lawman finally responded by ordering that the target practice cease.

Only then could the "stadium" come into focus. To the Bears it looked more like a little league park, with small, wooden bleachers on each side of a field that resembled a mowed, parched cow pasture.

Things didn't go especially well once they were inside the stadium, either. Fans yelled intimidating slurs and threw ice from the stands. Bear supporters couldn't offer much encouragement or support because Rusty, the bus driver, was their only fan in the rickety old bleachers. A strong Snyder attack and sloppy Bear play prompted La Bowie to quickly lose its composure.

At the end of the first half, the Bears were behind. "I don't understand this," Coach Baty stormed. "We could beat this team if we played our game, but they're running right through us! What's going on?"

Nobody answered his question. But they knew the answer.

Those of us that had gone to the party felt guilty. We knew why we lost the game. We learned a good lesson.— "Rod" Rodriguez

They tried to play better in the second half, but they tired quickly. Snyder hit harder, ran faster, and got into the Bears' heads with demeaning insults, on the order of "We're kicking your tamale butts!" and "Go home, you greasy Meskins!" It was a lost cause. The contest could not end fast enough. Bowie was routed, 0–27.

After the final gun, exhausted and embarrassed Bowie players loaded single file into their idling bus. Just as Coach Baty strode in their direction, a drunken man stumbled toward him.

"You owe me money, Coach," he slurred. "I bet money on you and you lost. I want it back."

"Stranger," Coach Baty snapped, "you need to keep on moving." The gambler got the message and staggered away.

"That hombre is lucky he walked away," whispered one of the players.

The boys finished boarding the bus while Coach Baty stood by the doorway, red-faced. After a weighty silence, he passed his judgment on them. "You're better than you played tonight," he said. "You just quit. How come you quit?" His jaw clenched. "I don't like quitters!"

That got our attention. We had a long time to think about it and it left a bad taste in our mouths. He was right, and we knew it. We didn't like that feeling, and we vowed to never quit again. I never forgot that lesson.—Al Lujan

The players sat mute all the way back to the hotel.

• • •

"Ray, we got in a hole the very first time we got the ball," Baty had told reporter Ray Sanchez during his long-distance phone call to the *El Paso Herald-Post* immediately after the game. "And we never got out of it. The first time we got the ball, we fumbled and lost it."

The Bears would sleep that Friday night in Snyder and head back home first thing the next morning. However, long after the evening's curfew, one motel room's lights could be seen glowing dimly through its thick curtains. A poker game was going strong. Teammates Enrique Camacho, David Archuleta, Tony Franco, and Jesse Martinez were having a grand time. While they gambled and cut up, Enrique's big brother, Ed, lay sleeping soundly in his bed. Just as the poker game was about to close down, Tony, the practical joker in the group, suggested a prank. "I'll wake Ed up," he proposed, "and tell him it's morning and time to load the bus. Let's see what he does."

Everybody agreed. "¡*Simón*! (Heck, yes!)."

"¡Eduardo, Eduardo! ¡*Es tiempo de levantarse*! (It's time to get up!) Hurry! We're already dressed and ready to go. Hurry up or Coach will be mad!"

Ed jumped up, threw on his clothes, crammed his belongings into his duffle bag, and, still in a daze, charged outside. Eyes still half closed, he stumbled a few steps toward the parked bus, bag in tow.

"What are you doing?"

Ed jumped at the sound of Coach Baty's sudden, sharp words. "Coach, I thought it was time to go," Eduardo replied, obviously confused.

"No. You have four more hours. Go to bed." Ed eased back into his motel room, where he was greeted with nervous, whispered questions. "¿*Qué te dijo? ¿Le dijiste alguna cosa*? (What did he say to you? Did you tell him anything?)" Unanswered questions lingered about what Coach Baty was doing outside the door. "How did he know?"

Baty's presence at that hour would feed into his almost mythical reputation. "Baty doesn't sleep, he's always watching you," teammates and future players would hear. They wondered if he had also known about the Friday night party. The Baty legend grew.

During the following Monday's skull session, after a long drive home and a long weekend of worry for the poker players, Baty renewed the issue of the late-night encounter. In the room full of players, he asked, "Ed, can you tell me why you were outside the hotel at three-thirty in the morning?"

"Well, Coach, the guys woke me up and told me it was time to leave. I ran outside, and there you were."

The poker players shrank into their chairs. "*Quisiera que él no hubiera dicho eso* (I wish he hadn't said that)," the perpetrators whispered.

Coach Baty's stare traveled from Ed to his brother Enrique, then to David and Jesse, and finally to Tony. He said nothing. The boys squirmed. In the back of the room, behind the players, Coaches Simmang and Rosas concealed their smiles with their hands.

Punishment was doled out, but focus quickly shifted to the next week's game against Douglas. After three scoreless quarters, the Bears astonished the hometown crowd by exploding for three touchdowns in the fourth quarter to drub the Bulldogs. Douglas had been undefeated before this game, with four straight wins. Baty told Ray Sanchez, "We're pretty happy about winning this one." Bowie's record now stood at 2–3.

This strong-finishing victory removed most of the sour aftertaste of the Snyder game and reestablished positive momentum. Spirited junior quarterback Bobby Cordova was earning more playing time as he added an exciting dimension of play, and leadership, to the offense. Coach Baty had mentored him for over two years now, and Bobby was delivering. The pieces were starting to fall into place for another run at the crown. Leading up to the big district opener against El Paso High, Coach Baty told the *Herald-Post,* "I don't see how we can stop 'em, but I think we'll score a couple of times ourselves."

"The EPHS Tigers were heavily favored seven days ago but the odds have dropped considerably," wrote Ray Sanchez.

While talking with Sanchez before one of that week's practices, Coach Baty called over the team equipment manager. "Cachi, go find Lalo Ortiz and get him to practice. He needs to know our game plan because he's part of it. You know where he is . . . at his girlfriend's."

"Sure, Coach." Cachi sprinted down the street into the Segundo Barrio.

That Friday night, El Paso High nudged Bowie 14–7 in front of the largest crowd of the season. All the scoring took place in the second half, with Bowie making a run at tying the game right up to the end. The next morning's paper quoted the opposing coaches: "I'm glad that game's over," sighed a relieved Coach Terrell Yarborough. Coach Baty, always a good sport, said, "Our two lapses hurt, but El Paso High deserved to win. They outplayed us."

The Bears refocused and began preparing for their next opponent, Austin High. They were still in the thick of the race, but another loss would end their playoff chances. With an open week, they would have two weeks to prepare and to rebuild momentum. However, a storm was brewing.

Buryl was troubled. At the supper table on Monday night, he looked up from his plate at Bo. "This can only be interpreted as disrespect. I have to do it for the team." Bo nodded in agreement.

Certain players were acting as if the rules didn't apply to them. They had been seen walking girlfriends home before showing up late for practice and had missed important drills. Cachi, the student manager, had frequently been asked to go fetch one player or another. The coaches agreed that the unexcused absences and tardiness would erode team discipline, for this season and beyond, if they were not resolved. Of course, it's always easier to discipline a third-teamer than a first-teamer, but they had to draw a line in the sand.

At the end of Tuesday's practice, Coach Baty made an announcement. "We've had too many absences and late arrivals lately. You know who you are. If you can't get to practice on time, you can't play. Starting now, anyone who misses or is late for practice without a good reason will be dropped from the team."

The following day, Wednesday, he didn't ask Cachi to find or retrieve anybody, although more than one player was absent. Coach Baty called the team together just as practice was about to begin, and asked, "We're about to play important district games. Do you want team leaders who think they're above the rules, acting like they're more important than the team?"

Several boys spoke up, agreeing that they deserved the same dedication, commitment, and respect that they themselves were expected to demonstrate. They concluded that the team was most important. Absentees were voted off the squad.

> This was a hard decision that he put in our hands. It forced us to grow up a little bit, and not to be so cavalier about what it means to be a team. "Team" meant that we all rejoiced together and we suffered together.—Father Edmundo "Rod" Rodriguez

Bobby Cordova, one of the rising stars, had evidently not been listening when his coach's ultimatum was delivered. He had stayed home that Wednesday, without providing appropriate notice or an excuse for missing practice. When he showed up the following day, Bobby found his locker emptied. Nothing was said. No explanation was requested. None was given. He had been kicked off the team. Every player noticed the empty locker.

> I couldn't believe this was happening to me; I was crushed and felt very humiliated—I swallowed hard and went home. The last few games, I had to sit in the stands for "pep" assemblies and at the games, and felt like everyone was look-

ing at me. I remember being very embarrassed . . . and longing for the camaraderie of the team.—Bobby Cordova

That week, every sports fan in El Paso read of the incident. Ray Sanchez wrote this for the *El Paso Herald-Post:*

November 3, 1952
CORDOVA OFF SQUAD; BEAR SPREAD FACES
AUSTIN—BOWIE HAS LOST FULLBACK, HALFBACKS—
NOW LOSES QB

During the season, Bowie High has lost its first-string fullback,
its first-string right halfback and its first-string left halfback.

Therefore, it fazes Bruin Coach Buryl Baty not one bit that his
Southsiders will be without one of their two top-notch quarterbacks when they clash with the Poweranthers of Austin High Friday in R. R. Jones Stadium, in a game that will make or break the
Bears.

Bob Cordova, who alternates with Jesus Martinez at the man
under post and is considered every bit as good as (and in some
quarters even better than) Martinez, was forced to drop off the
squad.

Coach Baty just sighed, managed a smile and said: "We still
have Martinez, today, I hope we'll have him Friday."

Cordova's loss will hurt plenty. It's no secret that the Bears will
use a spread against the Golden Cats. . . . Baty planned to alternate Cordova . . . with Martinez. . . .

District 2-AAAA fans see the air-lanes as the only way the
Bears can pull an upset and remain in the running for the loop
crown. Of course, the spread is the best air method, if you have
the man to pull it off. Martinez could be the man.

More bad news followed two days later, and Sanchez continued the tale
of woe:

November 5, 1952
By the Way . . .
ORTIZ OFF TEAM; BATY SAYS NOTHING

Speaking of quitting, it's amazing Bowie High hasn't. The Bears have suffered so many losses this season it's a wonder what Coach Buryl Baty has been able to do with the squad. Buryl, incidentally, hates to admit the losses. Thinks it makes him look like he's making excuses. He tried to cover up the fact that Medardo Ortiz, a starting offensive end, has been knocked off the team along with Quarterback Bob Cordova. Can't help liking a guy like that.

That next week, Austin High took advantage of the distracted Bowie Bears, smashing them in front of eleven thousand spectators. They ran up a 35–0 lead before sitting back and watching the Bears score twice on their subs. The Bears were officially eliminated from the district race.

"Men, we just got beat by a very good team, and we have to respect them for that. I'll admit that we've had some bad breaks lately, but those 'breaks' are *not* the reason we lost this game tonight."

The coach paused. "The reason we didn't play well was that we allowed distractions to interrupt our concentration and resolve. But we also learned something; we learned to be stronger mentally and not to allow outside influences to take our eyes off the goal. Now, let's regain our focus and get ready to win next week against Ysleta."

At the supper table, however, Buryl shook his head. "Sometimes I wonder. I know we're doing the right things, but maybe that's not enough." He paused. "And this shameless discrimination . . . I'm not sure what to do about it."

"Like you say, 'It's a long journey,'" Bo responded.

The next morning, Saturday, Coach Baty learned that Guillermo Olivas, a promising young player, had been cut from the junior high team. He was not in the mood for this news. In a meeting after the morning's junior high game, Coach Baty pulled no punches. "Coach Rodriguez, your job is to keep his grades up and keep him in school and on the team. We owe it to the kid. You need to put Olivas back on the team. Now."

The varsity Bears had experienced two tough losses in a row, and they needed to bounce back into the win column. But the Ysleta Indians stood in their way. Coach Baty also held a grievance against the rival coach, feeling that he had intentionally run up the score in last year's game. Coach Baty fueled the Bears' emotional fire all week long, and his strong resolve was a powerful motivational force. After waiting nervously before the kickoff, the Bears got off to a good start. They scored early and often, and kept pouring on the steam. Starters remained in the game until the final whistle, delivering a clear message. For his role in this decisive victory, untested sophomore quarterback Sal Garcia was named Player of the Week.

Late the next Friday afternoon, taped and dressed, Bowie's varsity team boarded the bus. The jaunt from their locker room across town for the Jefferson game would be their last of the season. Helmets and shoulder pads, packed in individual duffel bags, were being loaded into the baggage compartment by Cachi, the team manager, and Rusty, the bus driver.

Standing sheepishly over to the side was Nell, humming the Bowie fight song. He hoped to catch Coach Baty's eye as the team boarded. After all the equipment was loaded and the players were seated, Nell heard Coach Baty's voice. "Okay, Nell, let's go!"

Nell bounced up into an empty seat. A spot had also been reserved for him on the sidelines for every home game. Coach Baty always told Nell that he brought good luck.

As linebacker, Rod Rodriguez anchored the defense, and as the starting center, he led the offense with his blocking up the middle. He took his job seriously. However, early in the game, Jefferson's huge noseguard was causing trouble. When the 250-pound Jefferson boy read the play going to his right, he would lean that way to plug up the hole. When he saw the QB moving to the left, the big boy leaned to that side with the same effect. This troubled Rod because Coach Baty trusted him to get the job done. He needed to figure something out.

As they formed the huddle for a new offensive series, Rod told the two guards on each side of him that "no matter what the quarterback calls, I'll stand the big boy up. Fernie, you hit him high from the right, and Oscar, you hit him low from the left." This plan worked to perfection. The big Jefferson High noseguard sat on the bench, injured, for the rest of the game. La Bowie finished with a second straight decisive victory. In the loud and joyous postgame locker room, players were summoned for a few words from Coach Baty.

"This has been a tough season. After starting off with high expectations, you learned some hard lessons about what it means to be a team, and to be responsible teammates. And you learned about focus and composure.

"Football is like life," he said, repeating his favorite analogy. "When you get knocked down, you pick yourself up and try harder. Seniors, you have a lot to be proud of. We all thank you for your leadership. And returning players, stay out of trouble, make your grades, and remember what we learned. Next year will be our year." After listening intently to their coach's comments, the players, feeling good, strutted confidently out of the locker room.

• • •

Football season was over. Coach Baty felt the familiar emptiness that he experienced every year at this time. It would be nine months before his competitive juices would flow again. For now, it was back to the daily job of school. As he sat in his office on Monday morning, he called his student assistant.

"Maria, here's a dime. Would you please walk down to the bakery and buy an empanada for me?" Every day she heard this request. "And just pick the flavor you think I'd like best. And here's another dime in case you see Nell. Buy one for him, too."

Maria walked to the Bowie Bakery, about a block away from the high school. It was and still is one of the best bakeries in El Paso. The aroma of just-cooked pastries filled the neighborhood and served as a magnet for everyone nearby. Fresh empanadas, apple-, lemon-, or cherry-filled pastries, *laberintos* and glazed doughnuts were standard fare. When Maria returned, Mr. Baty would invariably have changed his mind. "Maria, thanks, but I'm not that hungry anymore. Why don't you eat it?" Eventually, she realized what he was doing—that he knew her parents were poor and couldn't feed their kids very well.

Bo and Buryl always looked forward to their Christmas holiday back home in Paris. This year, they accepted an invitation from Zelma (Buryl's aunt—technically—who was his old playmate) to break up their trip halfway and stay overnight at her home in Lubbock. At Zelma's supper table, of course, the conversation worked its way around to the football team. Bo recounted Buryl's fight to get new equipment, the amazing spirit of La Bowie, and the humiliating discrimination he had battled on road trips. She described how angry Buryl had grown about the prejudice his team encountered.

"That's surprising, because I've known Buryl all his life, and I've never seen him get that mad," Zelma said.

Buryl jumped into the conversation, ending it: "Zelma, I hope you'll make this Ambrosia fruit salad every time we visit."

"I will Buryl, just for you."

Later, after dinner, they moved to the living room and made a fire. In front of the blazing logs, Buryl and Zelma laughed out loud recalling their childhood shenanigans. "Remember swinging from the garage roof on the rope swing your daddy made for us?" Zelma asked. And they laughed about shooting birds from the old mulberry tree with slingshots.

Zelma brought Bo back into the discussion. "Bo, let me tell you what Buryl said when he was in the first grade. We were walking home, probably his second or third day of school. He told me, he said, 'Sister, I found me a sweetheart today.' And I asked him, 'Is it the new girl?' I'd seen you, and your big sister Alta was in my fourth-grade class. 'Yep,' he told me, and it was you he was talking about."

"And Bo, from that day on, Buryl never looked at another girl."

Bo smiled as Zelma carried on. This made her feel good, and she put her hand on Buryl's. Still, she couldn't resist a lighthearted response. "Well, you'd never have known it! He used to throw rocks at me when I walked past him and his friends in the park."

"That just meant he had his eye on you," Zelma nodded. "Didn't it, Buryl?"

"That's exactly what it meant," Buryl said, grinning.

The conversation wound down, and everyone agreed that it was time for bed. But Buryl, the night owl, was mesmerized by the leaping flames. "Y'all go ahead, I'm gonna sit and watch the fire for a while."

Two days later, a voice on the phone said, "Let's go hunting!" James Jackson knew who was calling before the sentence was finished. He knew that Buryl was in Paris for the holidays, and in fact, James himself had already made a plan: for the two of them to hike down to the Sulphur River and hunt for two days. They left before dawn on a frosty Sunday morning, parked a short distance off the country road, hiked in with their guns, water, canned goods, and gear, hunted all day, and camped that night. This was the best part of the jaunt: sizzling wild duck meat over a crackling campfire, gazing at the stars, and then crawling into sleeping bags for a warm, sound sleep under a clear sky. After a full second day of hunting, the two trudged through the thick trees and brush out toward the road. As they walked, Buryl's thoughts turned back to football. He reflected on the just-completed season. He thought about what had gone wrong. He resolved that the next season would be better. He'd make sure of it.

21 We *Will* Get This Right

SPRING 1953

This was the most intense planning meeting the assistants could recall. Coach Baty had returned from the holidays in an inspired frame of mind, more determined than ever. "We have to do a better coaching job this year: with fundamentals, execution, conditioning, scouting, game prep—everything. After the banquet tonight, we'll focus all our energies toward next season."

More than two hundred people packed into the high school cafeteria on that cold early-January evening. The annual football banquet was always exciting for players, their families and friends, and the faculty. Coach Baty introduced the season's lettermen, saving departing seniors for last. Each received a beautiful royal blue wool sweater with a bright white block capital "B" on the left chest. One of the seniors, Rod Rodriguez, was honored in absentia. He had already left for the Jesuit Novitiate in New Orleans, after a midyear graduation, to enter the Catholic priesthood.

After awarding the players' letter sweaters and making a few comments about the season just completed, Coach Baty announced that he would make a special presentation. He pointed to an awkward boy standing in the back corner of the auditorium. It was Nell, the "honorary" team member, wearing an old "Property of Bowie Football" practice jersey that Baty had given him. "Nell, would you please come up to the stage?"

Nell climbed awkwardly to a spot next to the coach. After a few words of appreciation, Baty presented him an official Bowie Bear letter sweater, with Nell's name woven into the capital "B." The audience applauded and cheered enthusiastically. A huge smile wreathed Nell's face. From then on, that toothy smile appeared every time someone complimented his sweater, a frequent event.

Nell wore that letter sweater every day and everywhere, winter and summer, until the day he died.—Giya Olivas

In the next day's sports page, Ray Sanchez wrote, "No wonder Bowie's hopes for a big 1953 football season are running high. Coach Buryl Baty announced 19 lettermen last night at the school's annual grid banquet—and 11 of them will be back. What's more important, though, is that nine of the 11 returning lettermen are also returning starters."

And among the clippings from back home was one in the *Paris News* on January 5 from Bill Thompson's column "Billboard," saying, "Among Gainesville's applicants for [its] vacant head coach job is Buryl Baty, one of Paris High's greatest backs. . . . At present, Baty is head coach of Bowie High in El Paso but he'd probably welcome the chance to come closer to home."

But the Gainesville job was not to be. There were fourteen applicants, and when the Gainesville Board split over the decision between Buryl and Ed Dusek (who had been a teammate of Buryl's at A&M), and stayed split for two weeks, Buryl pulled out of the running.

The possibility of moving to Gainesville and being so close to her family had made Bo's heart beat faster. But she agreed with Buryl that if half the administration had wanted Dusek, those same people would second-guess her husband from the outset. Coaching was hard enough without having to watch your back. It was best to be where the whole town was behind Buryl.

Bo told him, "Honey, we're fine right here in El Paso."

. . .

Spring training seemed more intense and more advanced than in previous years. An extra dose of fundamentals training was dealt out: blocking, tackling, passing, catching, kicking, recovering fumbles. And conditioning—the boys ran lap after lap after lap. "You gotta *want it* more than the other team!" Baty yelled over and over. It was a grueling February. From the first, drills were in full pads and full contact. By the third day of practice, every muscle on the team was sore, and nicks and bruises covered the boys' bodies. It was painful to stand up, to sit down, to climb the stairs at school. It hurt to move. A simple touch resulted in a wince. And each subsequent practice brought renewed agony.

Quarterbacks were constantly mentored in field leadership skills. "You're in control of the huddle—you are the *only* one who should talk. You're also in charge of attitude and momentum. When someone makes a mistake or things aren't going well, you tell 'em to 'shake it off and get 'em next time.' Or, say 'way to go, let's do it again.' Encourage 'em, push 'em, fire 'em up, be tough when you need to be." Coach Baty had run a few huddles in his day, and he had learned from the best.

They also ran daily tackling drills, called "head-ons." Players from two lines, one the ballcarrier and one the tackler, would collide at full speed into each other, mano a mano. Then the second players in each line would collide, and so on. In one set of these drills, best friends Manny Morales and Leo Muñoz were pitted against each other. Leo was flashy, a good-looking kid with wavy black hair and sharp features, and he was popular with the girls. With a slight, 150-pound frame, however, he didn't pack much power. Manny, on the other hand, was strong and shifty. He could fake you out, outrun you, or run right over you. He stood only 5'9" but carried 190 mighty pounds. He even looked older than the other boys; his thick black whiskers required a close shave daily. Leo and Manny had never contested each other in this drill, until today.

At the sound of Coach Simmang's whistle the two friends ran toward each other, and just before impact, they flinched, resulting in a soft "thud." Coach Baty's loud voice immediately boomed, "*No!* Just because you're *brothers* does not mean you can take it easy. Do it again, and do it at full speed!" They returned to the front of their respective lines for a repeat and collided again, this time at full speed. Smack! Their pads snapped together, and Leo flew backwards onto the ground. "That's better! The team that hits the hardest wins the game," Coach Baty said. Leo decided to avoid Manny in future head-ons.

Baty continuously pushed his running backs with shouts of encouragement—"Run faster, backs, run faster!"—and on occasion hinted at his frustration: "Dadgum, dadgum! Where's the hole, Camacho?" Or "What's the matter? You afraid to break a few ribs?" But there was never a curse word.

The boys saw that Mrs. Baty frequently picked her husband up after practices, and many times she watched the final drills from a distance. Players noticed her waiting patiently in the school's courtyard with her small boy. She was always friendly, and she smiled at and greeted everyone she saw. The little boy seemed mesmerized by the activities on the field as his mother held him beside her. One afternoon Coach Baty introduced his son to every player individually, and after all the handshakes, he asked, "Son, have you ever seen so many ugly faces?"

Sometimes Mrs. Baty allowed her son to sit on the sideline bench while the team practiced, keeping her eyes on him all the while. Players always made a point to walk by and rub the top of his head, messing up his hair. "¡Buenas tardes, niño!" they greeted him. He looked up timidly at their big smiles.

> We noticed how happy and proud Coach Baty was of his son by the way that he hugged and held him.—Jesus 'Jesse' Martinez

Also that spring, Coach Baty noticed Tony Lujan kicking the football and called him over. "Try that again, Tony." Tony dropkicked the ball halfway to Juarez.

Baty looked at Simmang and said, "We have our kicker!"

"We'll call him the 'Magic Toe,'" Rosas said.

"Now, punt the ball a couple of times." Tony punted two long, low kicks. "Tony, you have a strong leg, but let me show you how to punt." Baty demonstrated with a towering spiral kick and then explained how it was done. "The more you practice, the better you'll be." At the end of spring training, Coach surprised Tony. "Take this football home to practice over the summer. But take care of the ball, okay?"

Tony was shocked. He had possession of a real football for the whole summer. His excitement and gratitude were obvious from his voice. "Yes, sir, Coach. Thank you!"

A few days after spring training had ended, a challenge was issued by a couple of kids from across the border. They wanted to play Bowie's Bears in a pickup football game on their home field in Juarez. The Bears' players accepted the challenge, mustered up enough manpower, and showed up on the appointed day. The south-of-the-border team kicked off, ran down the field, and tackled the Bowie kick returner to the ground. A couple of extra Juarez players piled on for good measure. The Americans were surprised, asking the tacklers, "*¿Pensavamos que iba ser juego de toque?* (We thought this was a touch football game?)"

"*¡Queremos jugar el fútbol Americano, con taclear!* (We want to play real football, tackle football!)" replied the Mexican nationals.

"*¿Estas seguro?* (Are you sure?)"

"*¡Sí!*"

The Bowie Bears shifted into "real football" mode and shocked their novice opponents with explosive blocking, tackling, and running. Suddenly the Juarez players were picking themselves painfully up from the ground. After a couple of quick Bear touchdowns and stifling defensive series, Leo asked, "*¿Estás seguro de que no deseas jugar fútbol de toque?* (Are you sure you don't want to play touch football?)"

"*Simón, juguemos fútbol de toque.* (Heck, yes, let's play touch.)"

. . .

Meanwhile, humming in the background, was the national sports news. On April 8, 1953, Buryl had his eye on a drama unfolding at his breakfast table in the *Herald-Post*:

PLAN TO PROTEST OUSTING OF CLUB FOR USING NEGROES

Hot Springs, Ark.—The Hot Springs Bathers, kicked out of the Cotton States Class C Baseball League for signing two Negro pitchers, plan today to carry a protest to Baseball Commissioner Ford Frick. . . .

Club directors urged Frick . . . to condemn the ouster and to award any damages suffered by the club.

League directors assert that the club violated a constitutional provision of the 52-year-old professional baseball loop by signing the Tugerson brothers.

That May, when school let out for the summer, the Batys took an overdue trip back home. They first visited Bo's sisters, Alta and Jean, and their families in Dallas. It had become traditional for the family to eat at El Chico's for the Wednesday-night specials. Buryl always finished his own and then all three sisters' dinners, so there was no need for doggy bags.

On the next leg of the trip, from Dallas to Paris, Bo and Buryl stopped to have supper with Luke and Betty Abbett, old Paris friends, at Johnnie Casey's Barbeque in White Oak. The women did most of the talking: about their kids, their friends back home, their families. Luke and Buryl did get a few words in about football and coaching. Buryl described a recent visit with Coach Berry, who had said that his son, Raymond Emmett, would be playing end on the starting team this year at SMU.

When he was in Paris, Buryl loved his long talks with Coach Berry. He had only to walk a couple of doors down from Bo's family home to sit in Berry's living room. There they talked about football, and Coach Berry always provided a few tips. "Not one kid in a thousand is aware of what he's capable of doing if he sets his mind to it. Everything I coach is built around this one principle. Some coaches beat their kids down, but I think you've got to convince 'em that they can do it. If they don't believe they can do it with all their hearts, they can't win. You've gotta build 'em up when you sense they might be getting down. But don't let 'em get too cocky," he advised. Buryl soaked it all in, as he had always done.

In addition to the two trips back to Paris that summer with Bo, Buryl had a busy schedule in El Paso, umpiring baseball games, working with kids, preparing for the next season. When he wasn't working, he and Bo enjoyed weekend backyard barbeques with El Paso friends and time with their two-and-a-half-year-old son. One week, Bo's younger brother Dub came to visit and the Batys took him across the border to the Juarez market. There they bought a pair of cowboy boots for Dub to wear home and a pair for Gaines to grow into.

But always in the back of his mind, Buryl's thoughts reverted to one thing. Day by day, his anticipation mounted. His favorite time of the year was coming on.

22 High Hopes

Last season's disappointments had proven that anything can happen. But this year's Bears were talented and experienced, and they had worked hard to ensure the best season possible. With a break or two along the way, this team had a chance to make a run at the championship. On August 31, Ray Sanchez speculated in the *Herald-Post* about the upcoming season's possibilities:

> COACHES SEE HOT GRID RACE: RATE BOWIE STRONGEST
>
> The Coaches rate Bowie and Austin the favorites. . . . Actually, Bowie is given an edge, but it's so small as to be insignificant. . . .
>
> Ordinarily, Coach Buryl Baty's Bears would be clear-cut favorites, for they have a roster that would throw fear into a Frank Leahy. The reason they're not is that local coaches have come to respect Austin's big advantage in enrollment and figure [they] will again have plenty of reserve power.
>
> Still, the Bears are plenty feared—and rightfully so. They've always been tough, but they've always been too small to win the title consistently.
>
> This year, however, they shockingly enough have that SIZE— and it should be spelled with capital letters. . . .
>
> "We'll be pretty strong," Baty admitted, "but I don't think we'll finish first. Maybe second or third." That first comment is a key to the Bears' real strength, for anyone who knows local coaches knows how pessimistic they usually are.

The boys enjoyed reading about themselves as the campaign approached. On the other hand, former quarterback Bobby Cordova winced when he read this report. He had thought about this season for almost a year. Just before the start of two-a-day workouts, he asked Coach Baty if he could rejoin the team. "We'd be glad to have you," replied the coach. Team rules didn't need to be emphasized to Bobby. He now understood the conditions of playing for Coach Baty. Word of his reinstatement quickly spread throughout the Segundo Barrio, and the *Herald-Post* was not far behind:

Sept. 3, 1953
BOWIE QB RETURNS

The City and District 2-AAAA high schools opened football workouts yesterday with all top hands reporting.

In fact, the big prep news of the day—and the season so far—was that a boy who WASN'T expected to show up, did.

He's Bob Cordova, who could make more difference in the coming district scramble than any other one player.

Cordova played for Bowie High for two years at quarterback. But he and Coach Buryl Baty had a run-in and Cordova was dropped last season.

Yesterday, however, Cordova showed up for workouts. He had apologized to Baty and according to the Bruin front office his whole attitude has changed.

"He looks like he wants to play ball now," Baty said. "He's promised to stay in line."

Cordova last year was rated every bit as good as Jesus Martinez, the Bears' all-district quarterback. Martinez graduated this last semester and the Bruins were hurting for a man-under. . . .

"Salvador Garcia is still my No. 1 quarterback," Baty said. "He's been working out with us and deserves the position. Cordova will have to show us he means business before he even makes the team."

Two-a-day workouts started off well, and despite the players' inevitable soreness and fatigue, they remained spirited and productive. Coaches again drilled fundamentals and emphasized conditioning, but this year was different. These players were more mature, their skills more advanced. The coaching staff pushed them to be better yet.

"Give it your best every day—everything you have!" Baty urged. "You'll never regret doing your best."

He also emphasized the mental game, especially with his quarterbacks. He tweaked the game plan to best exploit the next opponent's weaknesses, diagrammed the offensive and defensive alignments on the blackboard for discussion, and taught his quarterbacks how to manage the game. He knew he could nudge his two signal callers; they were smart. "First," Coach Baty explained, "call the 24, then the 23 Trap, and follow our planned sequence. And after seeing these plays gain yards a few times, their defense will adjust and the safeties will squeeze in closer. When you see 'em cheating in, what will you call?"

"Fake 24 Trap, 7 Pass," quarterbacks Cordova and Garcia replied.

"Perfect. And remember, look to the right to draw the defensive back to that side before you turn back and throw it to the left," Coach Baty reminded them.

He did the same for the defense by explaining, for example, "Look at the eyes of the offensive players to read where the play is going. Backs usually look at the hole they'll be running through, and blockers look at the players they want to block."

> He pushed us to do our best, physically and mentally. He was a perfectionist and instilled those traits in all of us. He made me think, and helped me to out-think the other team's defense. That made the game so much more interesting and fun. —Bobby Cordova

One Saturday morning during two-a-days, Coach Baty received a call from his old coach, Harry Stiteler.

"Buryl, I'm in El Paso. Would it be okay if I drop by?"

"Sure, Coach. I'd ask you for supper, but my sister-in-law Glenda and her husband Harry Foote are here from Albuquerque, and we have plans with them. But why don't you come by the house this afternoon, and we can visit?"

Stiteler agreed, and Buryl immediately called home to acquaint Bo with the plan. He could almost hear the frown of disapproval on her face, but she said, "Well, it'll be good for you two to get together."

That afternoon, as "The Yellow Rose of Texas" played softly from the radio, Buryl jumped to answer the doorbell. His former coach's dark-blondish hair seemed to have grayed considerably since their last encounter. While Glenda and Bo served snacks and coffee, the men talked about football and reminisced about old times. Eventually, Buryl asked, "Well, Coach, what brings you to El Paso?"

"I'm out here on business, Buryl, and I was hoping to talk with you about it. When I left A&M, I started selling kitchenware: pots and pans."

He paused. "I figured you might consider joining up with me to cover the West Texas territory. Let me tell you, you can make a lot more money in sales than you can in coaching!"

Buryl shook his head. "Thanks, Coach, I appreciate the offer. But I enjoy what I'm doing."

. . .

The Bears travelled without their injured star Manny Morales, who was back in the game after a season of ineligibility, to play the reigning New Mexico state champs. Las Cruces would be heavily favored, and Bowie's coaches knew from experience that their boys would encounter discrimination on the trip, the kind of treatment that could cause a huge mental disadvantage. But Coach Baty would not allow his kids to buy into any of that. He coached them to ignore such nonsense and to focus intently on what they were there to do.

In the halftime locker room, the score was tied at zero. Coach Baty first advised his quarterback, "Attack number 78, and stay away from number 56." He seemed to know exactly what every player did on each play. He knew how to react—right now—based on what was happening on the field. Then, just as they were about to run out for the second half, he addressed the entire team: "You're a year older and stronger now," he said. "Play your hardest and your smartest right to the end, and you'll win this game." Bowie played tough defense and scored a second half touchdown to finish on top 7–0. This was an impressive road win. After stopping for a "victory ice cream cone," the Bears bussed back to El Paso at 1 and 0. However, their nemesis loomed ahead.

Bowie would host Snyder, the source of their worst nightmares the previous season. This promised to be a real test. Ray Sanchez predicted that Snyder would win by two touchdowns.

His account of the game praised the Bears' ferocity:

El Paso Herald-Post, September 25, 1953
BOWIE PROVES STRONG—BUT "DUMB" PLAYS WORRY
BRUINS' FANS

Bowie High's Bears, nursing bruises and bumps but none serious from their collision with a smashing, crashing Snyder team, today were disappointed but not unhappy over their 14–12 loss to the visiting Tigers last night in R. R. Jones Stadium.

Buryl Baty's Bashers were happy because they lived up to their press billing, giving the powerful Snyder Bengals fits and displaying to the nearly 6000 fans a team that's going to be awfully hard to handle in District 2-AAAA warfare. . . .

But at the same time there was disappointment over the mental miscues that may be difficult for Coach Baty to correct. They were mistakes of the mind and it cost the Bears a probable tie.

The Bruins called wrong plays, took penalties when they shouldn't and in general didn't look too much like a "smart" team.

But as Baty said:

"Sure, we made mistakes. But I'm not going to criticize my boys. They were hustling and giving it all they had. That's all I can ask of them." . . .

The Bowie 'line' was outstanding. . . . It was a line that was simply ferocious, tackling and blocking like pros.

But the Snyder powerhouse could not be denied in the fourth quarter. . . .

On offense, Quarterback Bob Cordova carried the brunt of the Bowie forces. His passes were magnificent and he personally scored one touchdown on a quarterback sneak. He passed beautifully 12 yards to Leo Munoz for the other.

In another article in the same *Herald-Post* edition, Ray Sanchez congratulated Baty for his promotion to assistant principal. "We never knew [from] talking to the big, strong, silent guy," he said. "We had to find it out from other people. Baty had been offered the job because, according to the principal, both the teachers and the students look up to him." He had at first turned it down, because he was unwilling to surrender his position as head coach, but the principal had induced him to take it on by combining the two positions.

Another away game loomed. Coach Baty orchestrated these trips carefully because most west Texas towns treated his boys despicably. Too often they had been turned away from restaurants, motels, and movie theaters. Too many times they had played poorly in remote locations. The difficulties that any team has playing away from home—broken routines, uncomfortable surroundings, distracting home-team fans, and so forth—were multiplied for the Bears. Only the most composed or clearly superior teams can overcome such stacked odds. For Bowie, it was like journeying with a bull's-eye on its chest. Travelling to nearby Pecos was no exception.

After an early arrival, the bus stopped at a grocery store and the boys went in to buy snacks. But quickly, one by one and in bunches, they were rushed out by the proprietor as he shouted, "No Meskins!" On the downtown square, players couldn't miss yet another sign in a storefront window reading, "Welcome to Pecos—No dogs or Mexicans allowed." These words were not new, but they were still shocking to the players every time they read them. Later the team was escorted to the very back of a restaurant for their lunch. And afterwards, when they went to a movie to relax before the night's game, their requests for tickets on the main floor were denied. "Y'all can't sit down there. Meskins gotta sit in the balcony." The boys did start out in the balcony as directed, but they sneaked downstairs when the theater darkened.

"Don't let it bother you," Coach Baty said. "Always remember, you're as good as anybody."

That night, even the cheerleaders were victims of demeaning comments, and fans threw ice at them.

> We were humiliated. And our cheerleader sponsor acted like we were to blame. —Lucy Rivas Lucero, cheerleader

The Bears lost a well-played game to a strong Pecos eleven, 7–14. A quiet bus ride back to El Paso followed.

The next morning, as always, Coach Baty attended the eighth-grade game. After Guillermo Olivas ran circles around the opposing team, the coach approached him in the locker room. "Giya, I want you to get ready and stay out of trouble. Do that and you'll play on the varsity next year," he said. Giya's jaw dropped and his eyebrows flew upward. He was visibly thrilled.

Then Coach Baty walked across the room and delivered the same message to another boy, Ernesto Perea. "Keep your nose clean and make your grades, and you can be a great player, Ernie. You'll play in front of all the Bowie fans, and wave to them from the victory bus after games. But you can't continue to hang out with the same people. Those guys will get you in trouble. You have to be responsible and make good choices. Do you understand, Ernie?"

"Yes, sir, Coach!" Ernie exclaimed.

Next, La Bowie played a local opponent, Cathedral High. In his first game of the year and first play of his season, Manny Morales broke through the line and displayed his ten-flat speed to run eighty yards for a TD. However, a red flag lay on the ground back at the line of scrimmage. Guard Tony Franco had jumped offsides, and the play was called back. The team jogged all the way back to the huddle.

There, quarterback Bobby Cordova reflected on what he had been taught by his coach: if a play works, call it again and again, until it doesn't work. "Manny," Bobby blurted out, "let's go again!" Bobby called the same play and the huddle broke with a loud clap. Manny raced to the end zone again, this time for eighty-five yards.

"Penalty, offsides, half the distance to the goal line!" yelled the head linesman at the original line of scrimmage. Tony had once more flinched before the snap of the ball. He was embarrassed. A substitute came in for Tony, and Tony caught Coach Simmang's wrath. "You have to *think* to win games, Tony!"

The Bears began sluggishly, but eventually Manny again outraced the Irish defense to the end zone. A Cathedral player was overheard demanding, "How can that fat boy run so fast?" Bowie shifted into high gear for a 27–0 victory.

Coach Baty commented to reporter Sanchez, "I'm happy with the result, but we didn't play especially well. We'll have to play better than this to beat Douglas next week."

Late the following week, it was time to travel to Arizona. Bobby Molina had pondered his predicament all week. As second-string halfback, Bobby had played earlier in the season for the injured starter, Manny Morales, and he craved more playing time now. He recognized Manny's talent, but he thought that surely, given a chance, he could prove himself the bigger boy's equal. Bobby was tiny, only five-feet five, but he would mix it up with anybody; he had six feet worth of heart. An inspiration hit him about how to take Manny's place.

After watching him pack his equipment bag and walk out of the room, Bobby nervously eased over to remove Manny's cleats from the bag. He quickly threw the shoes behind a large trashcan in the corner of the locker room, then attempted to remain calm. He could hardly contain his excitement as the team climbed up into the bus.

At the Douglas High School stadium, players retrieved their gear from the baggage compartment. In the locker room, they had their ankles taped and relaxed for a while, as was always their pregame routine. A few minutes before warm-ups, they began to don their shoulder pads, jerseys and game cleats. Manny emptied his duffel bag, but he couldn't find his shoes. His heart raced; they were gone! He looked again. Surely this was a practical joke by one of his teammates. He moved frantically around the room searching for the missing shoes. Panicked, he yelled out, "Coach, I packed my cleats, but now they're gone. I can't find 'em!"

Coach Baty was quiet. He turned in Molina's direction. "Bobby, what size shoes do you wear?"

"Nine and a half, Coach," Molina squeaked.

"Then take 'em off and give 'em to Manny," the coach ordered.

Molina stood on the sideline in his dress shoes until the third quarter. When the Bears were well ahead on the scoreboard, Coach Baty told Morales, who had already scored twice, "Manny, give Bobby his cleats so he can play." The second-teamer was thrilled to put on the high-tops and step onto the field. He promptly scored a touchdown. Manny quipped after the game, "Your cleats made more touchdowns than either of us."

That night, the Bears drove back home with another big victory. En route to the high school field house, however, they made a victory run through the Southside, honking and waving. Families, friends, and neighbors clapped and cheered as the bus passed.

From early on, Coach Baty had insisted that Rusty, the bus driver, parade the team through the Segundo Barrio after every victory, blasting the horn and celebrating. Very few fans could travel to the away games, and even the home games were difficult to attend for those without transportation because the local stadiums were long two- to three-mile walks away. And Coach Baty had wanted to involve everyone. The new tradition had quickly escalated as crowds gathered along the streets in anticipation. When the bus showed up, it signified that "La Bowie" had won. Of course, younger athletes could not wait to grow older and play for this glorious team.

Sometimes the boys would see Mrs. Baty driving toward the football field with her son Gaines to watch afternoon practices.

"Uh, oh, here comes the boss, the police!" Ed Camacho would say when he saw her approaching. Mrs. Baty and the boy usually stood at a distance from the action, unless the youngster could convince his mother to allow him to stand near his father or to sit on the sideline bench. There, he was occasionally encouraged to fetch footballs or kicking tees on the field, and Bear players roughhoused with him gently.

Passing team members always shook hands with him, greeting him with, *"Buenas tardes, niño!"*

Sometimes the high school boys sat and talked with the coach's son. One afternoon after practice, while Coach Baty was working with the younger players, a few upperclassmen gathered around the boy on the sideline.

"How you doing, *niño?*" Leo Muñoz asked. "Do you like football?" The boy nodded eagerly.

"Are you gonna play football when you get big? I bet you'll be a quarterback, *sí?*" Ed Camacho asked. This question was met with a smile.

Manny Morales said, "Tell your papa that Tony here wants to play quarterback, too!" They all laughed, knowing that Tony Franco had been converted to an offensive lineman.

Tony appreciated Manny's joke, but he couldn't let the comment go unanswered. *"¿Qué, güey? ¡Besa mi culo, Morales!"* Then Tony continued, *"Niño,* tell your daddy that my friend Manny said *'Besa mi culo.'"*

Leo looked appalled. "Don't tell him to say that, Tony! If he tells his dad, we will die!"

"Oh, he won't tell him; he won't remember the words," Tony said confidently.

Needless to say, the three-year-old went home cursing in Spanish, and the next day was one of reckoning for the tutors.

· · ·

El Paso High, led by star quarterback Junior Ruiz, was favored to win the next game. Meanwhile, La Bowie, at three wins and two losses, had played well so far. Local media buildup was considerable. Coach Baty sensed that his Bears were especially nervous, and just before the opening kickoff, he addressed the team. "We've prepared for this game for the last two years," he said. "You're ready. This is gonna to be a tough game, and you're tougher than they are. Just *hit 'em hard* . . . and keep hitting 'em 'til you win it."

Bowie raced to a 19–7 victory. Excitement filled the night air as the triumphant Bears bussed and honked throughout the barrio. Happy players hung from open windows to wave and to greet their cheering families and friends. Even disinterested neighbors were drawn into the celebration. They might as well join the fun; they certainly could not have slept with all the honking, whistling, and cheering going on in the streets.

The following week at a school assembly, Coach Baty announced Jullieta Acosta as the season's football queen and awarded her a miniature gold football charm.

The Bears' win over El Paso High set up the clash against their archrival, the haughty Austin High Panthers. But this year, Austin's coach knew his boys would have their hands full. Both teams were undefeated in district play, and both practiced hard all week. The victor would be in the driver's seat for the championship. In an interview, Coach Baty told Ray Sanchez, "I don't see how we can possibly beat Austin. Their backs are capable of going all the way and I just don't know if we can catch up with them." Austin's Coach Red Harris, on the other side of town, countered with, "I don't see how we can possibly beat Bowie. They have too much." Both men knew to avoid billboard material.

The night of the game finally arrived. In the pregame locker room, Coach Harris reminded his boys, "This is an excellent Bowie team. Remember, you have to guard the pass *and* the run against them. They do both really well. And, it's important to concentrate just on what's happening on the field, not in the stands. Bowie's crowd will be big and loud; they have more subway fans than Notre Dame."

In the Bowie locker room, nervous players listened to their own coach. "Men, opportunities occasionally arise in our lives to do something memorable, something great. Tonight is one of those times. This is the night that we've prepared for. You'll remember this night for the rest of your lives." A quick moment of silence passed. The coach increased his intensity. "Do you hear those people out there in the stands? Those people are here to see you win. Let's give 'em what they came here for!"

La Bowie beat Austin going away, with another 19–7 win, improving its record to 5–2. It was a resounding victory. Ysleta remained as the next hurdle to Bowie's outright crown. Coach Baty and his assistants would spend most of the weekend in their offices, rerunning films on the old projector, focusing on the Indians. But first, Baty would focus on the future.

The next morning, Saturday, he stood on the junior high team's sideline, giving pointers to his future players. Of course, he watched one young quarterback very closely, and called him over between quarters. "Giya, don't always hand off the ball. Next time run a 'keeper'... fake the handoff to the halfback, and then run wide around the end for a touchdown." Coach Baty's suggestion worked. His suggestions usually did.

Baty insisted that all Bowie junior and senior high football coaches attend all games. The coaches then convened for hours at a coffee shop after the Saturday-morning games to critique and strategize. Then, during Monday-morning film sessions, they critiqued each other's performances, play by play, and drew up new plays to exploit the next opponents' tendencies and weaknesses. If they ran out of paper, they diagramed on napkins. Every coach learned from his own and other coaches' mistakes and successes and was expected to improve continually.

Everything from fundamentals to the next game's strategy was discussed. "Coach Rodriguez," Baty said, "I want you to teach fundamentals, first and foremost. Winning is good, but we want these kids ready to play varsity." He would give Coach Rodriguez the ten plays to work on in practice the next week and to run in his next game. Only once previously had a junior high or B-team coach chosen to run a different offensive scheme, in defiance of Coach Baty—he had been promptly fired.

That week, press coverage of the Bears intensified. The *Herald-Post* rated Bowie as the favorite—"Bowie has the pass attack and a better defense." "But footballs take funny bounces." Coach Baty argued. "As long as we have to go on the field to play, there's a chance of getting beat."

Excitement fed off excitement in the Segundo Barrio. Schoolyards, barbershops, churches, and locker rooms all buzzed with energy. Everybody talked about the chance to win district. Finally, the night of the game arrived. Players and fans were so nervous that many of them were literally shaking.

As Coach Baty paced the floor, he blurted, "I swear, you boys are going to give me ulcers!" This comment always brought smiles from the team. Then he continued: "Men, there's an Ysleta team sitting in that other locker room that thinks they can beat you. You're ready, but they're not going to give it to you. If you want it, you need to go out there and get it. You control your destiny. Do you want it?"

"Yes, sir!"

"Then go get it!"

Bowie Bears burst onto the field to seek their destiny. And from Coach Baty's words, they knew they had the power to achieve it.

Player of the Week Manny "Mule Train" Morales scored a touchdown on a sixty-five-yard run and set a new district record with 19.4 yards per carry. The Bears dominated, 26–6. Once inside the rowdy locker room, the head coach grinned and clapped and waved his fists above his head as he congratulated the team: "The Bowie Bears are District Champions!" Players noticed Coach Baty wiping tears from his eyes. With this victory, the Bears sported a 6–2 record and an undefeated district ledger. One district game remained, but the outcome would be inconsequential.

Bowie fans and players lingered to continue their celebration. The Bears had come a long way. They had finally arrived.

Ray Sanchez's account told the story:

El Paso Herald-Post, November 18, 1953
By the Way . . .

Every year in every sport, By the Way . . . writes an entire column about each champion. And this one belongs to Bowie High's fascinating Bears who clinched the District 2-AAAA and City football bonnets last week.

This Bowie team may not be the greatest the Southside school ever had, but if it's not it certainly ranks up there pretty close.

. . . There is something about this team that holds your attention—and admiration. It's a team that it's a pleasure to watch because it can pass, it can go through the middle and it can run around the flanks. On defense, it's just as wonderful. Why the Grizzlies won the championship is really very simple when you consider this:

Bowie had the boys and the coach. What other combination can beat that? . . .

. . . Buryl Baty, the Bowie mastermind, has endeared himself to El Paso. The former Texas A. and M. quarterback is called "the best coach in West Texas" by many, and I'm certainly not going to argue about it.

. . . His teams know how to run their plays, they know how to tackle and they know how to block. That's the sign of the coach.

Of course, this is also a reflection on Buryl's assistants, Line Coach Jerry Simmang and Backfield Coach Fred Rosas, and they, too, must come in for their share of the raves. . . .

I called the Bears "fascinating" at the start of this column. I think the name fits, don't you?

In the final game against Jefferson, several starters were held out so that lingering injuries might heal. Still, the Bears outmanned the Silver Foxes. They celebrated by hanging out of the bus, waving and cheering in the Segundo Barrio.

It was on to Bi-District.

Much of the city celebrated. This championship was embraced not just by La Bowie; it brought joy to Hispanics across the city. This was what the team had worked toward, but it seemed surreal. This was rarified air. The Bowie Bears were the best team in El Paso!

23 The Playoffs!

As expected, Odessa finished their season undefeated by beating Plainview. Immediately afterwards, in Odessa's coach's crowded office, Coach Baty flipped the silver quarter off his thumb. Odessa's coach yelled, "Heads!" The coin clanged and bounced and spun on the concrete floor before settling with tails up. As the winner of the flip, Baty chose El Paso for the site for the playoff game. Odessa would bring a big line, a fast, crushing backfield, and a well-balanced attack, and all but one starter was a senior. The Bears, on the other hand, would pin their upset hopes on a brilliant defense. They boasted one of the finest defensive records in the state; in nine regular season contests, Bowie had allowed just sixty points. In no game had the Bears allowed more than fourteen points to be scored against them.

Game time approached. Nerves were tightly strung as the Bears, taped and dressed in their royal blue uniforms, made their crosstown bus ride. They drove for three miles past sidewalks filled with Bowie students and fans and with most of the barrio walking to the stadium and singing the fight song all the way. The streets were packed.

Normally, banter eased the drive to the stadium. On this trip, however, except for the shifting of gears and the low, vibrating hum of the bus's motor, there was silence. The Bears had good reason to be nervous.

As the boys fidgeted before kickoff, only the crowd's noise from outside the locker room could be heard. Eventually, Coach Baty spoke. His voice was calm.

"Men, we are here for a reason. We are here because you've played your game all season long and because you have not given up. Games like these are the reason we play football; they're the reason why we showed up for two-a-days. Games like these, with the butterflies in our stomachs, are what we've worked for." He paused. "Today, you're prepared. Just play hard and smart like you've played all year long. If something bad happens, come back with something good. Play it to the end. Play to win."

The Bears burst out excitedly before their cheering fans on a bright autumn Saturday afternoon. But Odessa looked like a college team compared to Bowie. Derogatory slurs flew in the Bears' direction from the start. Still, the Bowie boys kept their composure. After several unproductive series for each team, Odessa finally finished a drive with a nineteen-yard touchdown pass.

Down 0–7, the Bears knew they needed to answer, but the Broncos were not in a giving mood. They stuffed Bowie's offense play after play. Finally La Bowie mounted a short drive to earn a measure of field position. However, faced with another fourth and long, Tony Lujan, the Magic Toe, punted the ball deep into Bronco territory. Odessa began their offensive series with a conservative running play. As the play unfolded, it appeared that victory might be in the cards for the Bears after all.

"Ball! Ball!" echoed players' shouts to the tallest point in the stands. A fumble rolled on the ground with a mad scramble in its direction. Bowie's Benny Landin won the race, and he wrapped the bouncing ball up tightly. At last, a break for the Bears.

On the first play from Odessa's fourteen-yard line, a defender broke through the line to drop the Bear runner for a two-yard loss. Quarterback Bobby Cordova recalled the play that he and Coach Baty had discussed in skull sessions that week. He called the number. Lalo Ortiz caught Bobby's pass and lunged across the goal line. Touchdown Bowie! After the extra point, the Bears were back in the game, 7–7. The entire Bowie sideline and crowd went crazy—laughing, screaming, clapping and shaking hands.

After the ensuing kickoff, Odessa put several positive plays together. Sixty-eight yards later, the ball was punched across for a 14–7 lead. Momentum shifted back to the visiting sideline.

In the halftime locker room, the Bears were shaken. They had fought hard to catch up, only to allow a long scoring drive to steal their momentum. Coach Baty buoyed their confidence. "We're in a dogfight, but we're doing fine. We'll make a few adjustments, and the second half is where your extra laps and sprints will pay off." He paused for a second before continuing, "Men, we have twenty-four minutes to play . . . and a lifetime to remember. Give it all your heart, and fight to the end."

When the game resumed, Bowie's defensive adjustments were successful. Royal blue jerseys swarmed the ball. Nearing the end of the third quarter, both offenses had been stymied. Something had to give. Every person in the stands stood and shouted encouragement for their team. Trying to make a big play, Odessa's signal caller dropped back to pass under heavy pressure. The ball barely left his hand before he was slammed to the ground. A long wobbly pass hung in the air . . . and hung, until a Bronco receiver caught it at full-speed and outraced the defense for a seventy-one yard touchdown. Stunned Bear fans watched quietly as the Broncos celebrated on the visiting sideline. Odessa now led, 21–7. In the fourth quarter, Odessa's size and depth took over, and they won going away.

As Odessa faithful cheered and sang their team's fight song outside, cleats click-clacked on the Bears' locker room floor. The boys didn't try to hide their disappointment. Long faces and hushed voices permeated the room. They had just lost the game they had dreamed of winning. Abruptly, the heavy metal door slammed as the coaches walked into the room.

Coach Baty quickly broke the silence. "We're all disappointed, but we were beaten by a better team that should go deep in the playoffs. But this game takes nothing away from what you've accomplished. You've done something special this year. You went undefeated in district, and came close to being undefeated for the season. You've come back from adversity. You've become a better team. You've become better students. You've become better men.

"You'll remember this championship for the rest of your lives. You seniors will apply these same winning principles from now on. And we'll miss each one of you. For you underclassmen, I want you to remember the success we've had this year. Winning championships is now our tradition. Next year we'll win this game. And next year, or the next, we're going for state! Until then be proud, but also be gentlemen. Make your school and your parents proud."

Coach Baty held both fists high and displayed one of his hitched smiles. "Now let's hop on the bus back to Bowie and celebrate our great season!" he yelled. Rusty drove the bus across town to and through the Segundo Barrio, honking all the way. The team celebrated, with lots of noise.

Coach Buryl Baty was again named District Coach of the Year. Seven Bears were named to first-team All-City honors: David Archuleta, Fernando Lara, Manny Morales, Enrique Camacho, David Holguin, Pete Salvidar, and Benito Landin. Lineman Archuleta was named District MVP. Coach Baty called each of these players, including "Peanuts" Avilla, an All-District second team selection, into his office for personal congratulations and to give each player a picture of the All-District team.

It always hurt to lose the last game of the season, and the familiar postseason emptiness always followed. However, classes resumed as usual on Monday morning. Life would not wait.

At school, Assistant Principal Baty ensured that things ran smoothly, and he maintained discipline across the campus. It was safe to say that he commanded the respect of the entire student body. As Ernie Perea said, "He could swing a mean paddle." No student wanted to hear his own name on the public address system, demanding that he "report to the assistant principal's office." This was generally considered to be a worst-case scenario.

> Me and Carlos Gonzales got in trouble for admiring the girls in the library, and we were sent to his office. He looked at us and we knew what was coming . . . no questions asked.—Juan "Baca" Mendoza

Mr. Baty chaperoned at school dances and special events, enthusiastically greeting every student at the front entrance. His presence almost guaranteed a trouble-free event. Even the gang members behaved themselves. They knew what Baty's response to horseplay would be, and they wanted no part of it.

As always, the Batys made the long drive back to northeast Texas for the holidays. This year everyone met at the old Hutchinson home in Paris for Christmas Eve. It felt so good to the sisters, especially Bo, to feel the warmth of home, even though their upstairs bedrooms were very cold. The family had a great evening exchanging gifts, snacking, sipping eggnog, and laughing out loud about memories of their younger days. The girls reflected upon Christmases of not that long ago: eating the apples and oranges and bananas that Santa left for them in the year's only reprieve from their usual limit of one piece of fruit per day. Eventually all the kids were put to bed. Parents needed to prepare for the night's visit from Santa.

Santa brought Gaines a miniature metal model of a fire station, complete with accompanying model trucks, cars, and other accessories. The only problem was that the fire station had to be assembled. Over fifty pieces and two hundred screws and bolts were discovered in the box, along with a badly written instruction sheet. Buryl and his brothers-in-law Harry, Clyde and CI (Santa and his helpers) assembled the toy station until four o'clock on Christmas morning. Of course, all the children were up at the crack of dawn to find what Santa had left for them.

On the day after Christmas, the sisters followed their long-standing tradition of dressing up in high heels, gloves, coats, and hats to go shopping in downtown Dallas. They always debated whether they should go to Titche's or Neiman's first. These girls loved to shop, though they did more looking than buying. Seamstress Bo always critiqued the merchandise. "The seams on this expensive dress are sewn badly," she would say.

Rumors soon spread in Paris about Coach Baty. On December 30, in an article by Bill Thompson, the *Paris News* advised its readers, "Don't be surprised if the name of Buryl Baty, former Paris High grid star who was El Paso's Coach of the Year this season, pops up in connection with the vacant Longview High football coaching job.

"Baty produced a district champ for Bowie of El Paso in Class AAAA this season and was voted the Coach of the Year honor for El Paso. He wants to move closer to home."

In early February of 1954, word spread that the Aggies had hired Kentucky's coach, a man with an unusual nickname, "Bear" Bryant. It had been rumored that Bryant had staged full scrimmages on Saturday nights immediately after his Kentucky Wildcats' losses. He was acknowledged as a good, tough coach. "I wonder what Bebes Stallings thinks of him," Buryl pondered. Stallings would be a sophomore at A&M the next season.

In El Paso, a winning tradition was being established at Bowie. Spring training in '54 was intense as Coach Baty prepared his team for an encore.

In May of 1954, the family celebrated Buryl's thirtieth birthday, in anticipation of a bright future.

24 Nothing Can Stop Us Now

1954 SEASON

Headlines told the story. The district coaches picked Bowie to win the championship.

Buryl's favorite time of the year was just around the corner. Before the season arrived, however, he had just enough time to squeeze in a day of dove hunting. And this year, Bo acquiesced to his desire to take Gaines with him. She conceded that he was probably old enough to become Buryl's "hunting buddy." This would be the four-year-old's first time in the "country." The morning of the hunt, the boy was wide-eyed and almost as excited as his daddy.

Buryl drove a half hour out to the hunting field and then loaded the gear and his son for a hike. At almost daybreak they walked across high-desert terrain before encountering a deep, dry creek bed. "Wait here and I'll be right back to get you," he told Gaines. Buryl quickly leaped across the creek gully with his shotgun and the pack that held his shells and a sack lunch. He laid this cargo on the ground, then jumped back across the creek to his boy. "OK, are you ready?" It felt good to hold his son. It felt good to take him hunting. "Hold on to me tight, OK?" Small hands went to Buryl's perspiring neck and tightly gripped his shirt collar. The boy didn't know what to expect, but he felt secure with his father.

Buryl backed off, took a couple of running steps, and suddenly the two were airborne. The boy nervously watched scraggly grass, pebbles, and sandy soil flash past beneath him as the two flew over the crevice, and was jolted when his father landed abruptly on both feet. The scary jump was over as Buryl gently set him down. They trekked a little farther before the excitement of the actual hunt began. Gaines covered his ears as flying doves were shot in midair, and he helped his daddy find the fallen birds. Time passed quickly. On the way home, the two guys couldn't wait to tell Mom all about their day together. "Your mama will cook our birds for dinner. You'll love 'em!" Buryl promised.

It was finally time for football. The coach's preseason talk was similar to the talks he had delivered in previous years. The older players were accustomed to their coach's expectations, and this speech served as a clear reminder. The newer players, sophomores and freshmen on the varsity for the first time, were slightly intimidated.

"Men, you'll work hard every day to make your grades and to get better as a team. You will act like gentlemen at all times. You will obey the rules or you'll pay the consequences.

"That we're defending champions means *nothing*. The fact is that we've won *nothing* yet this year. This is a new year and a new team. You upperclassmen know what it takes to win, and we'll have to work even harder this year, because everybody will be gunning for us. You juniors and seniors will need to lead your team. Don't allow yourselves or your teammates to do anything but work your tails off and get better every day."

I was inspired every time he spoke to us.—Leo Muñoz

After this traditional dose of inspiration, players were issued practice gear: helmets, pads, jerseys, t-shirts, pants, jocks, and socks. "Property of Bowie Football" was stenciled in black across the white practice jerseys and tees. This labeling was intended to discourage theft of the jerseys. Actually, it made them more coveted. To wear an official Bowie football shirt was a source of macho pride for a player and generated considerable respect and envy in the barrio.

Coach Baty regularly drove through the Second Ward early on Saturday mornings en route to the junior high games. He always enjoyed talking and joking with his players when he saw them along the way. In the past, he had occasionally had to reclaim Bowie football jerseys he had seen drying on backyard clotheslines. This hadn't happened as much recently. However, during his first drive-through of the '54 season, he noticed a large family leaving the cathedral after the early mass. Four of the family members wore jerseys with the "Property of Bowie Football" stencil.

The next Monday at practice, Baty summoned Giya Olivas over to talk privately. "Giya, I want you to return three of the Bowie football jerseys." Giya looked at his coach, speechless. A few seconds of silence passed.

"But tell your grandmother that she can keep hers," Coach Baty added.

Another afternoon before practice, Coach noticed Giya's absence. He spoke at once with the team's equipment manager to send him on what must by now have become a familiar errand. "Cachi, go find Giya for me. If he's not at home, try his girlfriend's house." Cachi took off running down the street and eventually returned with his prey. He had located the missing freshman on his second stop. Giya ran punishment laps both during and at the end of practice, all the while very worried about what would follow. A happy-go-lucky boy with pitch-black hair, a big smile, and sleepy eyes, Giya was a continual challenge to Coach Baty. On one of his frequent troubleshooting walks through the halls, the head coach noticed that Giya was not in his English class (he had learned to notice such things). He immediately drove to Giya's home in the barrio, and peering through an open window, spotted him. The slumbering boy was jolted awake by a loud, strong voice. "Giya, why aren't you in class?"

The startled kid answered with the first thought that came to mind: "I'm sick, Coach."

"OK, get dressed and I'll take you to the doctor."

Within minutes they were on their way to the neighborhood doctor, who agreed to examine the "patient" and to send an explanatory note to the coach. It wasn't long before Giya showed up with a sealed envelope. Coach Baty removed the doctor's message and read it aloud: "Coach Baty, Guillermo has two ailments: Number one, he is quite nervous about this, and Number two, he is very lazy."

Coach Baty looked straight into the young man's fearful eyes and said, "This is going to hurt me more than it is you." He then administered several painful swats with the "board of education."

Afterwards he added, "And you'll run extra laps after practice. If you stop running, I'll clean out your locker and you will not be on the football team." Giya did exactly as his coach demanded. He loved playing football.

Coach Baty became very familiar with Giya's family. Many nights, at the 10 p.m. curfew hour, Baty's voice could be heard calling through the screen door, "Mrs. Olivas, is Giya in?"

It was simpler to monitor his players at school, where the environment could be controlled. To that end, Coach Baty worked hard to develop rapport with the faculty, and he asked each teacher to alert him to behavioral or academic problems with his players. They typically responded,

"Coach Baty, I don't think you have to worry about your players. They're the most disciplined kids in the school." Still, he knew to be proactive.

During a Thursday grade check, Baty found out about Giya's barely-passing 70 on an algebra test, and he paid a visit to the classroom. The math teacher sensed big trouble. "Oh, Coach Baty, he'll do better on the next test," she pleaded, attempting to help Giya evade punishment.

"I know he will, Mrs. Morgan," replied the stern coach. Giya experienced another confrontation with the coach's paddle and fared much better on the following week's math exam.

After only six strenuous preseason practices over a four-day period, everyone was sore and tired for the first game. This year's opener would be a tough test. Ray Sanchez predicted Las Cruces as the favorite by a 14–0 score.

In the Las Cruces visitors' locker room, Coach Baty said a short prayer and then added, "You boys are in for a tough game, but you can win it. Let's go!"

The team ran out to the largest Bowie crowd they had ever experienced for an away game. Even the Bowie High band was there. This out-of-town support by their Bowie fans and classmates was exhilarating.

At halftime, the Bears were tied 7–7, but they were exhausted. Simmang and Rosas passed out cold Coca-Colas as the team rested and waited for Coach Baty's comments. He usually had something pretty inspirational to say at halftime. But on this night, there was a difference. The boys sat on the edge of their chairs as the minutes passed. Silence. Baty finally sauntered into the dressing room and grabbed a piece of chalk. He said nothing. The only sound in the room was that of chalk scraping against the blackboard as he wrote "2X" in big letters.

More silence followed. The boys were puzzled.

Coach asked the team, "You don't get it, do you?"

"No, Coach, what's it mean?"

"It means you're twice as good as they are, and that you'll score at least two more touchdowns to beat them in the second half. You can do it—let's go!" The boys charged onto the field inspired, confident, and reenergized. Meanwhile, the head coach pulled his first-year varsity kick returner off to the side. He looked the boy in the eye and said, "Giya, they're kicking to us this half. If Juan gets the ball, he's going to reverse it and give it to you, just like we practiced. I need at least forty yards out of you. If you can't give me forty yards, I can't have you return kickoffs. Can you do it?"

"Yes, sir, Coach, I can do it."

During a game, he'd change the team's style of play from quarter to quarter. They'd be prepared for every possible scenario. If one style of play wasn't working, he'd change it up entirely. Opposing coaches were clueless about what to expect next.—Ray Sanchez

The kickoff came to Juan, who reversed his field to the left and handed off to Giya, who was running full speed across to the right. After a long return, Giya was dragged down deep in the opponents' territory. Two plays later, the Bears punched the ball across the goal. The second half went just as Coach predicted. The Bears dominated the second half, building a 25–9 lead before replacing the starters with subs. After this victory, La Bowie was on a roll.

What Coach Baty did was incredible. He had molded and motivated us into a winning team in just four days. Las Cruces' only loss that year was to Bowie. —Tony Lujan

For the remainder of the weekend, the coaches worked on the game plan for the next week's road trip. Snyder had dealt them nothing but misery in the past. With the scouting information that Coaches Rosas and Rodriguez had developed, the staff created a few new plays and tweaked a few more. These plays, originally diagramed on a paper napkin at some coffee shop, were devised so that the Bears could score immediately. They usually worked.

• • •

Meanwhile, news from College Station implied that its new coach, Bear Bryant, was conducting a "hell camp" during two-a-days in a town called Junction. Evidently, Aggie players were quitting and bussing back to campus in bunches. Buryl wondered how Bebes Stallings was making out.

25 Snyder Game

After the long, tiring drive from El Paso, Thursday night in Snyder had been rough. The Bowie coaches had planned for a worst-case scenario by preparing their players not to be surprised by anything that might happen—because plenty could. This was a fact made evident by their Snyder experience of 1952.

The Snyder game would nevertheless be an important measure of their progress as a team. A win here would be huge, and the Bears wanted it in a big way. But it would have stacked up to be a tough battle even under ideal circumstances, and these circumstances were far short of ideal. To begin with, their reserved motel had refused to accommodate them. The kids hadn't spoken about it, but they knew what had happened and why. After finally settling in at the second motel, Buryl had spent a fitful, almost sleepless night worrying about the game and the boys.

Early on Friday afternoon the team drove, with a police escort, through the square to the café where lunch arrangements had been confirmed. There, the handful of players standing outside the bus could barely make out the exchange between Baty and the huge café proprietor in his food-spattered white apron. It was obviously about whether he was going to honor the reservation, once he had discovered that the team was Hispanic. All of a sudden, the proprietor's voice shot up.

"Coach, them Meskins are not going inside my place of bui'ness."

"Yes, they are!" Baty shot back. "I made reservations here, and we are gonna eat here. If you don't feed my boys, we are gonna get back in that bus and head back to El Paso. And if we do, *there'll be no football game in Snyder tonight.*"

Shock registered in the faces of boys and proprietor alike. The boys could not appreciate the risk to his job that a coach could run by walking away from a game. But they did understand enough of how their coach felt about football to be astounded that he might actually cancel a game. They stared at each other, stunned and speechless. Meanwhile, the proprietor's mental cash register was busily ringing up the likely damages of the town's wrath.

After a moment of angry silence, the decision came. The proprietor jerked his thumb toward the kitchen door at the rear of the building.

Coach Baty shook his head. In a gesture of submission, the proprietor threw up his hands and stalked away, muttering, "Do what you want."

"*¡Órale!* (Wow!)" the players whispered to each other as they walked in through the front door.

The loud conversations in the café dropped to a whisper, and hostile stares followed the team to their table in the rear section of the dining room. The wait was long, but eventually they were served. As the boys began to eat, several Anglo patrons caught each others' eyes, stood up together, and pushed their half-full plates onto the floor. As they moved toward the door, one of them blurted, "It stinks in here! I ain't paying good money to look over my shoulder at wetbacks."

Coach Baty rose, an act that speeded the exit of the plate-dumpers. But his business was with the boys. "We don't need to put up with this," he said. "Take your last bite, and walk outside, right now."

The team had now met Snyder—where no dogs or Mexicans were allowed. In Snyder, the malice had somehow seemed *meaner* than what they had encountered elsewhere. That had been true when they had played here two years ago, and it was turning out to be true this trip.

As the boys climbed back into their bus, the big café owner in his dirty white apron watched from the back door. He had served them, so there would be a football game. The fact that they hadn't been allowed to eat in peace was gratifying, but that was thanks to his customers. It wasn't his doing.

Coach Baty stood in the front of the vibrating bus and looked at his team. They had just seen grown men pushing plates of food onto the floor to show their contempt for them. These were tough boys, but they were boys, with fragile adolescent egos.

"Men," he said, his eyes narrowed, "this is exactly the kind of thing we prepared for all week. You can be proud of yourselves. You conducted yourselves with dignity. How other people behave is not your fault. But listen to me closely. Don't ever let anybody treat you like you're inferior to them. You're just as good as they are, and you have the right to go after your dreams. Nobody has the right to stand in your way."

The coach paused. Nothing could be heard but the idling motor until he continued. "You also have the right to win this game tonight, and you can bring your anger to the field. But you have to control anger and channel it; you can't let it control you. I want a tough game, but I also want a *clean* game! Do you understand?"

"Yes, sir!" the boys yelled. Suddenly they were again inspired and focused. And they would need to be both. This trip had only begun.

. . .

Later, the Bears took another short ride, this time to the game. The stadium, like so many other small-town fields, had several sets of wooden bleachers and a press box on the home team's side of the field, and only a bench and a few small bleachers on the visitors' side. Also on the home side was a cinderblock building that housed restrooms and a refreshment stand. On the opposite end of the stadium stood a larger cinderblock field house, upon which was painted "Snyder Tigers," that contained home- and visiting-team locker rooms. "This field looks like a cow pasture!" a player wisecracked from the rear of the bus.

A Snyder school official walked up to the bus to meet Baty.

"Coach," he said, as the two shook hands, "I'm afraid we have a problem."

"And that would be—?" Baty asked warily.

"Well, we don't have lockers and bathrooms for you boys. Seems there's some plumbin' problems . . ."

The boys sat in the bus until it was time to take the field for warm-ups. This was a nerve-racking wait, as normal pregame jitters were worsened by jeers from hostile Snyder fans. A few Bears walked together over to the public restrooms, but they were denied entrance. Loud catcalls accompanied their return to the bus.

"It doesn't matter how many people are yelling, or what they're yelling," the Coach reminded his players. "All that matters is what *you do*. All you have to do is to play good football." As the Bears hustled down the steps of the bus, the coaches yelled, "Let's go!"

When they entered the fenced stadium and walked past the home team's bleachers, they could not help noticing Snyder's athletes, who were already warming up. These farm kids looked huge. Meanwhile, locals yelled derogatory comments and threw pebbles, ice, and lemons at the out-of-towners. At the back of the Bears' procession, out of sight of the coaches, a young Snyder fan boldly lifted up a Bowie cheerleader's skirt from behind. Her face flushed with embarrassment. Kids in the nearby stands laughed and cheered.

Locker room and restroom facilities were obviously available for the local team, but not for Bowie. The Bears formed a circle in the dark area behind the goal post to shield those who needed to relieve themselves before the game. "Plummer" Ortiz, the team's trainer, went over to the faucet to fetch drinking water, but was turned away by several big white guys, one of whom sneered, "You Meskins can't use this faucet!" When Plummer returned to explain his empty bucket, Coach Baty grabbed it and retrieved the water himself. But the Bowie kids kept their cool. They had been prepared by their coaches.

After the local minister completed his pregame prayer over the loudspeaker and the Snyder band broke into its lively fight song, the Bears circled around their coach. "Men," he yelled above the noise, "there are lots of potential distractions in this stadium. That's the way they want it. They want you to think about what they're saying to you and what they're throwing at you. They *don't* want you to think about the football game. But don't let 'em distract you. Just focus on what we came here to do. Play better football than they do. It's as plain as that. When the ball is snapped you gotta hit 'em hard, and then again, harder!" He paused. "And never quit, no matter what happens. Are you ready to do that?"

"Yes, sir!" they responded. *"¡Simón!"*

Finally the kickoff came. And not a moment too soon for the Bears. They had waited for this game and waited to let their play do their talking. The Bears were confident that they would outplay the host team on its own turf. Hometown fans clapped and cheered, and Tiger cheerleaders waved their pom-poms. Excitement filled the air. Snyder's Tigers were ranked #3 in West Texas, but La Bowie was ready to take 'em on.

Early in the game, Tony Lujan made a jarring tackle, then started back toward his defensive huddle. A Snyder player ran up and smacked him in the back of the head with a forearm. This flagrant foul clearly took place after the whistle had blown and should have warranted an unnecessary-roughness penalty. Tony responded with a retaliatory gesture, but quickly stopped himself and again started toward his team's huddle. A nearby referee jumped in his face. "Don't start any trouble, greaser, or I'll throw your Meskin ass outta this game!" Tony glared defiantly in return. This was not the first time these derogatory terms had been heard that night; it was just the first time they were heard from the mouth of a referee.

Several plays later, freshman safety Giya Olivas lay painfully on the ground with blood oozing from his nose and mouth. Under a pile of tacklers, a Snyder player had kicked him in the face. This was a dirty but common tactic in these days before face masks. The offender had then hissed, "Take that, you spic!"

"Do you want to stay in the game, Giya?" asked Coach Baty.

"Yes, sir, Coach."

A little later, on a successful sequence of plays, Bowie drove to the Snyder twenty-yard line. On first and ten, the 24 Trap was called. The Bears had practiced this play daily. End Tony Lujan and tackle Benny Landin cross-blocked each other's man, while the ballcarrier took a delay step in the opposite direction before bursting through the hole. It worked perfectly, gaining eight yards and moving ever closer to the goal line. Suddenly the umpire threw a red flag and blew his whistle. "Clipping!" he yelled. "Fifteen-yard penalty!"

Benny Landin heard the call and waved his hands in disgust. Again the whistle sounded and a red flag sailed up into the glare of the stadium lights. "Unsportsmanlike conduct! Fifteen-yard penalty!" called the umpire.

Bowie's coaches were beside themselves but managed to summon the referee respectfully to the sideline. "Can you explain what's going on out there?"

"We have a clipping penalty for fifteen yards, and then an unsportsmanlike-conduct penalty for another fifteen yards."

"Clipping?" Baty appealed. "We ran an Inside Trap play. There's no way to clip on an Inside Trap."

"That's what we called, Coach."

"Who did you call it on?"

"Number 73, right there." He pointed to one of the kids standing nearby.

"Number 73? Are you sure?" Baty asked.

"Yes, Coach, I'm sure. It was number 73."

"But, sir, he plays defense, not offense. Number 73, that kid right there, wasn't even on the field. Can we get the rest of the officiating crew over here to discuss this, please?"

The zebra paused for a couple of seconds, then pulled out his red flag and dramatically tossed it again—high in the air. "That's fifteen yards for being out on the field, Coach." It was quickly becoming apparent that the

Bears had yet another formidable opponent: the game officials. Coach Baty bit his tongue.

I don't know how the coaches kept their composure.—Tony Lujan

Consequently, the Bears went from second and two at the opponent's twelve-yard line to first and fifty-five at their own thirty-five-yard line. They failed to convert the first down and had to punt the ball.

Later, the Bears mounted another drive toward a potential score. Jogging back to the huddle, Enrique Camacho told quarterback Sal Garcia, "*Has la jugada con la ruta número siete.* (Run the play with the 7 route.)" He wanted to run the play with a pass route shaped like the number 7; he believed the play would work.

A whistle sounded and a red flag again flew. "Fifteen-yard penalty for speaking Spanish!" the referee barked.

Coach Baty objected. "Mr. Referee, can you tell me where the rule book says a player can't speak Spanish?" The official ignored the question. Coach Simmang wedged himself between his boss and the official. "This is not the last you'll hear of this, mister!" Baty yelled, and pointed. The drive was stalled.

At halftime, the Bears huddled just outside the glow of the dim field lights. Those who had seen action in the first half sat on the ground and rested as they drank from the passed water bucket. Several feet away, a few players created another standing screen for those who needed to relieve themselves.

The second half of play offered more of the same. The Bears ignored repeated and demeaning ethnic insults. By the end of the game, two Bowie touchdowns had been reversed due to questionable referee calls and six untimely fifteen-yard penalties were assessed to kill drives. The Bears had been well prepared for just about anything that might be thrown at them, but the officials' favoritism was too much to overcome. Bowie lost the game 19–0.

Coach Baty glared at the referees. Fearful for their safety, the officials demanded that a state trooper escort him out of the stadium and to the Bowie transport. The Bears were again pelted with debris by hometown fans as they walked from the field toward their waiting bus.

Standing in front of his shaken players, Coach Baty reflected on the experience before they pulled away. "Men, I'm sorry for what happened on this trip. You've been through a lot here. We've all been through a lot. But let me tell you something.

"First, you played a fine game tonight, well enough to win. You gained more yards, you made more first downs, and you held on to the ball. You should each be proud of the way you played. And, you should be proud of the way you conducted yourselves in the face of adversity." His intensity rose as he continued. "There were two contests going on here tonight: one of character and the other of football. You won the more important one."

"As far as the game is concerned, it's over. Forget it. For now, the only games that matter are against Douglas and Cathedral. These next two weeks will prepare us for our pursuit of the championship."

Gears jerked and the motor revved as Rusty pulled the big bus out toward the highway.

> Every time we went on road trips, Coach Baty had to deal with the same thing. No one wanted us because we were poor Mexicans. But he always stood proudly by us.—Giya Olivas

The Bears had endured shameless discrimination many times before, but this Snyder experience trumped them all. And the "loss" was demoralizing. But Coach Baty's resolve infused his players with renewed strength and purpose.

Rusty, the bus driver, had already ordered thirty-odd hamburgers and hot dogs for the boys to eat after the game, and the bus stopped at a nearby store for them to buy snacks and sodas for the long ride home. Inside, the shopkeeper angrily accused two boys of stealing his merchandise. He called the police, who found nothing from the store in the boys' possession.

Finally, the team got out of Snyder. Coach Baty quietly told his two assistants, "Guys, this problem is not going away."

Exhausted players quickly fell asleep to the hum of the engine and the hypnotic sound of tires spinning over the pavement. Meanwhile, Coach Baty stewed over the events of the past two days. He needed to stay awake anyway, to help Rusty keep alert for the long drive home.

APPRECIATION—Luling's businessmen appreciated Coach Buryl Baty's work with the Luling Eagles this season in winning eight games and losing only two, so they gave Coach and Mrs. Baty, shown above, the brand new auto shown here.—(Conley Photo)

Luling's businessmen appreciated Coach Buryl Baty's work with the Luling Eagles, winning eight games and losing only two, so they gave Coach and Mrs. Baty, shown above, the brand new auto shown here. (Conley Photo, Courtesy of the *Austin American Statesman,* November 26, 1949)

Bo and Buryl's El Paso home, 1950. (Family photo)

Bo and Buryl, 1950. (Family photo)

Coach Baty and Coach Rosas on the Bowie side-line. (Courtesy of El Paso ISD, Bowie High Yearbook—*The Aztec, 1950*)

Bowie Bears pictured in front of plane before 1950 flight to Austin. (Courtesy of El Paso ISD, Bowie High Yearbook—*The Aztec*)

Buryl holds his son Gaines in the front yard in El Paso, circa 1952. (Family photo)

Coach Buryl Baty shows junior quarterback Jesus Martinez how it is done as he prepares to take the ball from center Edmundo Rodriguez. The Bears, with four returning lettermen, began practice Monday for the district grid race. (Courtesy of *El Paso Times,* Staff photo, 1951)

El Paso Head Coach Buryl Baty, David Archuleta, and Line Coach Jerry Simmang. (Courtesy of *El Paso Herald-Post,* 1952)

REPLAN STRATEGY — Bowie High coaches quickly went over their strategy when it was learned Manny Morales, the Bears' star back of last season, will return to the squad soon. They are, left to right: Fred Rosas, backfield coach; Buryl Baty, head coach, and Jerry Simmang, line coach. The three coaches hope Morales will be back Friday, when the Bears face Austin in a District 2-AAAA game. The three Bowie brains will really have to do some thinking if they're to come up with a solution on how to beat the Panthers. The Eastsiders are heavily favored, whether Morales returns or not.

Bowie Coaches Rosas, Baty, and Simmang plan strategy. (Courtesy of *El Paso Times,* 1952)

CHAMPS! — Bowie High clinched the District 2-AAAA championship by whipping Ysleta last night 20-6 at Ysleta and here the players are shown whooping it up in the bus as they prepare to return to El Paso after the big game.

Bowie Bears celebrate on bus after victory clinching 1953 District Championship. (Courtesy of *El Paso Times*)

Bowie Bears team picture during Championship celebration dinner, 1953. (Photo source unknown)

Coach Baty pictured as 1953 Coach of the Year, and his All-District players. (Courtesy of *El Paso Herald-Post*)

Bo, Buryl, and son Gaines—Christmas at home in Paris, 1953. (Family photo)

Bo and Buryl. (Family photo)

Buryl in El Paso
yard with son
Gaines, 1954.
(Family photo)

The last picture taken of Coach Buryl Baty (far left) and Coach Jerry Simmang (second from the far right) on October 6 with the 1954 Bowie Bears team. (Courtesy of *El Paso Times*, Staff photo)

December 29, 1972—TECH'S BATY RECEIVES AWARD—Texas Tech player Gaines Baty accepts an appreciation award from Bowie High School Booster Club by Principal Luis Cortez, second from left, soon after the Red Raiders' arrival in El Paso. Baty's father was killed in an accident in 1954 while serving as Bowie's head football coach. Shown, left to right, are Ernie Perea, Luis Cortez, Gaines Baty, Assistant Coach Fred Rosas, and Club President Manny Morales. (Courtesy of *El Paso Times*)

At the 1998 stadium dedication. Coach Fred Rosas is wearing the black shirt. Gaines Baty is on his right; Larry Baty, behind and on his left.

Bowie team in the stands at the stadium dedication. Front row, Larry Baty, Coach Rosas, and Gaines Baty, 1998.

Mural honoring coaches displayed at the Baty-Simmang Stadium in 1998.

Baty grandchildren (Ryan, Jacqueline, Robbie) with Gaines at Baty-Simmang Stadium, before 2013 player reunion. (Family photo)

Larry Baty and Gaines Baty with Ray San-chez at Buryl Baty's El Paso Sports Hall of Fame induction in 2013. (Family photo)

SEPTEMBER 25, 1954

The balance of the short weekend was intense. After only a couple hours of sleep, Buryl convened with the other coaches early on Saturday morning to watch and critique the junior high and B-team games, review and grade films, and refine the game plan for the next varsity contest. Later, during his few hours at the house, he paced from room to room. Bo tried to calm him, but to no avail. "I'm sorry, Honey, but I just can't get it off my mind," he said. He had just provided a blow-by-blow account of the trip.

He brooded over the Snyder debacle all weekend. Early on Monday morning, he stepped into the office of Dale Waters, the Bowie Athletic Director. Coincidentally, Giya Olivas happened to be walking past, and he stood quietly in the hallway, eavesdropping on the loud conversation between Baty and Waters.

The coach scowled as he described the open discrimination and the outrageous referee rulings. "I've got the films and you can see the bad calls for yourself. Then, let's decide what we can do to resolve this."

Waters shifted uncomfortably in his chair, then replied, "Buryl, let's not make waves."

Baty leaned forward. "I've just described the BS that happened this weekend. This garbage has gone on ever since I got here. We've talked about it and talked about it. And it's getting worse." His tone deepened. "This is not something I'm going to sweep under the rug, Dale. It's not right!"

"I'm sorry, Buryl, but I just don't know what we can do about it," Waters answered.

Baty's eyes narrowed as he glared and pointed his finger at Waters. "Well, Dale, I'll tell you what we'll do about it. Before long—I'll have your job!"

Waters' eyebrows lifted. He was speechless as he searched for an answer.

Coach Baty stalked out of the room. Just outside the door, he almost bumped into Giya, nodded at him absently, and continued down the hall.

He would figure it out, somehow. But for now, dwelling on the past was unproductive. Instead, Baty refocused on the tasks at hand. The season was young, and another undefeated rival loomed in just three short days. His team needed to rebound.

That Friday's *Herald-Post* reported on Bowie's progress.

BOWIE SHOWS BETTER PUNCH, OCTOBER 1, 1954
Ray Sanchez

Everyone knew Bowie High was going to have a better offense than last year but, wow, no one knew it would be this much better.

In fact, in slamming Douglas 46–0 last night in R. R. Jones Stadium . . . the Bears scored more points than they had in any one game in seven years.

The big difference in the new Bruin scoring punch is, without doubt, Sal Garcia. The Southsiders seem to always have a top-notch quarterback but none has been any better than Sal.

At least the way Sal played last night.

He passed, ran and handled the ball like a pro. He completed six of seven passes for 74 yards and two touchdowns. . . .

On the ground he rambled for 93 yards in seven attempts (a dazzling 13.3 average) and turned in the run of the night. . . .

The entire Bowie defense looked superb, holding Douglas to 20 yards rushing.

Wow! These Bears looked strong. And they played mad. This rout would cause rival coaches to lose sleep over upcoming games against Bowie. Next up on the schedule was Cathedral High. This Thursday-night game offered the opportunity for the Bowie coaches to personally scout two future opponents on Friday night, October 8.

The entire team dressed out in game uniforms for Wednesday afternoon's Team Picture Day and posed proudly. A light practice followed. Bo called Buryl that afternoon at the field house. "Please don't be too late tonight. I'm cooking your favorite dinner, and I have something . . . " she paused. "I've got a surprise for you."

Later that evening, Bo, Buryl, and their son sat at the kitchen table over roast beef and potatoes.

"How were your practices this week?"

Buryl's face lit up. "We had a short week, but our drills were good. The boys have a lot of spirit after our win. I'm optimistic. I think we'll be pretty good, maybe better than last year, with a break or two."

Bo fidgeted and looked down at her plate.

"Is something the matter?"

"No, nothing's wrong." Then she looked up, directly into her husband's eyes, because she wanted to see his reaction. "I'm pregnant."

"Are you kidding? *Yee-haa!*"

Buryl's shout echoed through the house and out the screened doors into the neighborhood. He jumped over to Bo, lifted her up, and spun her around in a circle. They hugged, and then held Gaines between them, hugging him. Buryl's focus actually left football for a while. He reminded Bo that he loved her.

"We're scouting on Friday night, but I don't have to work as much this weekend, so I can spend some more time with you. We can go out to eat, just you and me. We'll talk about what to name him, uh, or her, and how we'll fix up the nursery." They sat back down at the supper table to finish eating. "Two down and three or four more to go, right?"

Bo looked up quickly to see Buryl grinning, his brown eyes fixed on her. She knew right away that he was joking. Sort of joking.

"I don't know about three or four, but we'll see," she said, also smiling.

They sat on the couch after supper. Buryl, with his four-year-old future quarterback in his lap, held Bo close to him.

"I know this isn't a glamorous life, and it's tough on you. I'll get you closer to home as soon as I can."

"We're fine here; don't worry about that. I just want our kids and our family to know each other. You're the love of my life. I'll live anywhere you need me to."

"If we can string a couple of championships together, we can have any job we want. We'll have a good year this year, and Bowie will be in a better position than we found it. We'll have finished what we started here. Honey, we have a lot to look forward to."

Bo squeezed his hand.

"By the way, I'm thinking about taking Gaines with us to scout Pecos on Friday night. What do you think?" Buryl asked.

Bo winced. "Why don't you wait until he's a little older? He'll fall asleep, and you might not be able to concentrate on your business.

Besides, he's sitting on the bench with you tomorrow night at the game."

"OK. But someday soon I want to take him with me."

The next evening, the Bears overpowered Cathedral, beating them decisively. After the game, they rode the victory bus through the barrio, horns honking.

Early on Friday morning, Buryl, Fred, Jerry, Coach Emrick, and Coach Rodriguez gathered in the school cafeteria for coffee and to analyze and critique the game. They reviewed what had gone well, what had not, who played well, who had not, and what needed work. A refined game plan and several new plays were drawn up for the next opponent, district rival El Paso High. As the meeting wound down, Baty looked up from his notes. Knowing that Rodriguez's baby had been ailing for two days, he said, "Rodriguez, why don't you stay home with your wife and baby tonight? You don't need to go on this trip. The three of us can check out Pecos. Take the night off."

"Are you sure, Coach?"

"Yep, get a little rest, and we'll see you at your eighth-grade game in the morning."

That afternoon, after running them through a few light drills to loosen up, Coach Baty addressed the team. "Men, you played well last night, and you kept it up in your drills today. We coaches are driving to scout Pecos as soon as we shower. I want you to enjoy this victory and take the weekend off, but keep your noses clean. Curfew is in effect. Everyone needs to do his homework and start thinking about our next game. We play El Paso High in two weeks, and we'll need to work hard to get ready." With a big smile on his face and his fist pumping above his head, he yelled, "See you on Monday!"

Loud clapping and cheering came in response. The Bears were fired up, and they were one, as if the same blood pulsed through their bodies. They had won two games in a row and were going into district play with great momentum. The only person who was more psyched was their head coach.

Before leaving the field house, Buryl called home. "Honey, we're about to leave for Pecos. We'll get back as soon as we can, and Jerry'll drop me off at the house. I'll spend lots of time with you and our two kids this weekend." His smile traveled across the lines and through the phone to Bo. "I love you, and I'm excited."

"Have a good trip. I love you, too." She paused. "And Buryl, please be careful."

Not too far outside El Paso, Jerry's new Plymouth pulled off the highway onto a gravel road and stopped in front of a farmhouse. They thought their old buddy, former Coach Jim Bowden, might want to ride out to Pecos with them. Jim was glad to see his old friends, but he declined the invitation. "Thanks anyway, but today's Friday," he said, "and it's payday. I won't have any help tomorrow if my guys don't get paid."

"Jim," Buryl joked, "if you have payday every Friday, maybe I should apply for a job. Would you consider hiring your old head coach?"

"Yeah, Bowden, and you can hire me as your translator," Fred Rosas quipped. *"Yo hablo Español."*

"Yo también. I'm not sure I'd want you seedy characters working for me. But if you boys want to fill out a job application on Monday, I'll think about it."

The coaches needed to get going, and the friends shook hands warmly. "Good luck guys, and be careful," Jim shouted, waving as his friends eased out of the driveway.

27 Let's Get Home

It was a clear West Texas night, one of those nights when the stars sparkle so brilliantly that they seem alive. The monotonous blur of passing white center stripes, the hypnotic sound of tires on pavement, and the glare of headlights approaching from a distance were broken only by rushing bursts of air as approaching vehicles sped past in the opposite direction, like stray bullets. Jerry's eyes grew heavy. It had been a long day—a full Friday of classes, football practice, a scouting trip to Pecos, and a long drive back home. The hour was approaching midnight. Jerry's eyes closed and his chin fell toward his chest.

"Coach, are you OK?" The alarmed voice from the passenger's seat broke the silence.

Only then did Jerry realize that he had nodded off. "Gettin' a little sleepy, Buryl," he mumbled.

"There's a gas station just up the road. Let's grab a cup of coffee."

"Good idea."

Within minutes, the car pulled off the highway and into a dimly lit service station. Gravel cracked under new tires as the Plymouth crept to the gasoline pump. At first the station seemed to be deserted, but eventually a young man in overalls lumbered toward them. The three coaches stepped out of the car. The cool air felt good. Summer temperatures were beginning to subside.

"Fill 'er up, please," Jerry greeted the attendant.

After paying for fuel and black coffee, the three coaches walked back out to the car.

Buryl said, "Jerry, you want me to drive?"

"No, I'm fine. I was getting sleepy, but I'm wide awake now."

"Hey, Buryl, why don't you switch places with me?" Coach Rosas suggested. "I'm happy to take the front, and you can stretch out in the back seat. I promise to keep Jerry awake."

"No, thanks, Fred. I'm fine. We'll be home in thirty minutes."

Just as he pulled out onto the westbound lane of Highway 80 for the final homeward stretch, Jerry took an extended look to the left to ensure that no traffic was coming. As he accelerated and turned his eyes back to his right, he was blinded by the sudden approaching glare of bright lights—*headlights*!

A thunderous crash broke the tranquility of the night. Shattered glass flew in all directions. Loosened hubcaps and random pieces of metal clanged loudly on the hard pavement. Soon, only an eerie ring hung in the darkness. And finally, there was silence.

28 The Longest Night

As the night wore on, Bo became increasingly nervous. She was restless every time Buryl was out of town, and she could never sleep until he was home. It was her nature; she was a worrier. This Friday, she had cooked dinner for her son, put him to bed, and occupied the rest of the evening by sewing curtains for the new baby's bedroom. Now she sat, twitching her forefinger over her thumb.

The phone rang. "Have you heard from the boys?" Ruth Simmang asked.

"No, and I'm getting worried."

Concern quickly grew to panic. They both got on the phone, calling the athletic director, local hospitals, and the police department. With every fruitless call and every passing minute, Bo's distress grew. Minutes turned into hours. Finally, a woman at the police department acknowledged the report of an accident on Highway 80.

"What can I do?" Bo asked frantically.

"Call us back in an hour, ma'am."

A little later, three Hispanic women knocked on the Batys' door. They were very upset. They had heard that the Bowie coaches had been killed in an accident. Bo's breath was taken away. "This can't be true. He'll call me any minute." The women tried to console her before leaving. Time stood still.

The phone rang. "A man was brought in a few minutes ago, ma'am," said the elderly lady from the hospital. "A tall boy brought him in."

Bo breathed a sigh of relief. "The 'tall boy' must have been Buryl. If someone were hurt, Buryl would stay with him," she thought to herself.

In another hour, and after what seemed like a lifetime of waiting, the phone rang again. "Two men's bodies have been brought in, and Coach Rosas is in critical condition in the hospital, ma'am."

"No! There must be a mistake! Please, God, let it be a mistake. Please let Buryl come home," Bo prayed.

Daylight approached. A loud knock broke the dark silence. Bo had dreaded this knock. She took a deep breath and opened the door. Two state troopers stood on her front porch.

"Mrs. Baty," they said, without preamble, "we regret to inform you that your husband has been killed in a traffic accident."

The officers explained that the three coaches were roughly thirty miles from El Paso when they had stopped at Fort Hancock for gas. Mr. Simmang had been driving, and Mr. Baty was in the passenger seat. Not long after pulling out onto Highway 80's westbound lane, they were hit head-on. A fully loaded grain truck, driven by a nineteen-year-old who had fallen asleep, had drifted over the center stripe and collided with Mr. Simmang's vehicle.

Mr. Baty and Mr. Simmang had been killed instantly. The car was mangled beyond recognition. After hearing Mr. Rosas's moans from the rear of the smoldering Plymouth, troopers had pried the trunk open in order to reach him. The backseat had been pushed back into the trunk by the sheer force of the collision, but Mr. Rosas had somehow survived. The young truck driver had not been hurt, but the policemen said that he was in "great despair."

Before leaving, one of the officers presented Mr. Baty's personal effects that had been recovered from the accident site.

Now alone in the silence that swallowed the house, Bo gazed at what she held in her hands. She had felt a glimmer of hope that somebody was mistaken and that Buryl would walk through the door any minute. But his personal belongings in her hands dashed that hope.

Images flashed through her mind: of her and Buryl on the front porch back home, of his return from the war, and of his joy about her pregnancy—just two nights ago. She sat in the hollow house, incredibly alone, sobbing uncontrollably.

She eventually gathered her strength to call her sisters. "We'll catch the first flight out," Alta said. "Hold on. We'll be there."

Noises from down the hall woke Gaines. Sleepy eyes opened to the dim light penetrating the predawn darkness outside his bedroom door. The little boy climbed down from his bed and walked toward the lighted front room. Peeking around the corner, he saw his mother slumped on the couch, crying.

"What's wrong, Mama?"

Startled, Bo took a deep breath, gathered herself for a second, and in a trembling voice said, "Come here, honey."

He entered his mother's outstretched arms for a long and confusing hug. "What's wrong, Mama?" he repeated.

"Honey." A long silence followed as she tried to compose herself and force the words from her lips. "Honey, your daddy won't be coming home."

She held her son close to her as daylight gradually filtered into the room. Dawn was beginning to break.

OCTOBER 9, 1954

Giya Olivas was walking home from early Saturday morning mass when the milk deliveryman slowed and yelled out at him, "Aren't you on the Bowie football team?"

"Yes, why?"

"Do you know that your coaches have been killed in a car accident?"

Giya looked back at the deliveryman, stunned. He could not believe what he had just heard. Without a word he turned and raced to the schoolyard to find B-team Coach Emrick before the morning's B-team and junior high football games. "There won't be any games this morning. We had some trouble on the field," Coach Emrick motioned as he saw Giya running toward him.

"I already know!" Giya snapped back. The coach saw tears welling in Giya's eyes, and nodded.

Tony Lujan's phone rang. It was Lucy Rivas, and she told him about the accident. "You're the first person I've called," she cried. Tony was stunned and confused. His father rested his hand on his shoulder and said, "Death is a part of life. It's hard to understand, but it's God's will." Tony was not consoled. He called several teammates and they agreed to meet at the school. When David Holguin heard about the accident, his mother had to hug and calm him until he was able to go meet with the team. There, at the school, Coach Emrick and Cathedral High School's Coach Flynn offered condolences to every player who showed up.

Ray Sanchez always went into his *Herald-Post* news desk early on Saturday mornings to report on Friday night's games. On this Saturday, Ray was summoned to his boss's office and told to head out to Fort Hancock to report on the coaches' accident.

"Oh, no!" he cried. "I can't believe it! Those guys are my favorites—they're my friends!" Ray rushed out the door. This would not be an easy assignment.

As word spread of the tragedy, a crowd of shocked parents, students, friends, and townspeople drove out to the accident site. While the smoldering, mangled passenger car had been doused with water and moved to a wrecking yard, remnants of the collision were eerily visible: hubcaps, broken glass, a chrome bumper that had been torn from the Plymouth. A huge truck lay on its side in the ditch beside the road. Details of the accident were whispered, and questions were asked over and over again. "What if they hadn't stopped for coffee? Maybe they could have passed the truck before the driver fell asleep." "What if they had stayed at the gas station longer? The truck might have passed while they were still inside." "Why did this happen to such wonderful men? They had such promising futures."

When Julio Jauregui arrived at work at Hotel Dieu Hospital that morning, a nurse told him about the accident. "One of the coaches survived, and he's here," she said, but she did not know which coach it was. Julio immediately rushed to find Coach Rosas unconscious in bed, bandaged from head to toe. Julio was the first one on the team to see him.

> After a light Friday afternoon practice, the coaches got the team together and told us to behave; then they departed in Coach Simmang's car. That was the last time we saw them.—Juan Mendoza

> It was announced over the loudspeaker and the entire school was quiet, devastated.—Enrique Camacho

> I read it in a newspaper clipping that was sent to me. I cried. I immediately got a 30 day leave from my Marine base in California to come home.—Leo Muñoz

> I was on a Greyhound bus coming home on a military pass from San Antonio when I saw the wrecked truck on the side of the road.—Arturo Lightbourn

Coach Baty had touched his players and students in a profound manner. He had given them hope that they had never experienced before. He had provided a beacon of light that now was darkened. The kids first felt confused, then cheated, and finally angry that he had been taken from them.

Bo was more than devastated. The love of her life, the father of her son and of her unborn child, had tragically and forever been taken away from her. What could she do now—alone, a twenty-nine-year-old widowed, pregnant mother?

Sister Alta and her husband CI caught the first plane from Dallas to be at Bo's side. Glenda and Harry drove immediately from Albuquerque. Their presence would be comforting to Bo, and they could help with the dreadful requirements of such a transition. Alta and CI stayed at the house with Bo, while Glenda and Harry stayed with friends.

Ruth King called to inform Bo's other family members and friends of the tragedy and of likely arrangements. She explained that Bo had originally planned to travel to Paris immediately, but that she had decided to stay for an afternoon memorial service on Monday in El Paso. "They loved him here, and this will give them a chance to say goodbye." She promised that Bo and Gaines would arrive in Paris late on Tuesday with Buryl's body.

On the following Monday morning, public address speakers delivered the terrible news. For once, Principal Pollitt's deep drawl received the undivided attention of the whole student body. This news, which everybody already knew, served only to substantiate what no one wanted to believe. Pollitt announced that a memorial service would be held at 3 p.m. that afternoon in the chapel of the Asbury Methodist Church. "Only the football team will be excused from classes to attend the service, and a bus will transport you from the field house at two o'clock. Students who are not members of the team will be expected to attend classes, as usual."

Attempting to console the excluded student body, he continued, "Tomorrow morning, we will hold our own memorial service in the school auditorium for all Bowie students and faculty."

The afternoon drive across town to the church was unlike any the Bowie Bears had ever experienced. This ride was quiet, somber. As their bright yellow school bus approached the church, Rusty slowed the vehicle to a crawl. Still two blocks away from the chapel, a line of cars was being directed toward available street parking by uniformed policemen. With the exception of the large space reserved for the team's bus, the church parking lot was already full.

Pedestrians streamed from surrounding streets to join a long line of mourners filing into the church. Many Bowie students walked among the adults. These teenagers, obviously disregarding their principal's instructions, had deserted their classrooms. Some rode the city bus, some rode bikes, some hitchhiked, and many walked all the way to the service.

A special seating section near the coaches' families had been reserved for the boys. Hymns played softly on the organ made the only sound in the quiet church as the boys moved through the crowd to their seats. The chapel was packed, with the crowd spilling out of the sanctuary and across the well-manicured front lawn. The streets nearby were so crowded that they had to be closed to traffic.

Two closed caskets lay side by side in front of the pulpit. Flower arrangements, large and small, filled the front of the church and left little room for the minister, the organist, and the speakers. Flowers had been sent not only by friends and relatives, but also by rival schools. Even the Snyder team sent their respects for Buryl Baty and Jerry Simmang.

When the organist broke into the familiar strains of the grand old hymn "Amazing Grace," the congregation did not need hymnals to sing the words:

Amazing grace, how sweet the sound
That saved a wretch like me;
I once was lost but now am found,
Was blind but now I see.

There was not a dry eye in the big chapel. Bowie Bears cried openly.

After the emotional service, the Bears stood in line to pay their condolences to Mrs. Baty and Mrs. Simmang. They felt as if they were part of these coaches' families, but they had no idea what to say. Those who could find words were barely able to speak. "Your husband was a great man. I loved him," they said.

As his turn came to speak to the family, Tony Lujan noticed Mrs. Baty's son standing beside his mother. He gave the boy a hug and whispered, "Remember to take care of your mother." A young Hispanic boy approached and handed Mrs. Baty a handkerchief full of small coins: pennies, nickels, and dimes. The players had taken up a collection of whatever money they had, and one of the younger boys was chosen to present the gift to her. It was not much, but it was all they had.

For an hour after the service had concluded, Bo and Ruth Simmang greeted a long line of mourners who paraded past to pay their respects.

Newspaper articles spoke for many who knew the two fallen coaches. The *El Paso Times Sports Log* wrote on October 11 that "El Pasoans lost two real friends Saturday. The tragic deaths of Bowie's Buryl Baty and Jerry Simmang will leave a huge void in the hearts of many. . . .

"Not once during the many visits Sports Log made to Bowie did he hear a cross word directed by either man to a player. They never used a verbal whip to get results. They had another method."

"It was kindness."

Ray Sanchez was open about his personal grief for these people he had loved and admired.

El Paso Herald-Post, October 12, 1954
By the Way . . .

EL PASO BADE FAREWELL TO Jerry Simmang and Buryl
Baty yesterday in Asbury Methodist Church and in so doing El
Paso also bade farewell to a wonderful—but so cruelly short—
football era here.

That is, El Paso bade farewell to their physical bodies. In spirit,
they'll remain in the hearts of each and every one of us that ever
met them. They'll remain there unto our own death.

Even now as this typewriter clicks away they seem to stand by
me—young, strong and handsome and those somewhat silly grins
on their faces. We're all alone in the night. (I really wrote this column last night because I knew I couldn't sleep until I did.) The
rest of the office force is gone, their working day over.

But we three are still here and I can hear Buryl's voice with
that familiar chuckle saying: "Aw, Ray, come on," just like he did
whenever I tried to tell him what a good team he had put out. And
Jerry saying, like he did when I told him how great his football
lines were: "Gosh, Ray . . ."

Yep, they're embarrassed about these words I'm putting down
as they stand here and read them over my shoulder. Like most
men of great ability, they're overly modest. And it's a kind of mod-
esty that is so sincere it's actually boyish.

I hate to embarrass you two fellows, honestly, but I really feel I
must.

WIN OR LOSE, BURYL AND JERRY WERE RESPECTED
THESE TWO YOUNG GOLIATHS became a twosome in
1950, the year after Jerry came to Bowie High. Buryl joined him
there in '50.

With them they brought new unthought-of glory to the school.
Before they came Bowie was considered just another football
team. The Bears were seldom taken seriously.

But, boy, did Buryl and Jerry change that. The very first season the two were at Bowie the Bruins finished first in the district.
The next two years were those of rebuilding but never were the
Southsiders' foes able to relax. Even when beaten the Bears looked
good.

I'll never forget the words of Red Harris after Austin beat Bowie by 35–14 in 1952. That year Austin won the district championship with a terrific team. By such a lopsided score you'd think Austin had little trouble with the Bears. No sir. Red praised the Bowie team, saying his Panthers had to play their best game of the year.

Which brings to mind an incident which happened only last Thursday—the last time I was to see Jerry and Buryl alive. The Bears looked bad defensively the first quarter against Cathedral. But in the second quarter the Bears smothered their opponents.

During halftime, atop the press box, was the Ysleta coaching staff, scouting the game. Fred Harvey, Ysleta's scout and coach said: "Did you notice how Buryl changed his defense to stop Cathedral's offensive strategy?" That was also praise for Jerry for he was in charge of the line.

THEIR FRIENDSHIP WAS WARM AND REAL

WHAT MADE THESE TWO MEN so fine that they were admired not only by their friends but by their opponents just as much? Henry Wheeler, former Ysleta coach, flew all the way from Galveston for yesterday's services. He had no less than three long-distance calls informing him about the accident.

It's difficult to put into words. They had that unknown quality that makes everyone feel welcome. Their friendship was warm and real and they offered it quickly to anyone.

They were perfect for Bowie and that's why the Bears ascended to such heights under them. Under their guidance Bowie finished first in the district twice in four years and there were many before their death that would have bet Bowie was going to make it three out of five this season.

The Southsiders, because so many of them come from unstable families, are unstable themselves. But Buryl and Jerry had that quality which made the boys feel secure and welcome. The team was like a big, happy family, playing together, joking together and fighting together.

Sure there were incidents. But Buryl and Jerry never yelled at their players, like so many might. The two coaches just erased the incidents quietly and without disrupting the feeling of security.

They didn't blame the boys, also like so many might. It would be easy to do because the Southsiders, if one must be frank about it, are often discriminated against.

The two just quietly went about their business. And the results were astounding.

THERE WAS A REASON—AND THEY DIED PROUD

WHY DID THEY HAVE TO LEAVE us—physically? I've often asked myself: "Why did it have to be they?"

Allen Thomas and Nemo Herrera, two very, very close friends of Jerry and Buryl had this to say, Allen speaking first:

"There was a reason. We'll never know why Providence should choose to put that truck on that spot on the highway at the very instant Buryl, Jerry and Fred Rosas were there. If the truck driver had gone to sleep a mile before, the accident might never have happened. As it was Providence made it happen at just that instant. There was a reason."

Said Nemo: "It does us no good to ask why. It was destined. But they died in a proud way. With their boots on, like they say. They died in the line of duty. What better way can a man go than that?"

THEY HAD A GREAT CAREER STRETCHED AHEAD

INDEED THE WORDS OF Nemo and Allen make sense.

Jerry and Buryl died proud and it's fitting that they did, for all great men should go that way.

It would have been wonderful to have been able to follow their careers. Both were sure to rise in their profession. They were in the prime of life and their "Glory Road" was just beginning. But one can't have everything in life and we, the living, must now go without the satisfaction of watching them progress.

That is, we must go without the satisfaction of seeing it happen in real life. Actually, we all know it would have happened anyway. There really isn't much difference.

Well, I'm finished. Come on, Buryl and Jerry, let's go up to the house for a cup of coffee.

On Tuesday morning a memorial-service assembly was held at Bowie High School. Students filed quietly into the rapidly filling auditorium, while several men in suits sat up on the stage. After the last seats were taken, late-arriving kids were instructed to stand in the rear of the large room, and Principal Pollitt took the podium to address the faculty and students. The microphone crackled.

We are assembled here this morning in memory of two of our faculty members. We at Bowie are a little bit closer than most places. We have a deep feeling for our school, for our students, and for our faculty. The loss that we are experiencing is great, and as time goes on, I'm sure that it will be even greater. We were very fortunate in having these two men as members of our faculty. They were role models whom we were very proud for you to fol-low. They were sincere, loyal, kind and good, and they always had the best interests of you and Bowie High School at heart. It is true that we've lost two fine coaches, the best in their profession. But it is also true that we have lost two fine men.

This grief is not limited to us; it is felt in El Paso and through-out all the areas where they are known. We have received many, many telegrams, cards, and letters of sympathy, and we appreciate those very much. But we especially appreciate the condolences that have been sent by our ex-students, from near and far. These will most likely continue for some time. I would like to read one of these cards from one of our ex-students, one of our graduates. On the front of the card, and in his own handwriting, it reads: 'On behalf of Mr. Buryl Baty and Mr. Gerald T. Simmang.' Inside the card, he has written the following: 'I am sharing the sorrow with you all, for those that we love. We will never forget them. A stu-dent of Bowie High School, Felipe Cabralas.'

These cards and telegrams are arriving continuously. At a time like this it's so hard to say the things that you'd like to say; we just don't have the words to express our feelings. But I think that all of us are going to miss these men more than we realize."

Next the El Paso school superintendent, Dr. Mortimer Brown, stepped up to the microphone. He was slow to speak:

"God moves in mysterious ways, and I think the early death of these two fine young men exemplifies the meaning of this expression. Those of you who attended the services Monday afternoon heard Reverend Watts say that at a time like this it seems rather futile to search for the words to express the feelings, because you're just not able to do it. On the other hand, there are certain things for which we can be thankful. I won't call them bright spots, because there are no bright spots in this tragedy. It's difficult to think of anything bright about it. But, there are some things for which we can be glad. We can be glad that these two men lived as long as they did, and we can be glad that they influenced our lives. I particularly remember Longfellow's 'A Psalm of Life':

Lives of great men all remind us
We can make our lives sublime,
And, departing, leave behind us
Footprints on the sands of time.

Some might think that Longfellow was speaking of great men in history. But greatness is a relative matter. To me, these men, too, were great, and they, too, left their footprints here in this community. I think they left footprints on the sands of time that will not wash away quickly. I know they'd be glad of one thing, that if they had to go, as God decreed, they went at a time when they were trying to do their best at the jobs that had been assigned to them. It was while trying to do that that they were taken. What a glorious way to go, when you must go, when you are sincerely and earnestly trying to do better and to help your kids do better.

That's the image that I like to think of when I think of these two fine young men. Things could be so much worse, so much worse. Another stanza of Longfellow's "A Psalm of Life" goes:

Life is real! Life is earnest!
And the grave is not its goal;
Dust thou art, to dust returnest,
Was not spoken of the soul."

Reverend Watts then stepped up to the podium. "I'm going to ask that we stand for a prayer in memory of these two fine young men. Let us pray.

Almighty God, Creator and Preserver of all mankind, Author of everlasting life. We thank Thee for the lives of Buryl Baty and Jerry Simmang. We thank Thee for their selfless devotion to beauty, for their concern for young people, for their willingness to sacrifice and work for their welfare. Above all we thank Thee for the assurance that these fine qualities do not end with the grave, that death is not the master of the house, but only the porter at the King's lodge, appointed to open the gate and allow the King's guests to come into the realm of eternal day. We thank Thee for this school, for these students that these young men loved so much. And we pray that somehow their spirit may continue to inspire and strengthen all who work and study and play together here. And so that what we do here may be a true and meaningful memorial to what they did here. In Jesus's name we pray, Amen."

"The assembly is now dismissed."[1]

31 Buryl Goes Home

"This must be a mistake!" Buryl's brother Albert cried in denial. "This can't be!"

Devastated siblings and family members rushed home to Paris. Al was so distraught that his wife Gwen had to help him into the car and drive him and their daughter Sheron back to Paris from their home in Wichita Falls. When they arrived, they joined the rest of the family to wait for Bo and Buryl's return. The wait seemed long, as word came that an El Paso memorial service on Monday would delay the arrival. Of course they understood, but they needed closure, and to comfort Bo. They were very concerned for her, especially now that she was pregnant.

On Tuesday, October 12, the Batys made a grueling trip back home. Buryl's body was accompanied by a military escort (good friend Jim Bowden was one of its uniformed members), as his veteran status warranted. James and Betty Jackson met the group at Love Field and drove Bo and her son the final two hours to Paris. A hearse followed with the casket and its military attendants.

Gerald Thomas Simmang, twenty-nine, was also accompanied back home by a military escort, his wife, and a son, and buried at the Fort Sam Houston National Cemetery in San Antonio, on October 13, 1954.

A huge crowd attended the Paris funeral service to bid farewell to their good friend and hometown hero. All had heavy hearts. Buryl's father slumped, while his mother sobbed. Coach Berry wept openly throughout the service. "I'd never seen Coach Berry, or any man, cry like that," Luke Abbett observed.

At the crowded gravesite was a monument that read,

ROBERT BURYL BATY: 5/24/24—10/9/54

THY LIFE WAS BEAUTY, TRUTH, GOODNESS AND LOVE.

In the following days and weeks, Bo could not overcome her grief. But caring for her son served to occupy her mind. She had to keep going.

Her son and unborn child depended on her. She again rented a house in Paris, on Clarksville Street, just a few blocks from Buryl's parents. Bo's mother tried to offer consolation: "You're still young, and you have lots of living left to do." But Bo did not truly grasp the real meaning of her mother's comment until she was much older and able to reflect back on her life. For now, she lived one day at a time, and the days were long. In Paris, everywhere she went and everywhere she looked, she saw Buryl.

Buryl's mother, Bobbie, was in deep shock over the loss of her beloved firstborn son. Her grief was intense. She would sleep for a while, then cry profusely, or sit quietly in a daze, staring. Al described his mother's despair as she lay on the bed crying, and his unsuccessful attempts to console her. She grieved unceasing for at least two years and never completely recovered from her son's untimely death.

Buryl's father, Burton, tried to remain stoic, as men of his era were expected to be. Those closest to him were aware that a part of him had died along with Buryl. But Burton had to carry on, to support the family. He continued to walk to work every morning and did so until he retired in the late 1960s. He did not express his feelings verbally, but everyone saw the sadness in his eyes.

Meanwhile, on October 15, the *El Paso Herald-Post* ran an article reporting on the driver of the truck that had brought so much grief to so many:

TRUCK DRIVER PAYS $500 FINE; FREED FROM JAIL

Robert Moore, 19, of Spur, who pleaded guilty of negligent homicide in the deaths of Bowie High School Coaches Buryl Baty and Jerry Simmang, has been set free from Sierra Blanca jail after paying a $500 fine.

Relatives paid his fine.

Moore was driving the truck that smashed head-on into the car carrying Coaches Baty, Simmang, and Fred Rosas on Highway 80 East, five miles east of the El Paso-Hudspeth County line Oct. 8.

Baty and Simmang were killed instantly. Rosas was injured.

Moore was charged with negligent homicide. He said he fell asleep at the wheel of the truck. Judge Tom Neely of Sierra Blanca sentenced him to a fine of $500.

Moore was hauling a load of cottonseed from Deming, N. M. to Spur for his employer, M. M. Copeland, owner of the truck.

Judge Neely had visited Moore's jail cell and determined that, because the nineteen-year-old was distraught and remorseful, he should go free. Robert Moore walked away the next day.

Life as the Bowie Bears knew it had come to a standstill. The person central to their identity as a team and to their developing sense of manhood was suddenly, inexplicably gone. All that remained was a gnawing emptiness and their powerful memories. They began to realize that their relationship with their coach had run broad and deep; it had been about more than just football. And the question that hung on every lip was, "What now?"

Giya was in a daze, totally shaken. The first week after the accident, standing glassy-eyed outside the gym at lunch break, he overheard one gang member saying to another, "It's good that Baty's gone. He won't be around to bother us anymore." Within seconds, Giya was on top of the kid, slugging him mercilessly.

> I beat the hell out of that kid. Two people had to pull me off him.—Guillermo "Giya" Olivas

Coach Rosas was in critical condition in the hospital. Both legs and an arm were suspended in casts. With his shattered jaw he could barely speak, but he repeatedly asked about his fellow coaches. He received no answers. Finally, Mrs. Rosas decided it was time to tell him the bad news. "Oh, no! Oh, my God!" he cried.

Nemo Herrera and Lou Robustelli were named interim football coaches, and they were determined to do their best. Herrera announced that he was "going to make some changes." A number of players protested. Bomba Gonzalez yelled above the crowd, "This is Baty's team, and we don't want to change anything!" Coach Herrera and Coach Robustelli stepped away for a few moments, then returned. "Okay, have it your way," Herrera agreed. "I'll just show up." The boys practiced intently for the next game. But the locker room felt strangely empty.

The Bears resolved to win all of their remaining games for their departed coaches. Coach Rosas and his wife listened, sadly, to the radio broadcast of the next game from the hospital room. Their Bears led at halftime. Just before the second half began, the solemn, melancholy tones of "Taps" sounded across the stadium. On the field, players cried before gathering themselves to continue the game. Coach and Mrs. Rosas wept for the entire evening.

Ray Sanchez described the show that Bowie put on at halftime in the Bears' game with the Tigers:

El Paso Herald-Post, October 27, 1954
By the Way

That was a beautiful show put on by the Bowie band and corps during halftime of the Bruin-El Paso High game Friday.

The stadium was packed. It was one of the biggest—if not THE biggest—crowds ever to watch a prep game in El Paso. The huge crowd in itself was a tribute to the late Buryl Baty and Jerry Simmang. It was because of them many turned out.

The most impressive part of the crowd was the magnificent silence of it while the Bowie band performed during the half. Imagine, over 14,000 people gathered in one place and not a solitary sound out of it.

And there probably wasn't a dry eye in the lot either. Many cried unashamedly while the Bowie band marched, without music and with drumsticks beating only on the rim.

If the harder-hearted ones weren't choked up by the silence or the marching they finally broke down when two Bowie trumpets went into action at the end of the performance.

One boy stood at the high part of the stadium and blew taps while another boy stood across the stadium in the lower section and echoed the music.

Everyone there felt the presence of Jerry and Buryl at that moment.

After the band's heartrending performance, the game was effectively finished. El Paso High won the game in the second half. The Bears lost their competitive edge, and it was gone for the rest of the season. Their intensity and focus were pushed aside by grief.

The outcome of the game generated a flood of emotion. Players were devastated that they had let their former coaches down. And the feeling was not limited to the players. After the game, the band and cheerleaders boarded their bus for the trip back to the south side of town. One distraught girl shouted angrily, "Why didn't the team win this for the coaches, in their memory? The team let them down!" Another girl stood and punched her in the eye with a right fist.

For the rest of the season, in an effort to rekindle the Bears' doused fire, Robustelli would repeatedly shout, "Play the Baty game!" But the Bears' heart was gone. Robustelli and Herrera were fine coaches who were in an almost impossible situation. Basketball and baseball were their games, not football. They tried, but they could not develop the credibility or rapport of the previous coaches. The players resisted changes, and hostilities toward the substitute coaches festered. Segundo Barrio priest Father Rham (who had watched Baty's drills for four years) led prayers in the locker room and tried to help guide practices. But these well-meaning men were unable to buoy up the players' fragile emotions and confidence. The team was rudderless.

Coach Rosas had months, and years, to reflect on the loss of his good friends. During many subsequent discussions, he recounted his offer to exchange seats with his boss that night. "If Coach Baty had not declined my offer . . . *Sin la gracia de Dios, yo iria alli*. (There but for the grace of God go I)." Rosas repeated these words for the rest of his life.

For years Nell, wearing his letter sweater, continued to wait outside the locker room for Coach Baty on Friday afternoons.

33 Lots of Living Left to Do

Bo enrolled in Paris Junior College. As a single mother, she would need a degree. While she attended classes, Burton and Bobbie took care of their grandson. Burton took Gaines on long afternoon walks and shared in his boyish enthusiasm for the evening TV episode of *Gunsmoke*. June frequently accompanied them to the neighborhood park for entertainment. There children rode in the passenger cars of a child-sized train pulled by an engine and followed by a red caboose, on a track that circled the park. In addition, a miniature golf course was a magnet to kids from blocks away.

Meanwhile, Coach Baty was still remembered in El Paso, where on April 30, 1955, he was honored posthumously at a dinner for retiring coaches:

El Paso Herald-Post
KLEINFELD TO RECEIVE BATY PLAQUE

Saul Kleinfeld, one of El Paso's leading boosters of sports, will receive the late Buryl Baty's plaque at the Coaches' Dinner Tuesday in Franco's Café.

Mrs. Baty, who is now living in Paris, Tex., was to receive the plaque. However, because she is expecting a child, she will be unable to attend. She wired Mr. Kleinfeld, a friend of the Batys, to accept the plaque in her honor.

"I'm thrilled to do it," Kleinfeld said.

Mrs. Baty, in her wire, said: "He (Kleinfeld) was a very good friend of Buryl's and one to whom I am deeply grateful for his kindness and courtesies to me. May I also take this opportunity to thank all the nice people of El Paso who have helped in so many ways to make my burden easier to bear. God bless each of you.". . .

Sisters Alta and Glenda returned to Paris to support Bo during the birth of her second child. Lawrence Buryl Baty was born June 1, 1955. When the blanketed newborn was carried from the nursery for display to the family, Alta began to weep. The nurse implored her, "Don't let Bo see you crying!"

The next year, the Buryl Baty Award was established at Paris High School to acknowledge each year's best athlete. Bo and Gaines attended the first award dedication. Coach Berry spoke with tears in his eyes and through many long, silent, choked-up pauses. As he held the big trophy in front of the packed auditorium, he said, "Buryl Baty was a great player here at Paris High School—one of the best we've ever had. He became a great player at Texas A&M, a great coach, and a great man. Any student-athlete should be honored to win this award—not only because it will designate the best senior athlete at PHS each year, but also because it bears the name of Buryl Baty."

Buryl Baty awards were also established and presented at Bowie High School. Enrique Camacho and Tony Lujan, two of Bowie's best players, were honored and proud to accept these initial awards bearing Coach Baty's name.

Bo's family and friends marveled at how strong Bo appeared to be in the face of her tragic loss.

We never got over Buryl's death.—Glenda Foote and Jean Luttrell (Bo's younger sisters)

Bo was strong through all this. She was stronger than we were.—Alta Loven (Bo's older sister)

"In spite of what my sisters claim, I'm not doing that well," Bo confided to close friends, tears in her eyes. "I think of Buryl all the time. I don't know if I can live without him. What am I going to do?" She was overwhelmed by uncertainty and fear about her future. How was she to make it as the single mother of two boys? Although she masked her despair, seldom giving a hint of her emotions to other people, she nevertheless cried herself to sleep many nights, for many months, for many years.

The trial only made things worse. Bo, Ruth Simmang, and Coach Rosas had filed damage lawsuits against the trucking company whose driver had caused the accident and against the cottonseed company whose goods it was hauling. In July of 1955, the judge in charge of the case, Roy Jackson, refused to move the venue out of the county. Bo suffered painfully during the proceedings. In front of a jury, the defendant's legal team referenced the payment that Buryl's father, Burton, had received when he lost his arm, and claimed that "the Baty family has plenty of money and does not need more." In reality, Burton's minimal injury compensation was completely irrelevant to this case. Ultimately, the jury decided in the company's favor, and Bo was granted nothing. Zero. Bo's lawyer vehemently contended that "The seed company is clearly in the wrong. This should have been an open-and-shut case." Bo never talked about the trial, and nobody in the family knew if she had won or lost the case. She pushed forward.

On October 9, 1955, the one-year anniversary of Buryl's passing, Bo asked her sister Glenda to join her for a movie. "I just can't sit at home alone tonight." Their mother, Opal, babysat with the children while the two sisters went out. They ate at the only open restaurant in town and rushed to the movie. It happened to be a sad one—not a good choice for that particular night. "We both cried like babies," Glenda remembered.

There were days when Bo felt so distraught, so alone, and so hopeless that she could barely find the strength to climb out of bed in the morning. She felt like giving up. But she had two young boys who needed her. She had to keep going. Sometimes that meant just putting one foot in front of the other, confronting one day at a time.

Bo persevered. She continued her schooling, and after graduating from North Texas State University, she bought a home in Dallas and became a teacher at Samuel High School. She would later earn her master's degree at SMU.

When Bo remarried in 1960, she was careful to choose a man who would be a good father to her sons. This man was Gene "Red" Hudson, a high school principal and a coach, and Buryl's former Paris High School teammate on the championship squad of 1941. Buryl's mother, Bobbie, responded to Bo's wedding announcement with the acknowledgment, "It hurts—but if you're going to remarry, we're glad it's Red. He's a good man."

Red was, in fact, a great man and a great father. He loved and guided Larry and Gaines as if they were his own blood. He made a good life for them; he did all the things Buryl had looked forward to doing—he loved them, provided for them, taught them to be men—he hunted and fished with them, taught them to play football and baseball, took them to carnivals and ball games and stuffed them with hotdogs there, corrected them when they were wrong, stood up for them when they were right. He set a good example, as evidenced by the fact that a Garland, Texas, middle school is named for him. He and Bo lived a good life together. They supported their two boys. They went to church, they socialized with many close friends, they traveled during summer vacations. Red loved and supported Bo until the day he died.

Bo surely had her fears and frailties, and a lingering sense of loss and longing. But she was a loving role model and always projected a strong resolve; she was a Rock of Gibraltar for her two sons. She did, as her mother had predicted, have a lot of living left to do. She and Red became pillars of their community. She taught and inspired students for twenty-eight years. And she loved Red.

Time passed. And some memories faded. But we did not stop thinking about Buryl.

34 Coincidence or Providence?

1966

Gaines Baty was sixteen when his South Garland High School football team travelled to Paris to play the Wildcats. South Garland brought a good team, which created its fair share of interest. However, much of the buzz around the game rose from the fact that Buryl Baty's son would be playing in his father's hometown against his father's alma mater. Paris was excited about the Friday-night matchup.

Bo was noticeably nervous all week long. This game, while she looked forward to it in many ways, had already reopened painful wounds and dug up sad memories from twelve short years earlier.

The Paris High stadium was packed on this cool Friday night. Many of Buryl's former teammates were in attendance, as were old friends and admirers. As Gaines waited in the visitors' locker room before the game, he was told that someone wanted to see him. Waiting just outside the door were Bo and Red, his stepfather, and an older man who was introduced as Raymond Berry, Buryl's former coach. Bo and Red had arranged the meeting at Coach Berry's request.

"You look just like your daddy," Berry said, clasping Gaines's hand with a grip that was still strong. "I understand you're a fine player, and I know he'd be proud of you. Good luck tonight, son." As Gaines shook Coach Berry's hand, he felt a stab of emotion, an unfamiliar emotion. Gaines brushed it off and hustled back to rejoin his team in preparation for the game.

As the teams took the field just before the opening kickoff, the play-by-play announcer's voice boomed loudly through the public address system. "Ladies and gentlemen, we have an important announcement. Tonight, playing for the South Garland Colonels, will be one of our own. Wearing number 44 and starting at linebacker is Gaines Baty, the son of former Paris Wildcat great, Buryl Baty."

The crowd responded with a loud, long standing ovation.

After the game, Coach Berry again shook Gaines's hand outside his team's victorious locker room. "You played a fine game, son. You have a great future ahead of you."

Not only Coach Berry's comments, but also his warmth, clearly demonstrated a strong connection with Gaines. Perhaps he related well with Buryl's son because he had, at eight years old, also lost his father. More than twenty years later, the coach closed a letter to Gaines with the words, "I have always been proud of you, and feel like you are also one of my boys."

1970 and 1972

The family was in a state of high anticipation awaiting Gaines's first varsity game at Texas Tech. Bo, Red, Larry, and Aunt Alta and Uncle CI drove to Lubbock to see it. As the opening kickoff neared, Tech's colorful and spirited pregame fanfare buoyed their excitement. Then the band struck up the dramatic chords of the Raider fight song. To the delight of the cheering crowd, the mascot black stallion and masked rider reared up, and then galloped onto the field with the Red Raiders close behind. Among the red-clad squad was Gaines, unaware that the number he was wearing, 84, had been his father's number at Paris High. Bo, watching in the stands, felt a rush of emotion. The coincidence was not lost on her. Or was it coincidence?

Gaines's Texas Tech squads went on to earn postseason berths in the Sun Bowl in El Paso in 1970 and then again in 1972. On the first occasion, December 30, 1970, Bob Ingram of the *Herald-Post* recalled Buryl to his readers:

> It was a pleasure to meet Gaines Baty, 197-pound defensive end for the Red Raiders. Baty is from Garland, Texas, but was born in El Paso. His father was Buryl Baty, who was fresh out of Texas A & M and coached at Bowie High School about 20 years ago.
>
> He was one of the brightest and most popular coaches El Paso has ever had in fact. Gaines was only four years old when his father Buryl and another coach here were killed in a car wreck while they were on a scouting mission. The tragedy cast a cloud of gloom over El Paso athletics.

On the second appearance of Texas Tech at the Sun Bowl, in 1972, Coach Fred Rosas and several of Coach Baty's former players greeted Gaines at the airport, and in front of newspaper photographers and reporters, presented him with a plaque honoring his father—a special tribute to their beloved coach. On it was inscribed:

BURYL BATY
1950–1954
APPRECIATION AWARD
ON BEHALF OF THE BOWIE BOOSTER CLUB
FOR SERVICES RENDERED TO BOWIE HIGH SCHOOL
AND ITS COMMUNITY BY A GREAT LEADER AND COACH
PRESENTED TO HIS SON
GAINES BATY
12–28–72
EL PASO, TEXAS

The Tech team was then paraded to their hotel in fine limousines that were labeled "Texas Tech Red Raiders." Signs on the passenger doors of the limo in which Gaines was driven read: "Gaines Baty, son of Buryl Baty."

Well before he had even arrived in El Paso with the Red Raiders for the game in late December, a faithful friend of Buryl's, Sam Jenkins, had reminded the city of the event with a letter to the editor in the *Herald-Post:*

December 14, 1972
Editor: Long time fans of Bowie High School football will be interested to hear about one of Texas Tech University's fine football players who will be playing in the Sun Bowl December 30. Gaines Baty is a first string defensive end who has been honored on All-Southwest Conference teams this year.

Gaines is the son of Buryl Baty, who was a quarterback at Texas A&M in the late 1940's. After graduating from Texas A&M he came to El Paso to coach at Bowie High School in the early 50's. He and an assistant coach, Jerry Simmang, were killed in an unfortunate automobile accident while returning from a scouting mission for their team and school. Coach Fred Rosas, another fine coach, survived the accident.

I had the privilege of being a close and personal friend of Buryl Baty, both at Texas A&M, and in El Paso in the 1950's. I can honestly say that this man was one of the finest persons I ever knew, and anyone who attended his funeral and saw the grief felt by the Bowie Football Team at that time, would know the type of leader and man that he was.

It is a well known fact in El Paso that Bowie football fans support their team to the utmost. I trust they will be interested in this information on Gaines Baty.—Sam Jenkins.

During the days in El Paso leading up to the bowl game, old friends and former players of Buryl's, and countless other well-wishers, introduced themselves to Gaines as friends of his father's. And the night after the actual game, a number of former Bowie players hosted a reception at a restaurant in the Segundo Barrio. There many stories were exchanged about the good old days with Coach Baty. This was an eye-opener to Gaines, a connection to the stories his mother had always told him.

Summer 1998

In the early summer of 1998, as Madine Bailey was pushing her tray in the line of an El Paso cafeteria, she overheard the conversation of three Hispanic men just in front of her. One of them said, "We need to find the Batys. They might want to attend."

Mention of the Baty name captured Madine's attention. She and her husband Alton (an Aggie himself) were originally from Paris and had lived in El Paso since college. They had frequently socialized with Bo and Buryl in El Paso and had hosted Glenda, Harry, and their daughter Anita during the nights immediately after Buryl's death.

She bent around to catch the eye of the speaker. "I don't mean to eavesdrop, but you're looking for the Batys? Do you mean Buryl Baty's family?"

"Yes, ma'am. We played on his team at Bowie High, and we're dedicating our stadium in his name. We'd like to find the family and tell them about it."

Madine shook her head. "I don't know if this is a huge coincidence or a stroke of providence, but I know his family. One of my best friends is Mrs. Baty's sister Glenda. I can get a phone number for you." Within a day, Madine had sought out Bo's, Larry's, and Gaines's numbers and passed them on to the former players from La Bowie.

It was not long before Gaines's phone rang. "My name is Raul Gonzalez," said a Hispanic voice on the other end. "I played on your dad's football team at Bowie High School."

Gaines was speechless. The El Paso football team had never seemed entirely real to him. It had been far away in both time and place, and even his brief encounter with the Bowie players at his Sun Bowl game was twenty-six years past. But now the past was reaching out to him over a telephone line.

"After forty-four years of trying," Raul said, "we've finally gotten approval from the school board to name our stadium after your dad and Coach Simmang. We're having a formal dedication this fall, and we'd like for you and your family to attend."

That October, Gaines and Larry flew to El Paso for the dedication, which was staged around the Friday-night homecoming festivities. Raul and Mary Gonzalez met them at the airport and drove them to the stadium. "We still think and talk about Coach Baty," Raul said. "We still love him. He's still with us."

Several hundred energetic people were in attendance at the stadium. Personal cameras flashed while television cameras and reporters recorded the events of the evening. Bowie's principal, the school-board president, and the city mayor all gave speeches. Coach Fred Rosas shared a few words from the heart. Many men wore white football jerseys with royal blue numerals, indicating that they had played on "Coach Baty's" team. These men offered warm handshakes to Coach Baty's two sons and treated them like celebrities. This was clearly a great occasion in El Paso. It was reported that more people showed up at the dedication of Bowie High School's stadium to Buryl Baty and Jerry Simmang than attended George Bush's Texas gubernatorial debate that same night in the same town.

All the local television stations swooped in on the event. The features they ran that night focused on a lively, diverse crowd of people laughing and talking and enjoying themselves, with cheerleaders cheering and the lively brass sounds of a band in the background. KVIA Television's ten o'clock news observed that among the celebrants on the occasion—Bowie High School's seventy-fifth anniversary—were Buryl Baty and Jerry Simmang's players, who were here to see the stadium renamed and rededicated in their coaches' honor.

The next afternoon Gaines and Larry attended the pregame home-coming activities at Bowie High. Dozens of Hispanic men in their sixties introduced themselves. It was as though they were close family members, and they held the sons in great esteem. Of course, it was not the brothers, but their father who was revered. These men were honoring Coach Baty in the only way available to them—through his sons. And, although no one realized it at the time, they were fueling Gaines's curiosity about his father.

The former players all told stories about their beloved coach. For many, when they talked about him, about the shock of his death and the sense of loss and emptiness that had followed it, tears welled in their eyes. They laughed heartily when describing their experiences with his paddle. And their pride in what they had accomplished together was unmistakable.

Coach Baty had helped develop the kids of so many years ago into winners. He had shown them how to succeed. He had refused to tolerate their mistreatment at a time when they could not fight the battle themselves. He had given them tools with which to pursue and fight for what was rightfully theirs.

And these men had persevered. As leaders of the community, they were not the victims they might have been in their parents' era. They could now speak out vigorously to make themselves heard. And one thing they had long wanted to make heard was their gratitude to their old coach. They had wanted to honor him in a meaningful and lasting way. And they had finally won what they had pushed so hard for. It had not been easy.

Bobby Cordova, Leo Muñoz, Tony Lujan, Raul Gonzales, Manny Morales, Ernie Perea, and many others made the renaming of the stadium possible. Previous attempts had come to nothing. Finally, these former players had gone en masse to a school board meeting and presented a resolution. The stadium's renaming was approved, but no funding was granted to make it happen. Consequently the alums had put up over $2,000 of their own money to defray the expenses that were later reimbursed with the proceeds of a fund-raising dance and reunion of classmates from the era. Expenditures included an artist's magnificent mural rendering of their three Bowie coaches, a crane that was required to hang the mural, and the cost of painting the sign on the top of the stadium. To the former Bowie Bears' credit, the Baty-Simmang Memorial Stadium dedication was a grand success.

It was on this occasion that Gaines first became consciously aware of seeing his father "through the eyes of others" (as Bob St. John's *Dallas Morning News* story in 1998 headlined it).[1]

October 2004

Gaines was referred to Red Burditt, one of Buryl's former Aggie teammates and friends, in the summer of 2004. As the organizer of 1940s-era Aggie team communications and get-togethers, Burditt invited Gaines to a 2004 Texas A&M old-timers' football reunion. There Gaines was introduced to Aggie traditions, spirit, and former football lettermen. He met and talked with several of his father's former teammates, and got a small taste of what it might have been like to be an Aggie. And of what his father might have felt like going back to a game for a reunion. Many of these old players' recollections are embedded in this book.

March 2013

In 2013, Coach Buryl Baty was elected to the El Paso Athletic Hall of Fame. Larry and Gaines Baty accepted the award on their father's behalf, with several former Bowie Bears in attendance. These included Tony Lujan, Leo Muñoz, Giya Olivas, former Coach David Rodriguez, former manager Carlos "Cachi" Torrez, and Bobby Cordova (the former quarterback who had been thrown off the 1952 team). Reporter Ray Sanchez attended and wrote of the event in the next day's press. About his old friend Coach Buryl Baty, he concluded:

"He began an amazing and glorious era here. His name lives on."

35 Found Treasures—A Look into a Soul

2002

After a happy, full, and productive life with Red, her two sons, her extended family, and many loving friends, Bo was diagnosed with Alzheimer's and passed away in March of 2002. During her final weeks and months, consistent with this disease, she frequently mistook her sons for her beloved Buryl, asking them about his train trip in the military or about his players, today's practice, and the upcoming football game.

Shortly after her death, sons Larry and Gaines discovered a small package in her safe deposit box that Bo had kept hidden for all these years. Stashed away for safekeeping, and for her eyes only, were Buryl's personal effects that the state troopers had handed her at the end of that terrible night in October of 1954.

These personal effects included Buryl's wedding ring, his Texas A&M senior ring (Class of 1946), a pocketknife, and his wallet. The wallet contained military credentials, football plays diagramed onto a small sheet of folded paper, a clipping of a prayer, and pictures of his wife and son.

On the back of her picture, Bo had written a note to Buryl:

How can I think of anything sweet enough to say?
To the one I Love.
Yours, "Bo"
P.S. Guess you already know that I love you.

The prayer in his wallet had been clipped from a magazine:

An Athlete's Prayer
My God, my one Head Coach Divine,
Guide me through my life's playing time.
Teach me how to play the game

Only in a sporting vein.
Endow me with the will to win,
With a spirit striving from within.
And Coach, teach me as I live and learn
To expect, only, what I rightly earn.
Quitting never, though discouraged be,
Ever true to self, to team, to Thee.
Keep me clean in speech and thought,
In doing, and in living as I ought.
Of hate and envy keep me free,
For a more deserving man than me.
Prepare me now in friendly strife
On the playing field of life.
And someday, Master Coach Supreme,
Let me play on your great team.

Buryl Baty now plays on this great team.

Afterword

I have only vague memories of my dad. I faintly remember a few experiences: his last Christmas, standing on the Bowie practice field, our hunting trip together, and walking in on my crying mother on that fateful night. I still feel the sense of longing that began at that moment.

I've always felt a spiritual connection with him. And, in a way, I've felt his presence. Perhaps he was looking over me all these years. And, I feel, during the writing of this story.

Since I was a child, I have heard brief comments about his character and heroics: "Your dad was a great man" or "Your dad was a great player." My mother briefly described, with pride, highlights of his accomplishments—his touchdown pass to tie the Longhorns, and the Snyder restaurant incident. But I didn't ask many questions. And my mother was discreet out of sensitivity and respect for my step-dad, himself a fine man and father.

I always wondered why. Why was this great man taken from us? He was full of life, passion, and dreams. He was strong and inspired almost everyone he met. Was it simply a random, unfortunate event out on some dark road? Or was there a reason?

I wondered what he was like, how things might have been different had he lived, how I might have been different.

And while growing up, I had a sense that I would die young, like my father. I perceived this as my destiny.

As I grew older I talked of learning more about my dad. Still, life called with a family to feed and raise, my kids' teams to coach, and a business to build. And a round of golf. One day I'd do it, though.

As time passed, a series of unrelated incidents built momentum for my quest to learn more. At my step-dad's funeral in 1986, an older man extended his strong grip and said softly, "I feel like I'm looking at Buryl. You're the spittin' image of your father." I wasn't sure who was speaking to me until he introduced himself as Coach Raymond Berry. I was so taken aback that I couldn't respond. I could only nod and smile back at him. We did talk on a couple of occasions afterwards, and I have a beautiful letter that he wrote to me. But I wish I had asked more questions.

Later, the announcement of the 1998 El Paso Bowie stadium dedication seized my full attention. Raul Gonzalez's words on the phone that night slapped me in the face with a lost chapter in my life. Or, more accurately, a missing piece of my soul. At the dedication, every player's anecdote revealed a little piece of my dad, for whom I'd longed my entire life. These men had shared an intimacy with him that I could only envy. They provided me with a connection to him, and stimulated a flood of dormant emotions from deep inside. Until that day, this part of my life—the part shared with my father—had not seemed real.

Also at the dedication, a quiet gentleman introduced himself to me: Coach Fred Rosas. His still-black hair and dark features might have associated him with the former players in attendance, but he seemed to have a more mature presence. I knew he had a unique perspective, and I wanted to speak with him longer, and while alone. However, our time was brief and hurried. I greatly regret not talking with Coach Rosas in more depth when the opportunity presented itself.

Third, in 2004, a 1940s-era Aggie player reunion facilitated another set of perspectives with which to fill my huge void of information. My dad's former Aggie teammates all had memories to reflect upon and stories to tell. I gained meaningful insight into who my dad was and validation of what he stood for.

Then, I read a book titled *Twelve Mighty Orphans*, by Jim Dent. Seeing mention of my father's name in this book hit me like a brick. "My dad's story is as inspirational as the one I'm reading," I decided.

And on the night of November 13, 2008, Buryl Baty's name was blasted out on the Paris High School stadium loudspeakers . . . again. A young Paris Wildcat quarterback had finally broken one of his sixty-seven-year-old passing records.

These "signs" repeatedly pressed me. Finally, it was clear that I needed to meet my dad. And to tell his story.

So began a new journey to a place that had subconsciously possessed me since childhood. It has been an enlightening and emotional journey that may never be fully completed.

I had no preconceived notions about this story, its structure, or its themes. I simply felt that something could come from it and documented everything I could learn. I interviewed over one hundred people—family, friends, teammates, classmates, players, students, fellow coaches, opponents, various news reporters, and fans. Every event mentioned in this narrative actually took place—as described by written documentation or someone's firsthand, if hazy, knowledge of the incident. I merely pieced the facts and stories together. The rest took care of itself. But it was not me writing the story. Something or someone else flowed through me.

I was touched on many levels:

- Memories—Through it all, I couldn't help reflecting on that fuzzy, distant memory, that of the most significant event of my life.
- Curiosity—What was my dad like? How did he think? What were his weaknesses? His faults? What part of me is really him?
- Excitement—when I learned about him, talked to someone who knew him, heard of his influence and legacy.
- Inspiration—I was inspired by what he stood for, the words he spoke, and the lessons he taught. I also realized that these same inspirations could be valuable to my own kids, and their kids.
- Emotion—Even the simplest of comments could bring tears to my eyes—such as "You look just like your dad," or "He would have been proud of you."
- Questions—Was this early and untimely death in reality some sort of an 'exclamation point' for those so touched and inspired by him?
- Closure on my repressed sense of loss—My wife, Keri, suggested that since I was at the time so young and so protected from the tragedy, I may be finally experiencing the grieving process. I believe that she is correct.

During my research I spoke with Ms. Jo Nell Tenney, a 1949 Luling High School student of my dad's. Coincidentally, she'd lost her father at age ten. In late 2009, at age seventy-eight, she told me she had "missed her dad for sixty-eight years." I could relate. I had missed my dad since I was four years old, almost sixty years ago.

Upon reflection now benefited by time, I believe that this tragedy did serve a great purpose. An ordinary man in an ordinary job had induced extraordinary changes in people's lives. Many uncontrollable forces shape human lives. On the other hand, some individuals are strong forces in self-creation. He was one of these people. His shocking loss, from that day forward, permanently etched these lessons into his players' hearts. Those stunned boys clung to their experience of him all their lives, and player after player told me, unprompted, that he had passed on Coach Baty's principles to his own children. In Longfellow's words, he left his footprints on the sands of time.

Coach Baty stood for his players like no one had before. With courage and leadership in confronting his contemporaries, and possibly his own upbringing, he fought prejudice and the apathy that kept it afloat. From this genesis, the boys realized that they had rights and should fight for them, and that no one should inhibit the lives they wanted to live. No one could stand in the way of what they wanted to achieve. And they could achieve anything. In a profound manner, good had triumphed over evil: respect, dignity, honor, and sportsmanship over discrimination and contempt.

Again, through reflection, I remember my mother waiting up for me late into the night, many nights. As a teenager, I'd enter the back door as quietly as possible, hoping to sneak into bed unnoticed. There, at the kitchen table, she'd be waiting. She never scolded me. She never seemed mad. I sensed only nervous concern, and a hint of sadness. "It's dangerous out late at night. Something bad could happen to you," she would say. At the time, to a self-centered kid, her concern seemed to represent only a worried mother's unfounded protective instinct. Until now I never realized that my late-night arrivals likely forced her to relive the nightmare and fear of that fateful night in 1954. I wish I could take those nights back. Mom, I'm sorry for doing that to you.

I also understand now why she chose not to return to El Paso for the stadium dedication. As proud and strong as she was, participation would have thrown her headfirst into the middle of her most painful experience and brought back her most feared emotions.

Fortunately, family and friends of family have felt compelled to help me understand my history. Still, many details remain sketchy, or lost. I regret that many close to my parents are no longer with us. At the same time, I'm amazed at the number of people who knew or knew of Buryl Baty, and who still speak so highly of him. His influence should continue.

I did not know my father well, or for very long. Now, I've finally met him. I realize that he is alive inside me, and inside my children. And he has inspired me. This man lives in the hearts of many, and in eternity. I'm proud to pass on his inspiration to future generations.

I'm proud to be his son.

Acknowledgments

My Thanks to . . .

Robert Buryl Baty—for lifelong inspiration and strength. May your legacy live on.

Bettie "Bo" Hutchinson Baty Hudson—for your love and strength, and for keeping me in touch with my dad.

Larry—this is a gift to you: Our father, through the eyes of others.

Gene "Red" Hudson, my second father—for your quiet example, love, strength, and guidance; for loving and leading us as your own, and for allowing us to be who we were.

My many great coaches—who pushed me to my limit, and provided many of the lessons my dad wanted to teach me.

Buryl's family, friends, teammates, players—for sharing your knowledge of and your devotion to my dad. Former Paris teammates and friends who were instrumental include James Jackson, Luke Abbett, LV Morrow, JW Ashmore, James Barnett, Ollie Jack, and Bill Booth. And, of course, thanks to Raymond Berry for his insights into his father and the great Paris Wildcats of that era. Aggie team members who helped include Jim Cashion, Bob Gary, Warren Gilbert, Sam Jenkins, Butch Butchofsky, Red Burditt, Herb Turley, Charlie Royalty, Sam Moses, Barney Welch, James "Radio" Wiley, Don Nicholas, Charles Yeargain, and Hulin Smith.

Special gratitude goes to former Bowie players, coaches, and managers—for keeping the fire alive: Tony Lujan, Bobby Cordova, Juan "Baca" Mendoza, Enrique Camacho, Albert Lujan, Ernesto "Ernie" Perez, Daniel Baca, David Archuleta, Alfonso Del Toro, Raul "Bomba" Gonzales, Carlos Gonzales, Tony Carmona, Leo Muñoz, Julio Jauregui, Juan Mier, Eduardo Camacho, José "Joe" Cordova, Eduardo Reyes, Fernando Gonzalez, Jesus "Jesse" Martinez, José R. Turrieta, Ed Turrieta, Arturo Lightbourn, David Canales, Pete Salvidar, Guillermo "Giya" Olivas, Tony Franco, Father Edmundo "Rod" Rodriguez, Bobby Molina, Miguel Vasquez, Refugio "Cuco" Martinez, Frank "Panchito" Martinez, Juan Aranda, Oscar Duenez, Juan Antonio Ortiz, Alfonso Burciaga, Hector Peña, Francisco Avila, Salvador "Sal" Garcia, Antonio "Tony" Lara, Fernie Lara, Joe

Jordan, David Holguin, Manny Morales, Benny Landin, Jerry, Manny and Bobby Maldonado, Don Melendez, Medardo "Lalo" Ortiz, Tommy Zepeda, Mike Vasquez, Narcisco Trillo, Carlos "Cachi" Torret, and many others, and to Coach David Rodriguez, Coach Fred Rosas, and Mary Louise Rosas. This is your story.

Contributing former Luling Eagle players—including Eddie Halford, James Knippa, Ralph Smith, Charles Bullock, Larry Hoskins, and Jerry Patillo.

My family—Keri, Ryan, Robbie, and Jacque for your patience, assistance, critiques, encouragement, inspiration. Thanks also to my parents' family members Glenda and Harry Foote, Alta Loven, Jean Luttrell, Dub Hutchinson, Zelma Baty Barrett, Al Baty, and June Alexander for your help. This is written for you all.

My outstanding editors, Susan Rolfe and Margret Kerbaugh—I appreciate your friendship, your passion for Buryl Baty, and your great work.

Those who helped with this book in important ways—Joe Foran, Ray Sanchez, Raymond Berry, Michele Smyers, Bill Reed, Fran Vick, Russ Ingram, Roger Beynon, Jim Rolfe, Lana White, Donna Ingham, Skipper Steely, Ted Paup, and many patient manuscript readers.

Reflections of those touched by Coach Baty

"We still talk about his influence, to this day."—Raul Gonzalez

"He probably saved my life."—Ernie Perea

"He taught monumental lessons to me that have guided my life."
—Bobby Cordova

"We'd never considered the possibility that discrimination was wrong. Coach Baty showed us that we could, and should, stand up for ourselves. He was a true hero to us."—Tony Lujan

"He always stood up for us. For that he got more from us. We wanted to play hard for him."—Albert Lujan

"He confronted me about smoking, and what I smoked, and always checked up on me."—Enrique Camacho

"He gave us character and confidence. I continue to live by this and have tried to teach my own children the same. I believe his words are what helped me succeed in life."—David Archuleta

"He was a great man, a gentleman. He inspired me every time he spoke. He taught us to be proud, gave us hope. Buryl Baty was the best coach Bowie High School ever had. He is still with us."—Leo Muñoz

"We still talk about him. I taught my kids what Coach Baty taught us."
—Eduardo Camacho

"I went to Bowie to play football, and Coach Baty made me a better person. We loved him, and he loved us."—Juan Mier

"He changed our attitudes. He inspired us. I tasted victory and success, and learned that I could compete with others on the same playing field. He touched my heart and changed my life . . . my confidence, work ethic and ambitions. He was a role model for me, and I tried to follow his example."—José "Joe" Cordova

"We lost a hell of a man. I still dream of him."—Eduardo Reyes

"He was my hero then . . . and is still my hero now."
—Jesus "Jesse" Martinez

"He had a great impact on my life."—Arturo Lightbourn

"I try to live up to his example every day."—David Canales

"He was like a father to me. He taught us the difference between good and bad."—Tony Lujan

"It was a blessing that he came here to us. Coach Baty had a lot of heart."
—Pete Salvidar

"He left an important and very difficult decision up to us. This 'life lesson' helped us to grow up considerably."—Father Edmundo "Rod" Rodriguez

"I've played or watched games here for fifty-five years, and I'm sure that Coach Baty was the best coach ever in El Paso. He had a profound impact on my life. I passed those lessons to my kids. I pray that I'll see him again in Heaven, and that I'll be playing on his team."
—Guillermo "Giya" Olivas

"He turned my life around. I and my sons owe a lot to him. Coach Baty was sent to us from Heaven."—Alfonso Burciaga

"I preached to my kids the things I learned from Coach Baty."
—Salvador "Sal" Garcia

"He molded the moral fiber and determination in me that was the foundation of my life."—David Holguin

"He was our leader and beacon of light. At Bowie, we'd always been made to feel like we were second-class compared to the other schools. Coach Baty stood up for us and fought for us. He instilled pride in us. I appreciated his personal battle against prejudice. He brought hope, and helped us to believe that 'we're just as good as anybody, or better!'"
—Lucy (Rivas) Lucero, cheerleader

"Other coaches accepted discrimination as the norm. He fought it, which took guts."—Joseph Shepherd, Cathedral High School football player

"I was in awe of and learned so much from him. I played for several fine coaches in high school and college, and worked with and observed many more during my thirty-five-year coaching career. But I've never observed a better organized program and practices than Coach Baty's. He was a true leader. I believe he was the best football coach in El Paso history."
—Coach David Rodriguez

"Buryl Baty was 'legendary' . . . maybe the greatest football coach that Bowie ever had. When he came to Bowie, they were the football doormat here. He made an immediate difference. He created a glorious era for the team and school. He did more with less talent than any coach I've ever seen. He outthought and outfoxed opposing coaches. It was beautiful to watch. It was unbelievable how he captured El Paso's heart."
—Ray Sanchez

Coach Baty on Sports and Life

"Always strive to be better."

"The way you practice is the way you play. There is no substitute for good preparation."

"If you work harder and play tougher you can beat anybody. The same thing holds true in life."

"To win, you have to think . . . just like in life. And when you do, you can beat anybody."

"Sports is life in a nutshell. You get out of life what you put into it."

"You can go to hell for lying as well as for stealing."

"Never quit—keep fighting, keep going."

"With hard work anything can be accomplished."

It's called responsibility and accountability—you've got to do it—your teammates are counting on you."

"This will be a tough game, but you are tougher than they are."

"Hit 'em hard! And keep hitting them until you win this game!"

"Let's do what we came here to do."

"Are you afraid to get a few broken ribs?"

"Keep your nose clean. Go to church."

"You can make it on the outside, but first you need an education. Education is the way to rise above it."

"I don't want any dropouts on this team. I want you all to finish high school and go to college."

"Don't eat junk food . . . eat lots of fruit and vegetables."

"The game of football is like life . . . when you get knocked down, you get back up and go again."

"Do the right thing always."

"No matter who you are or where you're from, respect is where it all starts. Be respectful and respectable at all times."

"No matter what happens in your life, always stay positive and keep going."

"Sportsmanship: working hard and still having fun, accepting the good and the bad—as in life, and working through it all."

"There are no heroes-just players on a team . . . give respect to everybody. Work as a team."

"Always be on your best behavior. Be a role model. Set an example for others."

"Always play hard, but play fair and square."

"If it's hard, try harder."

"Just like life, there are only two ways to play: the right way and wrong way."

"You boys are going to give me ulcers."

"Rod, this is going to hurt me more than it is you."

"Never discriminate against another person, and never let a person treat you like you're not as good as him . . . but be under control. Never lower yourself to his level."

"Show these people that you're as good as they are."

"Nothing comes easy; you have to work for what you want. Without hard work you get nowhere."

"Give the best you've got, all the time, to achieve your goal. You want it . . . go get it!"

"Work hard and you'll appreciate your successes even more."

"Be strong mentally; don't allow outside influences to distract you from your goals."

"We have to learn from our mistakes and improve every day."

"Football is like life, and life is tough sometimes. But we will persevere."

"Go make your parents proud. Make your school proud. Make yourselves proud!"

"You can do anything if you believe in yourself. Go at it with all your heart, and never give up—you can do it!"

"Give it your best every day—everything you have! You'll never regret doing your best!"

Notes

Chapter 4

1. Raymond Emmett Berry did eventually emulate his childhood heroes by donning a Paris Wildcats' uniform and playing for his father. He later played college ball at SMU and professionally for the NFL Champion Baltimore Colts, subsequently being inducted into the NFL Hall of Fame. He also coached the New England Patriots to an AFC Championship and to their first Super Bowl. Throughout his successful career, Raymond Emmett Berry considered his father, Coach Raymond Berry, his greatest mentor.

Chapter 5

1. Quoted in Jim Dent, *Twelve Mighty Orphans: The Inspiring True Story of the Mighty Mites Who Ruled Texas Football* (New York: Thomas Dunne Books/St. Martin's Press, 2007), 227.

Chapter 9

1. See John A. Adams, *Keepers of the Spirit: The Corps of Cadets at Texas A&M University, 1876–2001* (College Station: Texas A&M University Press, 2011).
2. Ibid., 7.
3. Ibid., 81.
4. Tim Taliaferro, "The Rise, Fall, and Return of the Texas Cowboys" (*The Alcalde*, University of Texas Alumni Magazine, September/October 2008), 35.
5. Adams, *Keepers of the Spirit*, 81.

Chapter 10

1. In 1949, after a student vote, the name of the yearbook was changed from *The Longhorn* to *Aggieland*.

Chapter 12

1. Sergeant Baty's wartime journal was titled "My Diary" and began with an undated account of leaving Camp Maxey on the last of November, 1944. The final entry was August 15, 1945.

Chapter 13

1. General Patton stated, "Give me a company of West Pointers and I'll win a battle. Give me a handful of Aggies and I'll win a war." He commented that Otto Weygand (A&M Class of 1923, former Captain of the Aggie Band) was "the best damn general in the air corps!" [Henry C. Dethloff and John A. Adams, *Texas Aggies Go to War: In Service of Their Country* (College Station: Texas A&M University Press, 2008), 103–104.]

Chapter 14

1. In 1929 the Carnegie Foundation's report on football revealed subsidized athletics in 75 percent of all US colleges. Of course, football was the fabric of the southwest. Competitive schools' alums interacted in executive offices, country clubs, nightclubs, and churches. Many an alum lived and died by his school's football fortunes, and bragging rights were coveted. Red-faced alums were compelled to do whatever it took to change the pecking order, and their pocketbooks were their strongest levers. Nobody wanted to be on the bottom of the dog pile.

Chapter 15

1. H. C. Byler Jr., *Life at Aggieland in the 40's: The Life of a Cadet at Texas A.&M. College in the 1940's* (Bloomington, Indiana: Author-House, 2006), 50.

Chapter 17

1. This was in 1950, when the 1918 State of Texas "English only" law was in effect, well before the days of bilingual education. Principal Pollitt dictated that the law be enforced at Bowie High. Coach Baty was encouraging the type of behavior that would keep his athletes out of trouble and in school. The law was repealed in 1969.

Chapter 18

1. Carlsbad won the New Mexico State Championship in 1950 and 1951.

Chapter 19

1. This comment was originally credited to former Notre Dame Coach Knute Rockne.

Chapter 30

1. Transcript of memorial service recorded at Bowie High School's auditorium on October 12, 1954.

Chapter 34

1. Bob St. John, "Sons Get to See Dad through Eyes of Others," *Dallas Morning News,* November 24, 1998.

Sources

Books

Adams, John A. *Keepers of the Spirit: The Corps of Cadets at Texas A & M University, 1876–2001.* College Station: Texas A&M University Press, 2001.

Byler, H. C., Jr. *Life at Aggieland in the 40's: The Life of a Cadet at Texas A.&M. College in the 1940's.* Bloomington: AuthorHouse, 2006.

Cashion, Ty, and Bum Phillips. *Pigskin Pulpit: A Social History of Texas High School Football Coaches.* Austin: Texas State Historical Association, 2006.

Dent, Jim. *Twelve Mighty Orphans: The Inspiring True Story of the Mighty Mites Who Ruled Texas Football.* New York: Thomas Dunne/St. Martin's, 2007.

Dethloff, Henry C., and John A. Adams. *Texas Aggies Go to War: In Service of Their Country.* College Station: Texas A&M University Press, 2006.

Steely, Skipper, and J. T. Davis. *The Raymond Berry Years.* Paris, Texas: Wright Press, 1983.

Also Consulted

MAGAZINES

Taliaferro, Tim. "When the Smoke Cleared: The Rise, Fall, and Return of the Texas Cowboys." *The Alcalde,* University of Texas Alumni Magazine, September/October 2008.

ARCHIVES

Baty, Buryl. "My Diary," 1944–1945. In the possession of the author.

Hutchinson, Bettie Jo ("Bo"). Diary, January 1, 1939–June 15, 1943. In the possession of the author.

Memorial service at Bowie High School. Recording made October 12, 1954. In the possession of the author.

NEWSPAPERS
Austin American Statesman
Big Spring Daily Herald
Bryan-College Station Eagle
Dallas Morning News
Dallas Times Herald
El Paso Herald-Post
El Paso Times
Luling News Boy
Paris News

YEARBOOKS
A&M yearbook (*The Longhorn* until 1948; *Aggieland* thereafter)
Bowie High School yearbook: *The Aztec*
Paris High School yearbook: *The Owl*

Index

University of Arkansas (Razorbacks) games, 65
University of Texas (Longhorns) games
    1946 season, 61
    1947 season, 66–67
    1948 season, 77–81
    A&M rivalry with, 66, 118–19, 177
    Bowie students attend Tar Heels game, 109
    Shorthorns (freshmen), 44
    See also gallery 1
US Army Corps of Engineers, 48

vandalism by opposing teams, 27, 65
victory drives through Segundo Barrio, 158, 159, 166, 184
violence, gangs in El Paso, 123
violence in/at games, 27
    Baylor half-time brawl 1926, 65
    racist incidents, 125–26, 135, 176, 177–78, 179
    University of Texas, 66–67, 77
    vandalism, 27, 65

Waco, Texas, 65
Walker, Doak, 65, 70, 73, 74, 75
Waters, Dale, 181
weather issues

heat, 3–4, 8, 25, 94
Philippines, WWII, 55
wintry conditions, 16–17
wedding, 49
Welch, Barney, 74
Wesson, Euel "Pappy," 42–43
Wheeler, Henry, 197
whipping, 38, 42
White, Gus. *See* gallery 1
White, Jack, 32, 34
    See also gallery 1
wild oats incident, 118–19
Wiley, James "Radio," 43–44
Winkle, Jedge, 86–87
Woodruff, Bob, 65
World War II
    Axis strengthening, 34
    Baty's military career, 51–56
    draft reinstated, 16
    Japanese surrender, 56
    Nazi surrender, 52
    Nazi's near Paris, France, 20
    Pearl Harbor attack, 31
Wright, Charley, 73, 74, 79

Yarborough, Terrell, 138
Ysleta High School (Indians) games, 115–16, 126, 141–42, 161–62